God Loves Diversity and Justice

God Loves Diversity and Justice

Progressive Scholars Speak about Faith, Politics, and the World

Edited by Susanne Scholz

LEXINGTON BOOKS
Lanham • Boulder • New York • Toronto • Plymouth, UK

Published by Lexington Books
A wholly owned subsidiary of The Rowman & Littlefield Publishing Group, Inc.
4501 Forbes Boulevard, Suite 200, Lanham, Maryland 20706
www.rowman.com

10 Thornbury Road, Plymouth PL6 7PP, United Kingdom

British Library Cataloguing in Publication Information Available

Library of Congress Cataloging-in-Publication Data
God loves diversity and justice : progressive scholars speak about faith, politics, and the world /
edited by Susanne Scholz.
pages cm
Includes index.
ISBN 978-0-7391-7318-3 (cloth : alk. paper) — ISBN 978-0-7391-7319-0 (electronic)
1. Religion and justice. I. Scholz, Susanne, 1966–
BL65.J87G63 2013
201'.7—dc23
2013005254
ISBN 978-1-4985-5711-5 (pbk : alk. paper)

In fond memory of
Dr. Gholam H. Sadrzadeh-Ardebili
(1927–1994)

Contents

Introduction

From Progressive Theological Discourse to Changing the World

Susanne Scholz

God loves diversity and justice. This catchy theological statement makes a normative claim. It asserts to know something about God and God's relationship to diversity and justice. It assumes there is a god—in fact, one God—and that this one God loves diversity and justice. The statement openly acknowledges conviction in its theological position. According to some of my mostly Christian students, this is just what progressive religious discourse lacks: simple and clear slogans that articulate a theo-politically progressive perspective. In their view, progressively inclined professors make things too complicated when they analyze, deconstruct, or historicize Christian theological discourse, sources, and doctrines. Instead, my students yearn for theological language that helps them to think theologically in simple and clear terminologies, as they prepare to serve as ministers and teachers in theo-politically conservative contexts. They recognize that the Christian Right's discourse shapes the minds, hearts, and lives of people in many Christian congregations. Thus, they find it difficult, if not impossible, to start with complex theological explanations. What they want are substantive but unencumbered statements about progressive faith perspectives for their sermons, Sunday school lessons, and conversations with parishioners. These statements ought to be memorable so they can be recited in moments of opposition and debate.

Admittedly, I felt surprised about this complaint, but then I thought about it and wondered: Are there not already many theologically progressive slogans out there? And isn't complicated theological discourse exactly what we need in our days of the pervasive either-with-us-or-against-us mindset?

Yes and yes. But then I also thought that concise theological statements are certainly valuable because they articulate in a condensed fashion what must then be parsed from all kinds of perspectives and directions. This book is the result of my effort to take seriously my students' observation. It aims to offer what they said they need: a concise theologi-

1

cal slogan followed by theological discussions that complicate what seems a bit too simple and too clear. The hope is that the following interdisciplinary, interreligious, and intercultural responses to "God loves diversity and justice" provide ample food for thought, inspiring numerous sermons and lesson plans for all kinds of religious communities and teaching contexts.

The initial conversation, later morphing into this book, took place in a public one-day conference at Perkins School of Theology in April 2011.[1] Most contributors to this volume were among the panelists. Let it be known that the conference ended in a celebratory meal in a lovely restaurant in Dallas, where we continued to indulge in the joys of sharing a productive intellectual day with each other and our audience. All of the participating colleagues lived and worked in driving distance to Perkins School of Theology because my ad-hoc budget was small and plane rides prohibitively expensive, so staying local was a "must." As this volume demonstrates, Northern Texas does not lack progressive theological brainpower! I am thankful to all of my colleagues for their spontaneous willingness to join the one-day conference and later to find the time and energy to expand their papers into chapter-length contributions. I am also grateful to three latecomers to this project who did not participate at our one-day conference. I thank them for their readiness to share their much-needed views on secularity, sexuality, and religious plurality. I am also grateful to the two respondents, one participating at the conference and the other hearing much about it later, for their reflections on the various positions presented in this volume. A big thank-you to all.[2]

It should be emphasized that the various positions taken in this volume do not claim or aim for comprehensiveness. They come from selective interdisciplinary and interreligious academic perspectives, giving voice to progressive theological reflection. It ought to be understood that this book does not include Christian conservative views because they are so widely heard in society. In fact, the public usually regards discussions on faith and religion as identical with theo-political and social conservatism, even fundamentalism. In contrast, the book illustrates that such a view is limiting. Progressive positions and theological analysis relate productively to each other, regardless of whether one agrees on the merits of the theological slogan promoted in this book. The contributions also demonstrate that theological complexity is vital to theological discourse on God and the world. After all, God (if there is one) gave humans a brain! Hence, whether the contributors refer to sacred texts, theological doctrines, or human experience in the world, whether they affirm or criticize the statement of God loving diversity and justice, whether they are Christian, Jewish, Muslim, Sikh, atheist, straight, transgender, feminist, black, or Asian, all of them agree on the importance of assessing this religious statement. Thus, the very acts of debate, explanation, and critique are progressive intellectual practices; they make living in the world worthwhile, even meaningful, as they inform, deepen, and enrich how we live our lives, our citizenry, and faith commitments. In short, then, the theological statement, "God loves diversity and justice," may be simple and clear but the conversations gathered in this volume provide lots of wholesome food for thought. Nothing is ever as simple as it seems initially. And this is very good.

ABOUT GOD

Much has been written on God. The slogan "God loves diversity and justice" assumes the existence of God, but opinions vary about this assumption. The debate about God's existence is often heated and emotions run high, as books written by Richard Dawkins or the late Christopher Hitchens illustrate.[3] One contributor to this volume, Pamela Milne, does not assert a belief in God. What is important, however, is the fact that few people feel indifferent about the noun "God." Whether they are believers, agnostics, or atheists, all of them have opinions, expectations, hopes, or disappointments. They often ask the theodicy question as a way into a conversation about God. How could God have allowed this or that terrorizing and murderous event to happen? Why did God not do something to prevent it, help the victims, or punish the oppressors? Novels, movies, and art are filled with such conversations about God. Why is there suffering when God is presumably omnipotent and good? Why do children die? They wonder if perhaps, after all, God cannot do anything about the injustice in the world. If so, perhaps God does not exist?

Marc Ellis poses the latter question when he mentions "Jewish atheists and rebels" who could not "reconcile injustice and God" (62). He asserts that we do not "really" know "about God, if God is, what God is, or what God wants" (67). However, he himself decides on a different route, and so he tells us, "My own response is personal. I would not recommend it to anyone. Simply put, I understood that exile without God was not possible for me" (62). Isam Shihada does not suggest a personal solution. He advises that people of faith regard God as "a symbol of justice and diversity" uniting "us as human beings to work against all forms of injustice in our world" (84). When we do so, we participate in building a world without tags.

The challenge is to not limit our expectations about God. Perhaps we need to think about the divine as being present even when we only feel absence. Or, as Milne advises, the point is that we do not focus on God at all but rather on the task at hand. In her view, religions and ideas about deities are "social constructs" (34) and discussions on who God is go nowhere. Thus she suggests, "If theists are motivated because of the way they understand their divinity and this understanding leads them to work on social justice issues, it is really their own personal choice. It does not have to be the motivation for secularists. And as a secularist, I would not say that there is a deity out there wanting or pushing us to do something. But if that motivates you to make the ideals of the Universal Declaration of Human Rights a reality, then we can work together to get the job done. . . . There is so much work that needs to be done. We should not fight over why we are doing it" (53). In other words, Milne recommends that working together toward social, political, and economic justice should be our collective effort, not sitting in divided camps because of theological disagreements.

The idea about our common goals as human beings is also important to Nikky-Guninder Kaur Singh's discussions on God in the Sikh tradition. She explains that the "spectacular diversity" of nature and life, as well as planets, stars, galaxies, and universes, are all "manifestations of the infinite Divine" (25–26), and the various religious traditions should not be viewed as competitors but as representations of "our human capacity for peace and love" (23). When we recognize the divine as diversity and justice, Singh contends, "we will viscerally experience the ontological continuity between that One, our society, and nature" (29). Then all discriminatory habits and conventions, "traditional patriarchal and colonial blinders" (15), will shatter and we will recognize that "humans are all one," as Guru Gobind Singh declared famously (23).

ABOUT LOVE

Then there is love, although the theological statement that God loves diversity and justice does not contain a noun but a verb. God is its subject; God is the one doing the loving. What is God doing when God loves? Marc Ellis asserts that, first and foremost, God loves the prophets and therefore "[t]he God of the prophets is not a God of rescue" (69). In his view, God's love is deeper, more profound, and more lasting than "any celebratory understanding of God siding with diversity and justice" (69). God is not on a rescue mission, and so the prophets believe in God despite "the failure to eliminate empire in the world" (68). Prophetic hope does not depend on worldly success but rests on "the willingness to suffer without the possibility of rescue" (69). Theirs is a "prophetic plea beyond mere complaint or issue activism" (69). In other and perhaps simpler words, the prophets love God even if they do not have proof that God indeed loves the world, as "the debris is all around us" (69) with little evidence of any divine love or rescue in sight.

The Protestant reformer Martin Luther thought differently about God's love. He suggested that God loves us before we have done anything. God loves us because of God's grace. God's love does not require our doing, and so Luther asserted that humans cannot earn God's love. It is already given to us and all that is left for us to do is to trust that God loves us. Yet our theological slogan asserts that God loves diversity and justice, sounding similar to the preferential option for the poor, as Latin American liberation theologians described God's love for the oppressed and marginalized. So does our slogan suggest that God prefers diversity and justice? This would not be such a bad idea. If more and more people of faith were to follow God's preferential option for diversity and justice, the poor would be the foremost beneficiaries.

This is how Susanne Johnson thinks about it. She writes that we need to cultivate a "vision of God as the 'Utterly Just One'" to give people of faith "more compelling and consequential witness to God's own mission of inclusive love and justice in and for the sake of the world and its full flourishing" (91). Such a vision, says Johnson, requires that we regard economic inequities and imbalances as detrimental to "the community of Shalom promised by God" (108). The vision of God's love for diversity and justice supports resistance toward asymmetrical power and privilege in society, challenging class oppression often almost invisibly operating and maintaining the exploitative status quo. This "matrix of domination" (102) intersects in complex and complicated ways with gender, race, ethnicity, and other social categories, fostering co-optation and complicity on every level in society. Thus, Johnson wants to see broad-based organizing that brings "people together across lines of class, gender, race, ethnicity, nationality, geography, immigrant status, and religion" (107).

In other words, transformative efforts across the spectrum of people's social locations may be viewed as an act of God's love. Not the privatized sentimentality of Valentine Day's kitsch but rather the concern for justice, the balancing of out-of-control inequities, gross exploitation, and outright oppression of people. Love signifies a bias toward those who suffer the most under the pervasive structures of domination. When we say "God loves . . ." it reminds those of us who believe in a god that we need to transform our societies toward justice and peace. As Isam Shihada states, "We should therefore promote a culture of justice, diversity, tolerance, and peace because we know there is no peace without justice and diversity, as peace is the natural conclusion of justice and diversity. Without justice and diversity, there will be no peace at all" (80). And further: "The conviction that God is a symbol of justice and diversity may serve to unite us as human beings to work against all forms of injustice in our world" (84).

ABOUT DIVERSITY

On October 10, 2012, the Supreme Court's Chief Justice John G. Roberts Jr. asked how much diversity would be enough in the University of Texas's admission process. His question was part of the proceedings as the Court began grappling with the affirmative-action case *Fisher v. Texas No.*

11-345.[4] In U.S. culture the term "diversity" is usually "a gauzy, unobjectionable way to talk about the combustible topic of race."[5] Yet this is a limited view of diversity. Until 1956, the phrase *E pluribus unum* ("Out of many, one") was considered the unofficial motto of the United States. The U.S. Congress adopted "In God We Trust" as the official motto in 1956.[6] In other regions of the world, "diversity" refers to cultural, linguistic, and historical diversity, as, for instance, in the European Union, which chose as its motto "United in Diversity."[7] The idea also appears in the Baha'i religion, which claims not to "ignore, nor does it attempt to suppress, the diversity of ethnical origins, of climate, of history, of language and tradition, of thought and habit, that differentiate the peoples and nations of the world," because "[d]iversity of hues, form and shape enricheth and adorneth the garden, and heighteneth the effect thereof."[8] In short, the concept of diversity goes beyond concerns about race and ethnicity, and its significance has been widely recognized throughout history. Consequently, issues of nationality, gender, sexuality, immigration, religion, and culture are also crucial elements in debates over diversity. More recently, we have come to include ecodiversity and species diversity as important facets for life on earth.

The contributors to this volume point to the various forms of diversity and, depending on their particular argumentation, they highlight benefits and challenges in theological and religious theory and practice. For instance, Joerg Rieger cautions against merely celebrating diversity for its own sake or, even worse, as a strategy to co-opt different cultures and subcultures to improve the bottom line of any business. He cautions us to not use diversity as merely another way to endorse the status quo of society. What is needed, says Rieger, is a connection of diversity with justice to make visible the power dynamics in "broken relationships" (118) and "to reject false notions of diversity that, often unwittingly, celebrate differentials of power rather than empower those who bear the brunt of unjust relationships" (126).

Even less optimistic is Sze-kar Wan's observation. He wonders if perhaps God does not love diversity at all, although he acknowledges that the idea of such a God is much needed today. To Wan, several well-known biblical texts illustrate that the Bible is "not immune to ethnocentrism" and God is found in the midst of it (141). Wan's discussions on Second and Third Isaiah as well as on Luke/Acts illustrate that the biblical tradition does not unambiguously present God as loving diversity and justice. Second Isaiah celebrates universalist ethnocentrism to justify the vision of Israel as "the agent through whom God's salvation will reach the ends of the earth" (134). This literary tradition descends into "tribalism" in Third Isaiah, in which converts are classified as foreigners, regarded as "second-class citizens to the returning Israelites" (136). Wan finds the disregard for diversity in the prophetic tradition challenged by the Lukan Jesus, who ultimately turns into "a divisive figure who ends up legitimating Christian chauvinism" (141). Still, Wan finds "a glimmer of hope . . . subtle, often buried intimations of acceptance and inclusion" in these texts (141). For instance, according to Wan, "[t]he Servant Songs speak of a universal God who bestows blessings upon all peoples irrespective of ethnicity and borders, and the New Testament writers extol a self-giving God who would rather empty oneself than claim divine prerogatives" (141–42). Hence, Wan goes back and forth on the selected biblical passages, as their meaning may ultimately depend on "all of us who take the biblical texts seriously to answer the question" of whether God really loves diversity.

ABOUT JUSTICE

Undoubtedly, justice has been a central theme in religious discourse and practice throughout the ages, especially in the Jewish, Christian, and Muslim traditions. Justice is a top moral value in the Bible and, as the *Encyclopedia Judaica* states, justice "singularly characterizes Judaism both conceptually and historically."[9] Debates about what constitutes justice rage in philosophy, theology, or politics. Sometimes characterized as a white liberal "social contract" model that is content with the contemporary status quo, John Rawls's proposal of *A Theory of Justice*[10] continues to shape contemporary thought on how justice ought to be distributed in society.[11] Liberation theologians of any religious persuasion center on the notion of justice. They insist that God's justice must find social, political, and economic expression in this world. As Gustavo Gutierrez provocatively and famously asserted, the biblical tradition advances a preferential option for the poor.[12] To liberation theologians, God's justice consists in bringing justice to the marginalized, despised, and needy in society. This idea caught on not only in Latin American liberation theology but also in black theologies, feminist theologies, queer and transgender theologies, postcolonial theologies, and other religiously and geopolitically influenced religious thought and practice.[13]

Predictably, then, the contributors of this volume respond positively to the noun "justice." They affirm its significance and defend its ongoing relevance for contemporary ethics, politics, and society. Serge Frolov, for instance, notes that the Hebrew term *tsedeq* occurs more than six hundred times in the Bible, but this terminological predominance does not guarantee that all biblical texts promote justice. A case in point is Deuteronomy 20, which Frolov examines carefully, trying to decipher its potential for promoting justice. The situation looks grim, as this passage seems to promote genocide. Frolov keeps wrestling with the difficulties of Deuteronomy 20 because he does not want to let go of this text, and in the end he comes up with a hermeneutical solution that makes justice possible in Deuteronomy 20 and elsewhere in the Bible.

Justice—more specifically, racial justice—is central in Maria Dixon's response. She explores the expectations that African American scholars be harbingers of justice for their "people," always asked to focus on advancing social justice and diversity in all of their work, as if their positions were not fundamentally different, privileged, and distant from "our people" (162). Dixon points to the difference in class locations among African Americans as an underanalyzed factor. She questions the idea "that our scholarship must serve as a voice for [our] people while wrestling with the very reality that the vast majority of the race is ambivalent and/or hostile to our very existence" (163). Her reflections remind us that "justice" is a complicated noun, that our efforts to contribute to justice in the world encounter complicating dynamics inherited by history, politics, and culture, and that our commitments to a just world are multifaceted even when they appear simple. Dixon's concern for justice is unabashedly strong, although she observes that she and other middle-class people, whether they are black or not, are often complicit with and coopted into "Nineveh." The best strategy is, according to Dixon, "to interrogate our own complicity and create work that is accessible not only to those in Nineveh but those sitting in the 'hood'" (175).

Justice is also central in Qudsia Mirza's discussion on Muslim law and gender equality in Islam and Islamic feminism. According to Muslim traditions, especially in the Qur'an, Allah loves justice, and so every Muslim has the moral duty to do justice in the world. The struggle is what our justice entails. Mirza details the complex traditional and feminist debates in Islam over justice and the reevaluation of the meaning of gender equality in our time. She explains that Islamic feminists make religious norms, values, and laws central in their calls for reconfiguring women's rights in Islam. To them, gender justice and the equality of women in Muslim societies are at the heart of realizing the ideals of Islam.

Another strong call for justice, in this case gender justice, comes from Gordene MacKenzie and Nancy Nangeroni. For decades, both of them have fought for gender justice in the United States, taking on leadership roles in the transgender movement and reenvisioning diverse gender expression and identity as a spiritually holistic practice. In their chapter, they share their gender journeys generously and openly, not hiding institutional and personal difficulties they encountered on the road. MacKenzie and Nangeroni highlight transgender activists doing transgender justice in the institutional Christian church, and they describe the gender struggles within the Wiccan movement. They mourn the victims of transphobic violence but find hope and strength among the Kindred Spirits, the oldest transgender-founded spiritual tradition in the United States. Theirs is a personal commitment to transgender justice with national and global ramifications. They keep up their love for justice as an effective agent of change. Indeed, God loves diversity of gender expression and transgender justice!

The respondents, Pat Davis and Victoria Fontan, write from the secularized positions of human rights work and peace and conflict studies, respectively. One of them wonders about the value of traditional scriptural references in a world that needs immediate and reliable aid. The other wants to retire God. Yet most of the world's humans do not live their lives in secular ways. They pray, burn incense, sing, and dance religiously, assuming a higher power of the universe, whether they call it God, Allah, Almighty, or Brahma. However, both respondents remind faith-oriented thinkers that the secular critique must be taken seriously. Where is God or the gods when the world keeps burning children and adults? Where are the religious leaders and where are the followers? How do we respond to the relentless and murderous violence in the world today, we who are not on the run from the empires of the world, we who are not yet threatened by drone attacks and military devastation? How do we speak theologically in a world haunted by religious hypocrisy, shallowness, and literalism, as well as genocide, murder, and violence?

Personally, I grew up with Grimm's fairy tales. The good news was that nobody ever expected these tales to report actual history. They were told to teach about life, love, and sorrow. They were meant to be understood on the symbolic level, nurturing a sense of wonder and mystery, but also teaching something about the world. As we may know, fairy tales invite a lot of interpretation, although as children we just listen to them. We soak them up, but later, if we are lucky, we find ways to rethink them and to be reminded of them decades after we first heard of them. Perhaps we even stumble upon some innovative interpretations.[14] Would our first response be "But they are not true"? Hardly, because we recognize that these interpretations enhance, deepen, and even nourish our understanding of the tales and the world.

Similarly, the purpose of this book is to nourish our thinking about the theological slogan "God loves diversity and justice," as analyzed by the contributors of various faith and secular traditions and academic disciplines, so that our understanding of the world is enhanced. To do this kind of critical reflection in the conversation with the scholars included in this book is an opportunity to take time, to stop, to sit down and read, and to rethink how we look at the world today. It requires quieting the mind, taking a break from the noisiness of our everyday lives, and conversing with the fourteen scholars who are sharing their responses to "God loves diversity and justice." The hope is that readers will feel nourished by the various conversations and take courage to make diversity and justice present in the world.

NOTES

1. The event was free and open to the public; for the flyer of the event, visit http://www.facebook.com/events/195845550438434/ [accessed on December 6, 2012].

2. I also would like to express my gratitude for the institutional support I have received for this project. The Dean of Perkins School of Theology, William B. Lawrence, generously supported the hosting of the conference in April 2011. A Perkins Scholarly Outreach Award supported the writing of this introductory chapter.

3. Richard Dawkins, *The God Delusion* (Boston: Houghton Mifflin, 2006); Christopher Hitchens, *God Is Not Great: How Religion Poisons Everything* (New York: Twelve Books, 2007).

4. Adam Liptak, "Justices Weigh Diversity Issue at Universities: Lawsuit Claiming Bias," *New York Times* (October 11, 2012): A1. For an editorial assessment of this lawsuit, see Simon Waxman, "Diversity Against Justice: How Diversity Came to Replace Anti-Racism," *Jacobin: A Magazine of Culture and Polemic* (October 15, 2012): http://jacobinmag.com/2012/10/diversity-against-justice/ [accessed December 6, 2012].

5. Adam Liptak, "College Diversity Nears Its Last Stand," *New York Times* (October 15, 2012): http://archive.is/1jG2 [accessed December 6, 2012].

6. See "E pluribus unum" at http://en.wikipedia.org/wiki/E_pluribus_unum [accessed December 6, 2012].

7. See http://europa.eu/abc/symbols/motto/index_en.htm [accessed December 6, 20120].

8. Quote is taken from "Unity in Diversity," a document at the Baha'i Reference Library, available at http://reference.bahai.org/en/t/se/WOB/wob-21.html [accessed December 6, 2012].

9. "Justice," in Encyclopedia *Judaica*, vol. 10 (Jerusalem: Keter Publishing House, 1971–1972), 475.

10. John Rawls, *A Theory of Justice* , rev. ed. (Oxford: Oxford University Press, 1999).

11. For additional information and references to the discussion, visit http://en.wikipedia.org/wiki/A_Theory_of_Justice [accessed December 6, 2012].

12. Gustavo Gutierrez, *A Theology of Liberation*, 1st Spanish ed. (Lima, Peru, 1971); 1st English ed. (Maryknoll, NY: Orbis Books, 1973).

13. See, for example, Rosemary Radford Ruether, *Liberation Theology: Human Hope Confronts Christian History and American Power* (New York: Paulist Press, 1972); Mary Daly, *Beyond God the Father: Toward a Philosophy of Women's Liberation* (Boston: Beacon Press, 1973); Letty M. Russell, *Human Liberation in a Feminist Perspective: A Theology* (Philadelphia: Westminster Press, 1974); José Míguez Bonino, *Doing Theology in a Revolutionary Situation* (Philadelphia: Fortress Press, 1975); Commission on Theological Concerns of the Christian Conference of Asia (CTC-CCA) (ed.), *Minjung Theology: People as the Subjects of History*, rev. ed. (London: Zed Press; Maryknoll, NY: Orbis Books, 1983); Naim Stifan Ateek, *Justice, and Only Justice: A Palestinian Theology of Liberation* (Maryknoll, NY: Orbis Books, 1989); Sharon D. Welch, *Communities of Resistance and Solidarity: A Feminist Theology of Liberation* (Maryknoll, NY: Orbis Books, 1985); Deane William Ferm, *Third World Liberation Theologies: A Reader* (Maryknoll, NY: Orbis Books, 1986); Marc H. Ellis and Otto Maduro (eds.), *Future of Liberation Theology: Essays in Honor of Gustavo Guiterrez* (Maryknoll, NY: Orbis Books, 1989); James H. Cone, *A Black Theology of Liberation*, 20th anniversary ed. (Maryknoll, NY: Orbis Books, 1990); Richard Cleaver, *Know My Name: A Gay Liberation Theology* (Louisville, KY: Westminster John Knox Press, 1995); Marc H. Ellis, *Toward a Jewish Theology of Liberation: The Challenge of the 21st Century*, 3rd exp. ed. (Waco, TX: Baylor University Press, 2004); and Miguel A. De La Torre, *The Hope of Liberation in World Religions* (Waco, TX: Baylor University Press, 2008).

14. See, for example, Kay Turner and Pauline Greenhill (eds.), *Transgressive Tales: Queering the Grimms* (Detroit: Wayne State University Press, 2012); S. D. Fohr, *Cinderella's Gold Slipper: Spiritual Symbolism in the Grimms' Tales* (Hillsdale, NY: Sophia Perennis, 2004).

Part I

About God

ONE

God *Is* Diversity and Justice

A Feminist Sikh Perspective

Nikky-Guninder Kaur Singh

The Sikh tradition originated and crystallized historically and geographically between the South Asian Indic and the West Asian Abrahamic/Islamic worlds. It should offer linguistic, philosophical, cultural, and aesthetic source materials for scholars specializing in both Western and South Asian religions, but unfortunately, it has not caught their attention.[1] Academic, political, and religious divisions have kept scholars splintered far too long. A feminist exploration helps to overcome these divisions because "women resemble one another, across cultures, in certain ways more than they resemble the men within their own cultures."[2] I am grateful to Professor Susanne Scholz for including my feminist Sikh perspective in her anthology.

PREFACE

I want to make two points at the outset. First, the term "God" does not fit in the Sikh context. The founder of Sikhism, Guru Nanak (1469–1539), articulated the Divine as a singular Reality—*Ikk Oan Kar*, literally "1 Being Is." Its standard translation, "There is One God," distorts the vastness, the plenitude, or the intimacy bursting forth in the original "One Being Is." Instead of an opening into limitless possibilities as envisioned by the founder Sikh Guru, Sikh scholars and translators have selected and structured and shaped the infinite Divine into an intimidating male God. As the feminist philosopher Mary Daly reminded us, the term

13

"God" is a reified "noun," which is static and laden with Jewish and Christian patriarchal assumptions. "God," with its "Father-Lord" connotations, has negative effects on society as it produces an unhealthy experience with the Divine, and unhealthy relationships among people.[3] Transcending languages, cultures, and religions, Guru Nanak's primary numeral 1 with its soaring geometric arc is a universal modality. In any translation, the 1-ness of the numeral must be retained, and I would say "Be-ing" (recommended by Mary Daly in a Western context), or even the "One Divine," works out quite well as an English equivalent.

Second, I am making a change in the title of my chapter from the verb "loves" to "is." My intention here is not to undermine the power and dynamism of love, our supreme human moral ideal, but rather to preserve Guru Nanak's intention that the Divine in its very being *is* diversity and justice. Any dualism between subject and object, the lover and the loved is overcome. Heidegger offers a valuable insight on the ontological import of the tiny word "is": "speaks everywhere in our language and tells of Being even where it does not appear expressly."[4]

Such a semantic shift redirects our attention from the *other* to *us*. Instead of looking for the Divine vertically up in the distance, we generate a momentum that incites us to access that One existentially in the diversity among us—humans and nature alike. This approach maintains feminist theologian Sallie McFague's "horizontal focus"—"[t]he focus of this eye is not on seeing God, but on seeing the tree (this particular tree) which, in its own way, as itself, is *also* in God."[5] So we begin to discern the singular Divine among us—in the diversity of races, genders, species, planets, universes. No longer do we expect to confront a figure in the future who will judge us and dispense justice after death in heaven and hell. Rather, we become incensed by the injustice all around us *here* and *now*: When the same One is us, how could we have such inequality and discrimination? Tackling our socioeconomic-environmental-political problems becomes ever so urgent.

Furthermore, my semantic change discloses the distinct Sikh theological perspective. The Divine is certainly One (*Ikk*), but it does not reproduce the conventional monotheistic model, which has been the standard view. Even eminent scholars from within the tradition simplistically identify Guru Nanak's statement with the first part of the Muslim *shahada*.[6] As a continuation of the Abrahamic traditions, Islam penetrated India with the concept of the "One God," which conflicted with the polyphonic imagination of the diverse schools of the Hindus, Buddhists, and Jains. In the Sikh belief there is no opposition between the One and the many, nor is there any antithesis between unity and plurality. Sikh scripture claims, "*ikkasu te hoio ananta nanak ekasu mahi samae jio*—From the One issue myriads and into the One they are ultimately assimilated" (GGS: 131). Unity becomes plurality and plurality eventually becomes unity. The Kantian dictum about totality being plurality regarded as unity echoes the same truth. Guru Nanak's is not exclusivist monotheism; the One in its diversity transcends all exclusions and negations. It is only when we rid ourselves of the traditional patriarchal and colonial blinders that we begin to see the phenomenal diversity championed by the Sikh Gurus. As history has it, the Gurus were followed by men like Chaupa Singh, who put a malestream exegesis into effect, which was reinforced by the British colonial machine. As Arvind Mandair exposed in his recent study, the "specter of the west" dictated a symbolic order on the colonized peoples, and made the indigenous elites psychologically receptive to its categories and polarizations.[7] Those patriarchal perspectives carry on in postcolonial times.

This chapter looks at the kaleidoscopic variety of the Sikh theological imaginary and its impact on issues of religion, gender, and the multiverse we inhabit. I see things from my feminist eyes—that of a Sikh woman academic living in the twenty-first century in the United States. My primary source is Sikh scripture, the Guru Granth Sahib (GGS)—a text of sublime poetry compiled in 1604. Its 1,430 portfolio pages reiterate the beauty and enchantment of our wondrous multiverse. The effective poetic lyrics have the power to go deep inside into our unconscious and give us a feel for the divine unity among us, here and now. I will also analyze an illustration of the founder Sikh Guru from an early manuscript, which visually concretizes his encompassing poetic voice.

For the twenty-five million Sikhs worldwide, Guru Nanak's word and lifestyle constitute the nucleus of their doctrine and ethics. In the United States itself, there are at least half a million Sikhs, with more than two hundred public places of worship (*gurdwaras*). Yet so little is known about them that they frequently end up as victims of hate crimes. The most recent case was the massacre during their worship at the *gurdwara* in Oak Creek, Milwaukee. The leitmotif of diversity should familiarize readers with the very essentials of the Sikh tradition. My goal is to expand the emotions and imagination of my readers so we can together fight discrimination and oppression. Literature and art have a way of transforming attitudes that laws and regulations fail to do. Real change comes from within. As we look around, our globe is rife with hegemonies and conflicts. Religious wars are aflame across the world. The ghastly partition of the Indian subcontinent in 1947 along religious lines continues to foment communalist ideologies and haunt the South Asian psyche and its politics. Our current globalization is extending Western hegemony. It privileges the First World, and its neoliberal policies perpetuate intolerance, white supremacy, discrimination against women, and the negative impact of climate change on the marginalized. The Sikh example of recognizing the Divine as diversity and justice could have enormous contemporary relevance.

KALEIDOSCOPIC THEOLOGICAL IMAGINARY

The Sikh Divine comprises every imaginable theological ideal! Hindu, Buddhist, Tantric, and Islamic views that were current in medieval India come together in the wide-ranging literary spectrum of the GGS. The stereotypical oppositions between the Indic and Abrahamic worldviews of the day are transcended: "Some call it Rama, some call it Khuda; some worship it as Vishnu, some as Allah" (GGS: 885). Interestingly, even the atheistic Buddhist Nirvana is not omitted: "Itself Nirvana, It itself relishes pleasures" (GGS: 97). "God" or "gods" or "no god" alike are recognized as part of the infinite One! "Always, always you alone are the One Reality—*sada sada tun eku hai*" (GGS: 139). Persian terminology is used to emphasize the unicity of being: "*asti ek digari kui ek tui ek tui*—Only the One is, there is none other; Only you, you only" (GGS: 144). Again, "*hindu turk ka sahib ek*—Hindus and Muslims share the One sovereign" (GGS: 1158). (The term "Turk" referred to all Muslims in this period.) Since everything is a manifestation of That One being, all the manifestations would be a part of it. No god, no body, and no thing is excluded from this all pervasive being. The arc flying off Oan in Guru Nanak's vision of the Divine launches the imagination to intuit the unintuitable One, and everybody is welcome to perceive that One in their own way. Blotting out conventional icons and images that created divisions and animosities, the mathematical One embraces the Tao, Yahweh, Allah, Ram, Sita. . . . This numerical symbol has the potential to end conflicts between *my god/your god*.

Furthermore, this infinite One is intimately experienced as *both* male and female: "*ape purakh ape hi nar*—Itself male, itself is female" (GGS: 1020). Beyond gender, "*hari ape mata ape pita*—the Divine is itself mother, itself father" (GGS: 921). In a socio-historic context that was extremely patriarchal, the GGS claims, "*tun mera pita tun hain mera mata*—You are my father, you are my mother" (GGS: 103; GGS: 1144); with a slight variation, "*tumhi pita tum hi phun mata*—You are my father and you too are my mother" (GGS: 1215), and yet again, "*mat pita bandhap tun hai tun sarab nivas*—You are our mother, father, relative, and you permeate us all" (GGS: 818). Through such emotionally charged verses we embrace the transcendent abiding in everybody in a range of family figures. The sense of plenitude strips off patriarchal stratifications. It blots out masculine identity as the norm for imaging the Divine, and widens the spiritual experience.

The maternal imaginary regularly turns attention to the primal home—the mother's body, the ontological base of every person. In particular, it honors the maternal space as a social utopia in which the fetus is free from hegemonic designations of class, caste, and name: "In the dwelling of the womb, there is neither name nor caste" (GGS: 324). The Sikh Gurus were acutely aware of their oppressive patrilineal and patri-centered north Indian society in which the family name, caste, and profession came down through birth. So the mother's pregnant body is envisioned as free from social hegemonies. Here the fetus is nurtured by *her* life-giving uterus; it is not suffocated by the father's name, class, or professional ties.

But subsequent commentators of Sikh scripture simply deem it unnecessary to remember *her* body or our origins, and so the unique emphasis of the Sikh Gurus on the divine constitution of female physiology and our integrated subjectivity has been lost. For instance, the GGS explicitly affirms that the divine permeates both the heart and the womb ("*ghati ghati vartai udari majhare*—It pervades every heart and flourishes in the womb," GGS: 1026). Eminent scholars like G. S. Talib and Gopal Singh register the heart (*ghat*) but utterly ignore the womb (*udar*) in Guru Nanak's feminist sensibility.[8] The particular female organ even gets altered into a generic "stomach"[9] or "belly."[10] The radical vision of the Gurus and their invigorating overtures thus remain unseen, unheard. Their womb-respecting, birth-oriented glimpses and melodies need to be remembered so that their lingering can make each of us more wholesome, and our world a better place.

The seriousness with which the GGS takes women's genealogy is quite remarkable. Images of conception, gestation, giving birth, and lactation are unambiguously and powerfully present. The mother's milk is acknowledged as full of biological and spiritual nutrients. Even the recitation of divine name is succulently experienced as milk in the mouth. The language of the Gurus joins in with the words of contemporary French feminist scholar Hélène Cixous, "Voice: milk that could go on forever. Found again. The lost mother/bitter-lost. Eternity: is voice mixed with milk."[11] Her milk is a biological necessity, keeping us from dying. So is the divine word (*bani*). By pouring the two together, the Sikh Gurus make knowledge essential for everybody, upper class and lower, Brahmin and Shudra. The textuality of the GGS lies in its physical sensuality—in drinking the words as though they were the mother's life-giving milk.

The maternal imaginary in the GGS is palpably reclaimed; it is not a matter of religious deification, because "she" is not idolized into some distant goddess—an object of worship. It is when the Divine is genuinely imagined as Mother that her positive characteristics begin to filter the mind and ignite respect for mothers, sisters, daughters, and wives. Thus, an authentic subjectivity is born. Women are regarded as life-and-blood individuals who partake in the qualities and powers of the divine One. They are thanked for their creating and nurturing.

It is critical, however, that the "mother" not be viewed as the only female symbol for the Divine either. Sikh scripture offers countless ways of imagining and experiencing the infinite One. Even in one short hymn, Guru Nanak imagines the Divine as the bride in her wedding dress, as the groom on the nuptial bed, as the fisherman and the fish, as the waters and the trap, as the weight holding the net, as well as the lost ruby swallowed by the fish! (GGS: 23). In a speedy tempo, his similes and paradoxes free the mind from narrow walls. Male is not the only way to imagine the Divine. Motherhood therefore is one aspect of womanhood, and surely all women are not mothers, and may choose not to be mothers. With the singular stress on the maternal paradigm, woman's creative powers can be misconstrued as an automatic and mandatory process.

The "mother" symbol from the GGS must not be abused to make women into reproductory machines to beget sons! It is important that we do not equate the maternal potential with physical conception or limit the maternal to the domestic world. As Luce Irigaray says, it is not necessary that women give birth to children; they can give birth to many other things, such as "love, desire, language, art, social things, political things, religious things." [12] The "mother" as a Sikh theological principle reveals the potential to create — physically, intellectually, emotionally, politically, and spiritually. It shatters the gender roles that assign production to men and reproduction to women; conferring a sense of reality on women's creativity, it enables everybody to cultivate meaningful relationships with their past and future generations, and with their geological and cosmic community.

RELIGIOUS PLURALISM

Rather than irreconcilable differences, Sikhism posits equality and convergence among religions, for just as humans conceive the Divine in multiple ways, so do they respond. Diversity of scriptures, ideologies, devotees, and their forms of worship is fully affirmed and profoundly respected.

The GGS validates diverse religious scriptures. We hear it respect the "Vedas" that connote Indic texts like the Puranas, Shastras, and Smritis; we hear it respect the "Qateb" that connotes the Semitic texts, the Torah, the Zabur, the Injil, and the Qur'an. According to the GGS, "Some read the Vedas, some the Qateb — *koi parai bed koi qateb*" (GGS: 885). Divine revelation (*qudrati*) is celebrated as Hindu and Muslim scriptures (*veda purana kateba*), and all modes of reflection (*sarab vicaru*) (GGS: 464). For the Sikh Gurus, the singular Source transcends all conceptual constructs. Hindu and Muslim scriptures written down and recited differently in Sanskrit and Arabic share the same Author, the same Voice. Guru Arjan, who compiled the utterances of the Sikh Gurus along with those of Hindu and Muslim saints into the Granth, declares the common vocal expression: "Vedas, Puranas, Simritis, and saints, utter this *bani* (language) in their tongue" (GGS: 1227). Hindus, Muslims, and saints of different religious traditions speak in countless vernaculars and dialects a universal language. The GGS praises various scriptures, without imposing any one text or specifying any particular mode of thought. For our dangerously divided and polarized world, there is an important instruction: "Do not call the Vedas or Qateb false; false are they who do not reflect on them—*bed qateb kahhu mat jhute jhuta jo na bicharai*" (GGS: 1350). In a sad tone Guru Nanak empathizes, "What can the poor Vedas and Qateb do when no reader recognizes the One—*bed qateb karahi kah bapure nah bujheh ikk eka*?" (GGS: 1153).

Clearly, from the Gurus' perspective, the problem of religious conflict does not lie in the sacred texts but in us humans who neither reflect (*bichari*) on the scriptures nor recognize (*bujeh*) the One (*ikk*). In scriptures lie our deepest moral and philosophical values, and yet most of us across the board cannot intimately read either our own scriptures or those of others. Reading is complex, comprising the visual, perceptual, syntactic, and semantic processes. Often we hold such reverence for our holy book that we get anxious about any intimacy with it. Priests, along with scholars and exegetes, officiate as readers and thus intermediate between the subjects and their text. Reading the holy books of others can be daunting in other ways, for some may unnecessarily fear that by doing so we may lose faith in our own. The result clearly leaves everybody alienated and impoverished. The GGS rejects intermediaries and urges everybody to read scriptures with lenses that see through the singular Divine. In its typical pluralistic pattern the GGS advises, "Gain the wealth of Quran and Qateb in your heart—*Quran Qateb dil mahi kamahi*" (GGS: 1083). Reading with and through our hearts endorses personal interpretations by every reader, whether male or female, upper class or lower. The GGS thus opens the way for a "hermeneutics of marginalization"—championing the feminist goal "to develop a more holistic methodology of interpretation, one that is crucial, experiential, dialogical, contextual and liberating."[13]

Likewise, the GGS values the different methods and techniques of worship and devotion to the Divine. This position does not imply relativism but underscores a pluralistic perspective in which no mode of worship is rejected or excluded. It describes "[y]our devotees standing together contemplating the Vedas and Qateb—*tudh dhianhrehi bed qateb sann khareh*" (GGS: 518). This vivid scene of the Hindu and Muslim devotees standing together challenges the either-or religious segregations and insularities normally practiced. The fifth Guru exclaims, "Millions and millions have been your worshippers—*kai koti hoe pujari*," "millions and millions of poets have reflected on you in their poetry—*kai kot kab kaab bicareh*," and "millions upon millions meditate on your ever new name" (GGS: 275). Countless ascetics are remembered for attaining liberation (GGS: 1125). Along with the diverse human devotees, Guru Nanak embraces the tiny sparrow joyfully calling for her Divine beloved: "*khudai khudai*" (GGS: 1286); his tenth successor observes, "From tiny blades of

grass and towering forest all proclaim your infinity!" The Being is extolled by humans in chorus with the myriad species. No*body* is put down.
The verses of the Gurus are suffused with an appreciation and respect for
the multifold devotees, their languages, their holy books, and their ways
of worship. They even accept the sheer impossibility of accounting for all
those who meditate on the Divine (GGS: 253).

The GGS itself is a testament of pluralism. In the making of the canon,
the fifth Guru (Arjan, 1563–1606) collected the voices of Sikh, Muslim,
and Hindu holy men from different social classes and different geographical areas, and gave them equal status. He voluntarily and consciously
chose to incorporate the different religious, social, and cultural paradigms of his day into the Sikh sacred text. It was important for the Sikh
Gurus that people would familiarize themselves with difference and diversity. The "other" could not merely be tolerated; the "other" had to be
engaged with, understood, and appreciated. The pluralistic spectrum
would intellectually, emotionally, and spiritually strengthen their diverse
society. Evoking profound respect for the faith of others, the GGS serves
as a significant literary medium for building bridges and relationships to
foster harmony and peace.

Guru Arjan set the multilingual, multicultural, multiethnic, and multi-
religious verses into musical measures so readers and hearers could aesthetically experience that Being conceived in different forms and expressed in different styles. Of course, the presence of various languages
and vernaculars makes comprehension of exact words difficult. Nevertheless, the melodies heighten the aesthetic experience and evoke a common bond amongst listeners. Most of the GGS is put into the ancient
Indian musical system of Ragas, which means both "color" and "musical
mode" in Sanskrit. This was the Guru's way of linking the scriptural
language with the cosmos at large. Each *raga* has a season prescribed for
its singing, it has a prescribed time of the day, an emotional mood, and a
particular cultural climate as each measure evolved in a specific region.
These thirty-one *ragas* do not impose classifications or divisions; on the
contrary, Guru Arjan utilized them as patterns, which harmonize the
verses with the natural rhythm of the day, season, region, and emotions.
Connecting humans with space and time, they bring out the intrinsic
force of the verses. They are not confined to the classical *raga* system
either. Folk musical patterns with elemental beats, as well as regional
Bhakti and Kafi forms with their own primal rhythms, and various other
musical styles extending all the way from Afghanistan to the south of the
Indian peninsula, circulate in the GGS. We recognize the meaning of *raga*
in the brilliant blush (*rang*) of emotions produced by their symphony. It
opens the possibilities for gaining intimacy with fellow humans and with
the natural rhythms of our days and seasons.

The GGS thus provides a vital ground for interreligious engagement
and harmony. The reading and listening of the different religious ideolo-

gies and practices of the Sikh Gurus, Hindu Bhagats, and Muslim Sufis in musical melodies actually puts the pluralistic process into motion. The GGS contains 4 hymns and 130 couplets composed by the first recognized Punjabi poet Sheikh Farid (1175–1265), one of the founding fathers of the popular Chishti Sufi order in India. Sheikh Farid's verse familiarizes us with his West Asian sensibilities. The angel of death and the fear of judgment are always hovering in his hymns. Much as we may stay alert with our eyes wide open, the angel of death sneaks in, "extinguishing the two lamps on his way out—*divre gaia bujhae*" (GGS: 1380). The introduction of Azrail leads the reader toward Islamic theology. Birds too—cranes, crows, egrets, swans, and hawks—mournfully point to the finality of death. As the birds hatch their young ones in the skeletal sockets (GGS: 1378), they graphically illustrate the eventual decay of the vibrant human body. In his constant reminders of death and the Day of Judgment, Sheikh Farid is close to his contemporary West Asian Sufis. The overall sadness of Sheikh Farid's consciousness and his asceticism form quite a contrast to the exuberance of the Sikh Gurus who valued life and living. For the editor and compiler of the GGS, "spiritual liberation is attained in the midst of laughing, playing, dressing up, and eating" (GGS: 522). Whereas the mother's breasts flow with invigorating milk in the Sikh Gurus' poetry, they are withered and dried up in the Sufi master's hymn. Sheikh Farid's religious prescriptions, his rigorous asceticism, his intense anxiety in this world, his fear of judgment, and his eschatological perspectives are all so different from that of the Sikh Gurus. Yet they are consciously included in the Sikh sacred book with full acknowledgment of their distinctiveness and difference. There are even several scriptural instances where the Sikh Gurus (Nanak, Amar Das, and Arjan) directly respond to and enter dialogue with the Muslim Sheikh.[14] We have here a fine example of an active and meaningful engagement with diversity.

Similarly, we encounter Hindu holy men whose literary prism ushers readers into the Indic religious and cultural world. They view the Divine from their polyphonic Hindu imagination, and offer an entirely different hue and vibrancy. Since many of them were born in the lowest rung of society, they offer a compelling protest against the ancient caste system, untouchability, religious divisions, and basic human degradation. And each one of them is an exalted saint in the Sikh scripture. Bhagat Namdev, for instance, has sixty hymns in the GGS. Just a short hymn, "I Come to You," opens up a vast horizon of classical Indian literature, including the Puranas, the Mahabharata, and the Ramayana. The Hindu Bhagat begins by addressing Vishnu as his father, as the husband of goddess Laxmi, and as his long-haired, dark lover. Agape and Eros mingle in his sentiments, as does his imagery of Vishnu, Krishna, and Ram subsequently. We get to see the epic queen Draupadi in Duhshasana's court. We visit the sacred Hindu city of Kashi and the playful gardens of Brindaban. We meet with Mother Devaki. We receive glimpses into Hindu mythology with the world unfolding from a white lotus. We learn about Hindu rituals and the performance of the ancient Vedic Horse Sacrifice. We are introduced to Samkhya philosophy with Purusha's Maya manifesting herself. And we sumptuously hear Krishna's "blessed flute" that seduces each and all. But underlying the universe is the beat of that singular, formless (*nirguna*) Ram. Everything stationary, everything moving, be they worms or moths, humans or flowers, elephants or ants, their pulse resounds with that One. The formless is seen in myriad forms (*saguna*). The divine is the formless Ram; the divine is the dark, handsome, long-haired Krishna performing his dances and music.[15]

The Sikh Gurus did not propagate any theory of incarnation or any mythological notions of creation. In fact, the Japuji categorically states that the One cannot be installed into any form; no myth explains when or how creation came to be. Yet it was the pluralistic horizon of the Gurus that drew them to people holding worldviews different from their own. Guru Nanak acknowledges that there are "so many stories of Krishna — *ketia kanh kahania*" (GGS: 464). There is a genuine intention to know and interact with people of other faiths. Hindu poets like Namdev introduce the indigenous Indian past just as Sufi Sheikh Farid opens readers to the West Asian universe. If Namdev relates to the One in the form of Krishna or Ram, there was no reason to exclude him from the Sikh sacred text. Since nothing, nothing whatsoever, could be excluded from the Infinite One envisioned by the founder Sikh Guru, his fifth successor confidently included the multitude of concepts and images. Namdev's presence in the Sikh holy book highlights its inherent pluralism and offers a true understanding of "monotheism." This pluralistic model actually seeks to know and understand people of different religious perspectives, with the goal that its readers overcome any sense of alienation or hostility toward the *other*.

Guru Nanak's ecumenical vision continued to be crystallized by his nine successor Gurus. Guru Gobind Singh (1666–1708), the tenth and final human Guru, who made the sacred text the Guru forever, even imposed a moral obligation:

> *manas ki jat sabai ekai pahicanbo. . . .*
> *ek hi sarup sabai ekai jot janbo*
> (Akal Ustat: 85)

> Recognize: humanity is the only caste. . . .
> Know: we are all of the same body, the same light.

Guru Gobind Singh makes it a human responsibility to know (*janbo*) that we all have the same body (*ek hi sarup sabai*) and are formed of the same spiritual light (*ekai joti*). He acknowledges the vibrant diversity, and explained that differences happen to be an effect of our different geographical regions and cultural locales: "Different vestures from different countries may make us different; nevertheless, we have the same eyes, the same ears, the same body, the same voice—*niare niare desan ke bhes ko prabhao hai ekai nain ekai kan ekai deh ekai ban*" (Akal Ustat: 86). In spite of our differences, then, we must realize that we are all equally human and have the same biological and spiritual ingredients. We can hear an urgency in Guru Gobind Singh's tone as he voices the two imperatives *pahican-bo* (recognize) and *janbo* (know). He does not want his people to be threatened by the other or merely tolerant of one another; rather, a close look at the different features, complexions, accents, and textures of hair would only reveal our fundamental resemblance. In another popular verse Guru Gobind Singh declares:

> Hindus and Muslims are one!
> The same Reality is the creator and preserver of all;
> Know no distinctions between them.
> The monastery and the mosque are the same;
> So are the Hindu form of worship (*puja*)
>   and the Muslim prayer (*namaz*)
> Humans are all one!

During the horribly divisive moment in India's political and religious history, Mahatma Gandhi recalled the pluralistic message of the Sikh Gurus. The Mahatma had a moving public prayer that was recited by the masses. According to Sarvepalli Radhakrishnan (the famous philosopher who also was the first president of the Indian Republic), the Mahatma got it from the tenth Sikh Guru.[16] We can hear the above passage from Guru Gobind Singh echo in the Mahatma's public prayer:

> *Ishvara allah tere nama*
> *mandira masdija tere dhama*
> *sabko san-mati de bhagavan*
>
> Ishvar and Allah are your names
> Temples and mosques are your lodgings
> May God grant us all this wisdom!

Living in our twenty-first-century global village with neighbors who live and profess different faiths and convictions, the Sikh verses touch on some of our chords too. As we read the inclusive poetics, theoretical and doctrinal oppositions dissolve. The more that singular Being surfaces, the more "Islam," "Hinduism," "Sikhism" (and other such "isms") appear as artificial categories. The GGS challenges scholars and theologians to reconsider their neat divisions and systematizations that have been constructed too simplistically and held up all too dogmatically. Images and symbols from different religious and cultural backgrounds represent our human capacity for peace and love.

GENDER DIVERSITY

Throughout the Guru Granth, the male Gurus identify with the female person. The male poets put on her dress and her jewels, they perform her jobs, they emulate her feelings, and they think with her. Indeed, they are the "men who are capable of becoming woman" and carry us into Cixous's vast elsewheres.[17] In their case, the human does not stand for the male but actually includes both male and female. The language of the Sikh Gurus is gender-inclusive, for they experience the Divine from her female presence with their own flesh.

> To identify with someone in Freud's rich sense of the term is to merge not only with that person's mental or physical being. It is also to assimilate his or her corporeality in its full emotional resonance.[18]

This identification with the female has been a popular literary trope on the Indian subcontinent. Like the Sikh Gurus, the male Sufis and Hindu Bhagats abundantly appropriated the feminine tone, psyche, and syntax to express their spiritual yearning.[19] So pervasive is this motif that in Indian Sufism, the male devotee in classical Persian Sufi literature is recast as a female. But to literally see that poetic motif is quite something else! In a very early painting of Guru Nanak (1733), we come face to face with the Sikh founder conversing with the Sufi Sheikh Sharaf dressed up like a bride. In this visual narrative of a transvestite with the outward signifiers of feminine embellishment, clothing, and jewels, the socially constructed gender paradigms are boldly questioned.

The painting by Alam Chand Raj is from an early illustrated Sikh manuscript, the B-40 Janamsakhi.[20] The Sufi Master Sharaf lived two centuries before Guru Nanak, but his popularity in the Punjab continued on. In the illustration he is a young, black-bearded saint ornately dressed like a woman with all her feminine accoutrement. In both content and form, it is an intriguing scene. The background, with single-, double-, and some even triple-storied buildings, and a fluted dome reaching up into the skies, gives the impression of an urbanized Muslim town (identified as Baghdad in the text). The balconies and windows are intricately latticed, and the walls are decorated with colorful arabesques. Closer, we get a side view of a mosque set in a compound with its entrance opening up to the right. Against this backdrop charged with Islamic aesthetics, the blue-robed Guru and the bride-like bearded Sufi are having their own discourse. They are sitting across from each other on their knees on the green grass.

The B-40 text specifies that Sheikh Sharaf is wearing the conventional "sixteen" adornments, including henna, black collyrium on his eyes, and fancy garments, all very visible to the naked eye. The jewelry bedecking the saint's body is absolutely lovely. There is the marigold-shaped *binduli* ornament on the Sheikh's forehead, the pearl *mang* worn in the parting of his dark hair, and the marigold (matching the forehead ornament) *karn-phul* (ear flower) as a part of the pearl *khuntial* (earring tapering in shape). Around his neck is the *guluband*, a choker consisting of several rose-shaped buttons of gold strung onto silk, and the *har*, a necklace of strings of pearls that glides down to his waist. The Sheikh's crimson scarf embracing his bearded face and upper body is drawn back just enough to show his elaborate ornaments. His image may disturb some, but the Sikh Guru is utterly unruffled. Actually, nothing seems out of joint in this picture. The live marigolds and daisies are reproduced on the Sheikh's scarf and jewelry, creating an intimacy between his embodied self and surrounding nature. The overflowing artistic rhythm and the lack of anxiety on the Guru's face visually spell out the textual question: *"babe puchia sekha eh kia saang kita hai*—Baba asked the Sheikh, what is all this dressing up for?"

The image is fraught with the issues of sex and gender. Did the Sheikh see himself as a woman? Was his notion of the self feminine? Was he simply following a prescribed gender ideology, or was he in touch with his unique individuality? According to the text, the saint replies that he wanted to please God and did whatever he could to win him. The Guru then instructs that the Divine is won only with truth and adoring love. He does not put down the saint for cross-dressing. In fact, Guru Nanak respects him as he invites him to sing *ghazals* for which he was renowned, and the Sheikh acquiesces by singing beautifully on the theme of love. The Sheikh is praised for his talent; he is not discriminated against for breaking any gender codes. Guru Nanak looks upon him, and as the story ends, the Muslim saint's agony is transformed into bliss. That there be total synchronicity between the internal self and the external is the moral of the narrative—both in the text and in the pictorial rendition. Without the experience of authentic selfhood wearing too little or too much, dressing up in the masculine garb or the feminine is utterly futile. That the cross-dressed Muslim Sheikh felt elated testifies to his validation by the Sikh Guru. This painting has become popular with the group for lesbian, gay, bisexual, and transgendered Sikhs as visual evidence that the progressive Guru Nanak did not condemn cross-dressing or same-sex relationships.[21] He is seen promoting freedom to live according to one's own gender identities. Such scenes have great relevance, and if their visceral impact were to reach wider audiences, there could be a real shift in the oppressive paradigms dominating contemporary society.

VARIEGATED MULTIVERSE

From the Sikh perspective, this spectacular diversity—the variety of plants, animals, and microorganisms, the enormous diversity of genes in these species, the various elements, our different ecosystems, our planets, stars, galaxies, universes—are but manifestations of the infinite Divine that can never ever be fully fathomed or encompassed. Struck with wonder, "Nanak says, the singular Being spreads out in myriad forms—*anik bhant hoe pasaria nanak ekankar*" (GGS: 296). The Guru marvels, "You are One but your appearances are numerous—*ek tu hor ves bahutere*" (GGS: 357). The Divine, humans, and nature are united, for every bit animate and inanimate is made up of the same divine ingredient: "*sabh mahi joti joti hai soi tis kai canani sabh mahi cananu hoi*—there is a light in all and that light is you; by your light we all are lit" (GGS: 663). Again, we are told, "*ekeh ek bakhanano nanak ek anek*—Speak of only the One, says Nanak the One is the many" (GGS: 250), and yet again, "One only Is, numerous are the forms—*ekeh ap anekeh bhat*" (GGS: 238). Sikh scripture continuously resonates with Sally McFague's insight: "The natural world is not a single entity but a marvelously rich, multidimensional, diverse and intricate collection of lifeforms and things."[22]

Repeatedly, the GGS deflects individuals from attending to their narrow self to something far larger. Its opening hymn, the Japji, heightens our awareness of the beauty and vastness of the multiverse we live in. Recited in the morning, it reminds us of our human responsibilities in conjunction with the cosmic rhythms:

> *Rati ruti thiti var*
> *pavan pani agni patal*
> *tisu vici dharati thapi rakhi dharamsal* (GGS: 7)

> Amidst nights, seasons, solar and lunar days
> Amidst air, water, fire and netherworld
> The earth is placed, the place for righteous action.

Eternity is not chosen over temporality. Each one of our nights (*rati*) and seasons (*ruti*) and dates (*thiti*) and days (*var*) is revered because it makes us aware of both the lunar and solar cycles and the harmonious movements created by them. We can feel the billions and billions of years behind us and the billions and billions yet to come. Our daily calendars with their narrow standards of measurement acquire a much larger vista, opening us up to the wonderful patterns of our wide universe.

We also realize that we are made up of basic elements—air, water, fire, and earth—and all of their compounds. By expressing the physicality of our environment, Guru Nanak incites us to think about the miniscule atoms that make up our cosmos. His two short verses above inform us of the interdependence of all life, and of our own microcosmic and macrocosmic interrelationship. We are made up of the same stuff as the rest of our universe. It is all equally good. There is nothing in this world that is bad or polluted, for in another scriptural passage he declares, "The earth is not false; water is not false—*jhuth na dharti jhut na pani*" (GGS: 1240). Our intricate and profound mutuality is characterized by the Divine, who upholds each and all. Rather than whisk us away to a transcendent world out there, Sikh scripture brings us face to face with the concreteness and reality of the chemical, biological, and material shapes and forms around. "However many beings, these are all yours—*jete jia tete sabh tere*" (GGS: 193).

Within the vast temporal and spatial axes, the earth is firmly located: "*vic dharti thapi rakhi dharamsal*—The earth is set within, the home for righteous action." These cosmic descriptions place special possibilities and moral responsibilities. We share our cosmos with infinite species, and we must act in ways that are not divisive or endangering. Our locus is neither anthropocentric nor hierarchical. As the passage continues:

> *tisu vici jia jugati ke rang*
> *tin ke nam anek anant* (GGS: 7)

> Within this infinite matrix are myriads of species,
> Infinite are their names and forms.

Plurality and multiplicity depict this colorful and vibrant world. The Guru goes to great lengths to describe the vast (*baho*) variety (*baho*) of ways (*bidh*) and patterns (*bhanat*) in which this entire (*sabh*) creation (*sisat*) is designed (*saji*) and created (*upavani*) in such brilliant colors (*rang*) and hues (*parang*)—"*rang parang sisat sabh saji baho baho bidh bhnat upavani*— You created this multicolored world in many different ways, in many different forms" (GGS: 1314). But he adds that the brilliance of each and every color "sparkles by your light permeating all—*sabh teri jot joti vici vartai.*" The diversity is reflected in an infinite number of species (*ketia khani*), including those born from the egg (*andaj*), those born from the fetus (*jeraj*), those born from the sweat (*setaj*), and those born from the earth (*utbhuj*). In another exquisite verse, the Guru utters the magic and mystery of our earth and that of the myriad species: "*vismad dharti vismad khani*—Wonderful earth! Wonderful species!" (GGS: 464). Without any monopolization or manipulation, the innumerable organisms must coexist harmoniously with one another. Directly and boldly, Guru Nanak raises the imperative of ethical regard toward our entire cosmos. Life on earth demands that we free ourselves from the fetters of self-interest, and that we be morally obligated to all those who share with us our cosmic time and space. Only by expanding our tunnel vision can we learn to *act* virtuously and purposefully toward our larger "family." And so we make earth (*dharti*) our home of morality and righteousness (*dharamsal*).

With the singular Being enlivening each and every one of us, how can there can be any disjunctions or divisions of gender, race, or class? We humans are provided with equal opportunities. Guru Nanak categorically says that there is only one Dharam duty or morality, "*eko dharam drirhai sach koi*—Rare is the person who believes in the one religion" (GGS: 1188). The crucial pan-Indian term *dharam* (used for religion, virtue, duty, propriety, morality, cosmic order, and law) acquires a whole new meaning in Sikhism. Though *dharam* retains its Sanskrit etymology (from the root *dhr*, to sustain, uphold, support—shared with *dharti* or earth), it does not carry any of the conventional regulations. No action is singled out or reserved for anyone. There is no stipulation of gender roles in Sikh scripture in any of its 1,430 pages. Nowhere does it specify professions in accordance with injunctions of the traditional Indic texts. The Sikh Gurus do not prescribe the customary fourfold division of Hindu society into Brahmins, Ksatriyas, Vaisyas, and Sudras. Nor do they institute a division of the stages of life into that of *brahmacarin, grahastha, vanaprastha,* and *sanyasin (varnashrama-dharma)*. In contrast to the fourfold societal hierarchy and its corresponding privileges, duties, and responsibilities, Guru Nanak and his successor Gurus emphasize equality. Everyone— male and female—is equally impelled to perform their ethical duty throughout their entire life. While the Sikh community frequently cites the GGS for affirming the equality of the four castes, it tends to forget that their Gurus got rid of gender roles as well. They did away with the ancient Indic code of *patidharma* or *pativrata*—a woman's primary mode of religiosity as her worship *(dharma)* of her husband *(pati)*. They rejected the customs of *sati* (the widow having to die on the funeral pyre of her husband) and *purdah* (women having to veil themselves). They respected both male and female *bodies,* and I would say the GGS is unique in world scriptures in celebrating the centrality of menstrual blood (GGS: 1022; GGS: 706).[23] Unfortunately, such radical affirmations find no place in mainstream patriarchal hermeneutics.

The four castes are based on *varna* (which literally means color or complexion), and the Guru categorically states, *"khatri brahman sud vais, updes cahu varna ko sajha*—Be they Ksatriyas, Brahmins, Sudras or Vaishyas, the message is shared by people of all complexions" (GGS: 747). "Complexion" is very relevant today, for though castes may seem of the past, color and race are vitally important issues that we still need to face. So the message, according to Guru Nanak, is shared not just by people of the four castes but includes people of all colors. The Guru Granth declares that *Dharam* succeeds when the entire earth becomes equal, literally one color: *"sristi sabh ikk varan hoi"* (GGS: 663). However, that is not to evade difference and diversity, for the Japji celebrates a multiplicity of cultures and languages *(ketia bani)*, a variety of political structures—the kings *(pat)* and rulers *(narind)*. Hierarchies and divisions have no place, and no one species or language or culture or country is put up higher than another. The GGS verses incite us to imagine, produce, and perpetuate a world full of fascinating differences, without social discriminations, cultural dominations, and imperial oppressions.

Like the Japji, the evening hymn Arati celebrates the cosmic choreography of the planets, and as it emotionally widens the inner circuits, it connects readers with one another across cultures and religions. Hindu,

Muslim, Sikh, Jewish or Christian, everybody is invited to worship that transcendent One:

> The sky is our platter; the sun and moon, lamps,
>   it is studded with pearls, the starry galaxies,
> The wafting scent of sandalwood is the incense,
>   the gentle breeze, our fly whisk,
> All vegetation, the bouquet of flowers we offer to you.
>   What a worship!
> This truly is your worship, you who sunder life from death.
>   The unstruck sound in us is the drum to which we chant. (GGS: 663)

The magic of infinity has tremendous physiological impact: it releases anger, jealousy, hatred, and other such poisonous stuff. Though universal, the GGS lyrics provide us with an outlook on particular social, economic, political, and religious problems that may arise at any historical moment. They come with an aesthetic energy crucial in shaping our worldviews, attitudes, and behavior. The rich plurality of images reaches into the visceral hub where dictatorial rules and regulations never quite make it. The mystery and thrill of reading scripture inspires us to fight the "isms" around us—be they racism, classism, sexism, or religious fundamentalism.

From beginning to end, the GGS serves as a powerful antidote to any divisive rhetoric. It is indeed hard to fathom what the ears of Wade Page were hearing as he rampaged with his gun shooting worshippers during the recitation of the GGS at the Oak Creek Gurdwara! He was musically attuned, but his "hatecore" music with his white racist band, the Blue Eyed Devils, had made him deaf to the music of a "mud-colored" race. In contrast to the hatred and divisions promoted by Mr. Wade's band, the GGS lyrics produce positive energy within the individual. Opposite to his racist ideology that divides humans into separate and exclusive biological entities, the GGS promotes the feel for the singular Infinite Creator, generating acts of love and compassion toward all siblings in the world.

Once we recognize that the Divine is diversity and justice, we will viscerally experience the ontological continuity between that One, our society, and nature. In this mode of being, we realize our interconnections and interdependence and value every bit of our marvelous multiverse. We will reflect on the mystery of the Divine present in this infinite diversity of ours and work to create equality and justice for everyone. We will take constructive steps to conserve biodiversity. Only when we get a real feel for that *oneness* we all share will we implement our social, political, economic, and environmental policies. The thought of the transcendent Divine permeating our multiverse energizes us to work for equality, health care, education, our ecosystem, and justice for each and all.

NOTES

1. Mark Juergensmeyer, "The Forgotten Tradition in World Religions," in *Sikh Studies: Comparative Perspectives on a Changing Tradition: Working Papers from the Berkeley Conference on Sikh Studies*, ed. M. Juergensmeyer and N. G. Barrier (Berkeley: Graduate Theological Union, 1979).

2. Wendy Doniger, "Sita and Helen, Ahalya and Alemena: A Comparative Study," *History of Religions* 37, no. 1 (August 1997), 97.

3. Mary Daly, *Beyond God the Father: Toward a Philosophy of Women's Liberation* (Boston: Beacon, 1985), 33–40.

4. George Pattison, *God and Being: An Enquiry* (Oxford: Oxford University Press, 2011), 6.

5. Sallie McFague, *Super, Natural Christians: How We Should Love Nature* (Minneapolis: Fortress, 1997), 172.

6. Gurinder Singh Mann, *The Making of Sikh Scripture* (New York: Oxford University Press, 2001), 101.

7. Arvind Mandair, *Religion and Specter of the West* (New York: Columbia University Press, 2009).

8. G. S. Talib, *Sri Guru Granth Sahib: In English Translation*, vol. 3 (Patiala: Punjabi University, 1987), 2098: "In each being's heart pervasive. . . ." See also Gopal Singh, *Sri Guru Granth Sahib: English Version*, vol. 4 (Chandigarh: World Sikh University Press, 1978), 979: "And he pervaded the hearts of all."

9. *Sabdarath Sri Guru Granth Sahib*, vol. 3 (Amritsar: Shromani Gurdwara Prabandhak Committee, 1964), 1026.

10. See http://www.gurbani.org, which for the most part is very thorough and accessible. Nevertheless, this translation uses "belly" for "womb" on page 1026.

11. H. Cixous and C. Clement, *The Newly Born Woman*, trans. B. Wing (Minneapolis: University of Minnesota Press, 1986), 93.

12. Luce Irigaray, *Sexes and Genealogies*, trans. G. Gill (New York: Columbia University Press, 1993), 18.

13. Silvia Schroer and Sophia Bietenhard (eds.), *Feminist Interpretation of the Bible and the Hermeneutics of Liberation* (Sheffield, England: Sheffield Academic Press, 2003), 33.

14. Pashaura Singh, *The Bhagats of the Guru Granth Sahib* (New Delhi: Oxford University Press, 2003), 54–73.

15. Nikky-Guninder Kaur Singh, *Of Sacred and Secular Desire: An Anthology of Lyrical Writings from the Punjab* (London: IB Tauris, 2012), 59–63.

16. Dr. Sarvepalli Radhakrishnan, *The Principal Upanishads* (London: George Allen and Unwin, 1953), 139.

17. Cixous and Clement, *The Newly Born Woman*, 98.

18. Cited in Janet Gyatso (ed.), *In the Mirror of Memory: Reflections on Mindfullness and Remembrance in Indian and Tibetan Buddhism* (Albany: State University of New York Press, 1992), 229.

19. Of course, some feminists may object to the longing bride as a model. They might see an inherent dualism in the relation between the bride and her groom, and the role of the bride seeking her beloved may be viewed as restrictive and stifling. In this case we must remember that it emerged in Sikh literature at a point in time and space when the Indian woman was humiliatingly subjugated, so to see *her* as the paragon of physical and spiritual refinement, and hear *her* desire being expressed, is significant. For details, see Nikky-Guninder Kaur Singh, "The Bride Seeks Her Groom: An Epiphany of Interconnections," in *Feminine Principle in the Sikh Vision of the Transcendent* (Cambridge: Cambridge University Press, 1993).

20. The B-40 is considered to be very important because it has extensive historical documentation. For more details, see Nikky-Guninder Kaur Singh, "Corporeal Metaphysics: Guru Nanak in Early Sikh Art," *History of Religions* (forthcoming in 2013).

21. Visit www.sarbat.net/nanak-b40janamsakhi.htm [accessed December 6, 2012].

22. McFague, *Super, Natural Christians*, 173.

23. Nikky-Guninder Kaur Singh, "Sacred Fabric and Sacred Stitches: The Underwear of the Khalsa," *History of Religions* 43, no. 4 (May 2004): 284–302.

TWO

As Long as You Are Doing Something

A Secular Feminist Perspective from Canada

Pamela Milne

On December 8, 2011, Susanne Scholz (S2) interviewed Pamela Milne (PM) on the phone about her views on the slogan "God loves diversity and justice." The following is an edited version of their conversation.

S2: Thanks so much, Pam, for taking the time to speak with me about "God loves diversity and justice" and to share your thoughts about this theological slogan from your secular, feminist, Canadian perspective. Is this slogan an anathema for someone with your convictions, and if so, how so?

PM: Well, the slogan "God loves diversity and justice" cannot really be an "anathema" because the word itself comes from a church context and it means a formal ecclesiastical ban or curse. Hence, on that ground alone it is not the way I think about the slogan. I know we use the term more generally nowadays to refer to something that is intensely disliked or detested. I would not deal with the slogan in that way. I do not detest the slogan. Instead, I am inclined to say that it puzzles me because when I hear a slogan like that within my secular context, it is hard to have a sense of its meaningfulness. The reason for that is that, as a secularist, I do not think of "God" as an extent reality, as an entity, something out there. I am an agnostic, not an atheist, because it does not seem productive to argue against the existence of something whose existence can only be claimed or hypothesized in the first place. So it is a pragmatic decision for me. And therefore a statement like "God loves diversity and justice" on one level is no different from a statement like "God hates homosexuals." From my perspective such a statement reflects the deity construct of the person who is making the claim. In other words, it does not tell me anything about the nature of a divine entity: it only tells me something about the thought patterns and values of the person making the claim. When someone makes a claim about the nature of a deity, I take that as an interpretive signal about the religious views of the person I am dealing with. For instance, if somebody is holding up a sign in front of an abortion clinic that says "God hates abortion" or picketing a funeral of a gay or lesbian person with a sign saying "God hates homosexuality," I draw some inferences about the values this person holds and how she or he understands a given religious tradition. But I do not draw any inferences about any divine entity.

S2: In other words, you do not draw any inferences that this statement says anything about God but rather about the human person who is using this kind of language.

PM: Exactly, because I do not think there is an entity out there called "God" about whom we could know anything. As an agnostic, I do not try to argue that there is no deity, but if there is I do not think we could really know anything about it or would be capable of grasping its nature. The concept of the universe just blows me away. The notion of the universe is beyond most people's grasp so if there is a divine entity, it should be even more unfathomable than that. If there is a divine entity, I sure would want it to be much more than any human could imagine or that human language could express. So I do not spend a lot of time thinking about deities or divinities because anything that is said about a deity is said from the human perspective. Our notions of the divine are just that: human constructs.

S2: So when you hear this slogan you basically get stuck at the very first word, "God."

PM: Right. I do not think we can know anything about a deity. Any descriptions we have in written religious texts like Bibles or Qur'ans are some human's ideas about a divine entity. I see religions and ideas about deities as social constructs. They are ideas that people construct and then they use those constructs to shape and guide their lives. Now, for some people, religious constructs are really helpful. It helps them get through daily life and any adversity that they might face. That is usually a benign function of religion as a social construct. Religions are just one among many social constructs we find in societies. Every social institution from education to politics is a social construct and reflects the values of those doing the construction. Institutional constructs are useful and necessary, but they change as the values change upon which they are based. Religions are somewhat different in this respect. Generally, people claim authoritative status for their religion. That is also a social construct. People make religion authoritative. The problem is that people, most often men, have constructed religious systems and deities that are reflections of themselves and their value systems. Then they use those constructs to authorize and justify their own actions, to present themselves as enacting a divine will and as being a reflection of the image of the deity. And for many religions that are text based, the men who constructed those texts lived a very long time ago so their ideas are not only gender specific but also culture and time limited.

S2: Do you then mean that the slogan "God loves diversity and justice" is indefensible for secular people living in contemporary Western and non-Western societies? How can Western secularized societies assert any ethical position about justice and diversity if they cannot say that "God" is on their side?

PM: Yes, that is what I am getting at. People make up or create religions, they construct them. They construct deities and then use those constructs to give weight to the position they argue. This is where Mary Daly really was so insightful when she said that "if God is male, then the male is God."[1] For me, this is a powerful insight, especially when we think of the Western religious traditions, though I am sure the Eastern ones have similar problems. The gods worshipped in these religions are created in the image and likeness of their male founders and developers and are limited by the limitations of those men. And so anything that is said about a deity can only be said from the human perspective.

Now when I hear a slogan such as "God loves diversity and justice," I think firstly that the person using the slogan images the deity as male because the word "god" is marked for grammatical gender. This is why English also has the word "goddess." Most people are so conditioned to the maleness of the deity image they are not conscious of the masculine form of the word, "god." Secondly, I think that the person using the slogan is probably drawing her or his notion of the deity from a range of sources, not just from one religious text like a Bible. Their deity concept is probably influenced by Western philosophical traditions from the Greeks, along with the person's own ideas about whatever deity they worship. Thus, if you get ten people saying the slogan, they probably have ten different constructs of what the deity is. Thirdly, the qualifying phrase of the slogan, "loves diversity and justice," does not really tell me anything tangible about a deity. Rather it suggests to me that the person who utters the slogan has a commitment to diversity and justice and, therefore, might be a social justice advocate.

S2: So in your view, the slogan does not tell us anything about the deity and everything is a human construct, whether you affirm this slogan or rail about homosexuality and abortion. However, if somebody asserts that "God loves diversity and justice," do you not expect this person to be less exclusionary, harmful, or hateful than somebody objecting to homosexuality?

PM: Yes, of course. The person who claims the deity hates things like homosexuality or abortion is going to be a person who opposes these things and projects those views onto the notion of the deity. Both sloganeers could be coming from the same religious tradition. They could both claim to be Christian or Jewish or Muslim, for example, and could be drawing on the same heritage. And both may have particular parts of that heritage that validate their views. This is exactly why it is so problematic to use religious texts such as Bibles authoritatively. Religious texts, like the Bible, are written over long periods of time by many different authors and are multi-voiced; they incorporate many perspectives. Even the Qur'an has the Mecca and Medina verses that seem to reflect different perspectives on social issues. People can, and have, been able to find material in religious texts to support views ranging from one end of the spectrum to the other on virtually every moral issue. Everybody can find something useful to support their opinion. If you want to promote slavery, that can easily be done on the basis of the Bible, since there are no biblical passages in which the deity condemns slavery as a practice or institution. In fact, up to the twentieth century, the Christian Bible was a useful document for people in South Africa wanting to justify apartheid and prior to that it was a useful text for whites in the United States to uphold the slave trade. The problem with a text like the Bible is that it can be used in many different ways and for many different positions. This is possible because it reflects the cultural values of the times and places from which it emerged. Since slavery was an acceptable social institution throughout the entire period during which the Jewish and Christian scriptures were composed, neither the Jewish Bible nor the Christian Bible critiques or condemns this practice. However, if we had a text that did not have any negative bias toward slaves, women, or outsider groups like "gentiles" or pagans, a text that was completely positive toward all those groups, such a text could not be used credibly to justify harassing, discriminating against, or even killing persons in such groups.

There are scholars who maintain that meaning resides completely in the reader and readers construct textual meaning.[2] This, however, is not my position. I think there is always an interaction between a text and a reader.[3] A competent reader constructs meaning from data in the text itself. A reading that is not supported by any data in the text cannot, in my view, be deemed competent. Thus, to me, both the reader and the text are accountable for meaning and, hence, the Bible has to be held accountable for its negative material that is still used by readers to promote such things as slavery or the idea that women are inferior to men or that one group of people is "chosen" over another.

Because the Bible is a canonical text its negative material cannot be simply eliminated. When there were laws in our countries that said it was legal to own slaves or that women were property not persons, those laws could be changed. Once our ideas evolved to a point that we came to think that owning other human beings as slaves or that treating women as property was unethical, we could do away with that law. But in an authoritative collection, like the biblical tradition, which has no problem at all with one set of humans owning another set of humans as a slave or with treating women as property and regarding them as inferior to men, one cannot simply change the text. This is the problem with a canonical text. When some people read it as authoritative, they can and do use it to justify practices and views that the modern world generally regards as unethical.

S2: Since people justify their positions with the Bible and you will not get rid of this text any time soon, is your solution to study this dynamic so that people at least know what they are doing when they are doing it?

PM: My strategy is to expose and critique the material in the Bible that I regard as unethical and unacceptable in the modern world. Most people have no idea about the content of the Bible. They generally think it is a benign book, "the good book," and many are shocked to learn what it contains. For example, when the Religious Studies Department at the University of Windsor was disbanded in 1996, a course I had been teaching on women and the Bible[4] was moved into the Women's Studies Program. This change of locale has made a considerable difference to teaching this course. Since then I have taught mainly feminist students, many of whom do not have any particular connection to religion. Some of them are hostile to religion, as many feminists understand, and in my view rightly so, that religion has been a bastion of male dominance. Religion has been one of the weapons used habitually and consistently against women for centuries. Most students, taking this course on women and the Bible as a women's studies course, have never read the Bible or any scholarly materials related to it. When they read the biblical passages assigned for the weekly seminars, they see some of the horrific stuff that it says about women. They also learn strategies for analyzing such texts, for identifying what problems the texts present for feminist readers and for dealing with them. The goal is to prepare students to go out into the world as feminists, where they will encounter such texts as being used to denigrate people or to deny them full human rights because they are women, or gay/lesbian, or not Christian.

Recently, we have had public debates in Canada on issues such as same-sex marriage during which religious conservatives trotted out Bible-based arguments in an attempt to stop legal recognition of same-sex marriage. My aim is to prepare my feminist students in such a way that they can participate in these debates and provide feminist responses to these uses of biblical materials. My students will have analytical tools for doing that. They can make the argument that a particular biblical concept or view ought to be irrelevant in a modern secular society. If people want to hold those views personally and privately, that is one thing, but they ought not to impose them on a secular society.

Hence, my task is to expose the problems and deficiencies that are in the biblical texts and to show that archaic texts like Bibles are inadequate and unacceptable ethical documents today. They are simply not up to modern standards. David Clines[5] points out that gender equality is fundamental to the modern world but this idea does not even exist in the Bible. There, women are property and not fully human. They are a subset of man, which is, or at least should be, an unacceptable view in the modern world. The problem for people who want to stay in the tradition is how to navigate the out-of-date and horrific ideas encapsulated in a text that is regarded as sacred.[6] Of course, the text itself is not sacred. People regard the text as sacred, and because they regard it as sacred, they use it as a form of power. Ultimately, this is what it comes down to: power. One slogan or another does not make a difference. The difference lies in the power of those who use a particular slogan for good or for bad.

S2: So how do you deal with religious fundamentalism then?

PM: Fundamentalism is, of course, an American invention given to the world.[7] Karen Armstrong defines it as a "global response to modern culture."[8] The Fundamentalism Project at the University of Chicago[9] provided much insight into this worldwide phenomenon. The Fundamentalism Project also identified a number of defining charac-

teristics, the first and most important one is reactivity.[10] Fundamentalism arose in the early twentieth century in the United States as a
reaction to scientific and secular modernism, including modern biblical criticism. Fundamentalists see the secular state as an enemy that
has intruded into all spheres including education, family affairs, and
religious practices. They see progressive forms of religion as having
been corrupted by liberalism and secularism. Another significant
characteristic of such movements is that they adhere to elaborate be-
havioral requirements and clear gender (and sometimes racial) hierarchies.[11]

Overall, fundamentalists represent a fairly small proportion of people
in North American societies and certainly in European societies. There
may be some societies in which they are more prevalent, but the key
issue is how much power they exert. For years, ultra-orthodox Jews in
Israel have exerted political power far in excess of their numbers. Very
recently, we have seen how they have expanded their power by pro-
jecting their views about the inferiority of women onto the wider society in Israel. If they have their way, women will be excluded from the
public sphere, restricted to the back of the bus, limited in how they
dress and their access to education. The recent harassment of an eight-
year-old girl on her way to school in Beit Shemesh highlights the
problematic use of religious traditions in a modern, presumably secular, society.[12] It is not enough for those ultra-orthodox men to practice
religion in their own way among themselves; their goal is to impose
their archaic views on everyone in the country. Secular and moderate
religious Israelis will have to address this challenge head on. When
the Israeli Supreme Court bowed to the pressure of the religious right
in 2003 and denied women the right to worship with a Torah scroll at
the Western Wall, it sent a disturbing message about the power of
religious extremism. It also promoted discrimination. Little wonder
the battle has escalated to a more wide-scale effort of restricting wom-
en's freedom.

If one looks at what has happened in the United States in the twentieth century, one sees fundamentalists trying to find ways to get power. Nancy Ammeran's article in the first volume of the Fundamentalism Project drove home to me the point that the history of fundamentalism in the United States and Canada is really a history of male
power struggles.[13] Fundamentalisms provided arenas of power to
marginalized, elite men who otherwise would not have held power in
mainstream society. The first strategy was to drop out of normative
society and to form separate communities. They also attacked public
education and promoted the home schooling movement. By the mid-
1970s, when these strategies had not attracted large numbers of peo-

ple, they tried a different approach. They promoted the idea that the United States should be a Christian nation and, as such, its military and economic power would guarantee their ability to evangelize the world. They began rubbing shoulders with influential politicians and having breakfast with presidents. Groups like the Moral Majority were instrumental in defeating the Equal Rights Amendment in the United States. So this approach has had some degree of success but not as much as they wanted. Nowadays they seem to pursue the strategy of running for political offices at all levels. In the long run, it will depend on whether secularists and people who think their deity loves justice and diversity will exert more power in society than people who think that their god hates Muslims, Jews, and homosexuals. It has come down to this. That is where it becomes meaningful to me.

S2: One could argue that within some religious traditions, at least those that align themselves with the Bible, always contained some groups that tried to work toward progressive causes. Think, for instance, about liberation theologians aligning themselves with the poor and oppressed in Latin America.

PM: Yes, also think of the Quakers and the Unitarian Universalists. Certainly you can see fringe groups like that taking a lead on social justice issues and using their religious traditions to bolster that position.

S2: Yes, there are such groups throughout history. Think about the earliest Christian groups prior to Constantinian Christianity whom we call "heretics" today, or the radical wing of the Protestant Reformation movement, led by theologians such as Thomas Müntzer in Germany. Some groups always tried to stay within their religious tradition and to nurture, develop, and empower liberatory and egalitarian principles in their respective societies. But they do not convince you as a secular thinker?

PM: The point is that such groups were regarded as "heretical" or "radical" and not mainstream in their religion. They lost in the power game. The existence of factions like these does not convince me that religion is necessary or essential in the struggle for social justice. The progressives and radicals constructed religion in a selective way, like anybody else, so you have a whole range of how religious positions are defined. Some of the fiercest and most vicious battles take place among groups within the same religion. All of them claim to use the same tradition. It depends on which part of the tradition they choose to emphasize. For me, therefore, it is not terribly reassuring that there are people within a religion that find liberatory or egalitarian principles in it. I am glad they do, but their views do not necessarily protect me from fundamentalists. From a feminist perspective, the Western religious traditions have been used far more often to bring harm to women, for example, than good. And the places in the world today where women have the fewest human rights are typically places with "religious" governments. The places where women have greater human rights tend to be strong secular societies. That is not to say that there have been no religiously committed people advocating gender, racial, or sexual orientation equalities. It is to say that such equality is much more likely to be safeguarded by secular law than by religious law.

Marieme Hélie Lucas has argued that the most serious human rights violations committed nowadays are done, not by states, but by fundamentalist movements. She argues that it is important to recognize these movements as political in nature, not simply religious. The failure to understand this will have major negative consequences for human rights and democracy, including the erosion of secular space and gender apartheid.[14]

The guarantee of equality and just treatment under the law does not depend on religion but on democratic society. The problem for me with text-based traditions, such as Western religions, is that the texts are frozen in time. They are traditions constructed by people in antiquity that are removed from us in time, custom, and place. Their notions of justice or diversity are limited by those times and places. Therefore, they cannot be completely functional and must be corrected and supplemented. That is what people have to do when they want to stay connected to such traditions. Modern societies developed beyond the base of what is contained in these texts. The texts weigh them down because they include some really negative materials which cannot be simply cut out and be forgotten.

The early work by liberation theologians, for instance, was pretty good in identifying issues of poverty and oppression but, for the most part, these male liberation theologians were blind to the gendered nature of those issues. It took feminist theologians, like Letty Russell[15] and Rosemary Radford Ruether, to point out this shortcoming.[16] But theologians like Ruether, for example, often relied on general notions of biblical prophecy without recognizing the horrific images and ideologies about women encoded in the prophetic books. The feminist critique, too, used biblical material selectively. The problem is that opponents of liberation theologies have used the Bible just as selectively, and if they have more power, they do more damage.

Hence, for me, the concept of justice is something that evolves over time. The contemporary understanding of justice is much wider and deeper than the biblical notion. Therefore, we have to have texts that are better than the biblical traditions. For me, the Universal Declaration of Human Rights is such a "better" text. It is far less ambiguous than the Bible or Qu'ran. It is clear cut in what it calls for in terms of treating all people in fair and equitable ways. It recognizes that rights are only as strong as the society that supports them.

S2: There is, of course, a critique of the notion of rights as a Western, individualistic construct.[17]

PM: Although I do not know the details of this discussion, I would stress that there are different ways of understanding it. There is certainly an interesting difference between the way "rights" are understood in Canada compared to the United States. In Canada we have, in the past, put much more emphasis on group rights than in the United States where there is considerable emphasis on individual rights to the negation of the group. The legal system in the United States seems to understand rights in the context of formal equality whereas in Canada we do not think that formal equality is adequate to protect human rights. We tend to emphasize substantive equality under the law. Substantive equality means that it is necessary to take into account differences to be equitable. For example, with respect to birth, our system has long recognized that childbirth has a different impact on women and men and hence, for women to have equitable access to employment, they need paid maternity leaves. In the United States a formal equality argument would say that if you deny maternity leave to a man, then it is okay to deny it to a woman, despite the substantive difference. After all, only a woman gives birth. Hence, in Canada we recognize that women's bodies are different from men's bodies, and so we treat women as a group differently from men as a group in some situations. Canadian law recognizes that the same treatment of men and women does not always produce justice and equality. Hence, we take group rights into account as well. This notion is also expressed in our federal employment equity legislation that pertains to the rights of four designated groups: women, minorities, aboriginal peoples, and persons with disabilities.

In the United States, individualism is stressed much more than in Canada. Also in the United States the idea of a "melting pot" is predominant. This notion suggests that everybody ought to melt into some amorphous "American" society. In Canada we think of diversity as a mosaic and people are encouraged to celebrate their cultures and contribute them to create a diverse and multifaceted society. We value that much more than in the United States, I think. Hence, even concepts, such as diversity, equity, or justice, evolve with time and may differ from place to place.

With respect to the idea of justice in the Bible, Job had it right: God is not just. We cannot attribute characteristics like that to a deity. Justice is a human responsibility. I do not need to appeal to a deity to act in an ethical way; it is my human responsibility. I do not have to have a god on my side. I need to try to understand how we have come to think about justice and use tools like the Universal Declaration of Human Rights or the human rights codes developed by secular societies. But then, as a citizen within a society, I have the responsibility to make sure that the governments we put in place respect those kinds of documents.

For me, one of the distressing things today is seeing Canada leaning more and more toward American models. Our current prime minister, Stephen Harper, is closer to the religious right than any other prime minister we ever had. Although he speaks little of his personal beliefs, he attends an evangelical Christian and Missionary Alliance Church. The foundational views of that church include such things as an emphasis on personal salvation, opposition to abortion, homosexuality, and women clergy.[18] The political party Harper leads used to be called the Progressive Conservative Party but it dropped the word "progressive" when it merged with the Canadian Reform Conservative Alliance, a party heavily influenced by right-wing Christians in 2004. Indeed, Harper's Conservative Party and government are now anything but progressive. Social justice concerns seem to have disappeared from the government's priorities, and women and minorities are feeling the impact most strongly. Human rights organizations and women's rights advocacy groups have been dramatically defunded. The long gun registry, legislation enacted after the murder of fourteen women at the École Polytechnique in Montreal on December 6, 1989, has been dismantled.[19] Under the Harper Christian-influenced regime, Canada has slipped from the seventh to the twenty-fifth position on the World Economic Forum gender gap index.[20]

Overall, I fear we in Canada are moving backward, away from social justice. People like Tommy Douglas, an ordained Christian minister who did much to advanced social justice in the mid-twentieth century, seem harder to find in Canadian politics today.[21] My point is that even though religious conservatives and fundamentalists are a very small part of our population, they have a significant influence on the shape of our society. Their influence does not take us toward greater social justice but drags us back to an archaic, inadequate, inequitable biblical model. On a political and social level, religion is negatively impacting the lives of women, LGBTQ persons, racial and ethnic minorities, first nations, and persons with disabilities, while it benefits white male heterosexual conservative Christians.

S2: Do you not think the notion of social justice is very Western, Jewish, and Christian? Sometimes I wonder if this idea of social justice has also developed in what we usually classify as Eastern religious traditions. Some people make the claim "justice" is a deeply Jewish concept that the Christian and Muslim traditions adopted later.

PM: Quite frankly, I do not think any ancient religion has an adequately developed notion of social justice. I think democracy has developed the notion beyond what it is in any of the world religions. Another problem I have with Western religions is that their model of "god" is monarchical. Therefore, you get images of god as king, lord, and Christ the king. Monarchy is based on hierarchy, and hierarchy is embedded in Western religions. In the Hebrew Bible, you find the Hosea/Gomer-YHWH/Israel marriage model that also carries over into the Christian Christ/church model. The early Christian Church adopted the hierarchical patriarchal household as its institutional model. These models are not models of equality or social justice. Just as Israel or the Church are never construed as the equals of YHWH or Christ, so wives can never be equal to husbands or women equal to men in the church. So the religions themselves are predicated on a hierarchical and monarchical model which goes against the move toward democracy. It should be a democratic principle to promote social justice, to make sure that every person has access to food, housing, and sustainable employment.

In Canada, we still have a relatively good social safety net, although it is being gradually eroded. The gap between the rich and the poor is not as bad here as it is in the United States, but it is growing. Ultimately, when this gap gets to a certain point, it will lead to social revolution. The Occupy Wall Street movement is a sign of growing discontent. Right now, the occupiers do not have enough power, but the gap between rich and poor is alarming in the United States. The wealthiest 1 percent currently owns 40 percent of the wealth of the nation. As that gap increases, there will be a tipping point. Joseph Stiglitz, former chief economist of the World Bank, draws on Alexis de Tocqueville's observation that a key part of the genius of American society is the notion of "self-interest properly understood." The last two words are the important ones. Stiglitz comments that "paying attention to everyone else's self-interest—in other words, the common welfare—is in fact a precondition for one's own ultimate well-being. . . . Throughout history, this is something that the top 1 percent eventually do learn. Too late."[22]

One of the problems I find with the biblical tradition is that any social justice material appears in the context of hierarchical ideas. In addition to the acceptance of monarchy as the normative divine/political model, there are other problematic ideas. For example, the notion that the first will be last and the last will be first is troubling (Matt. 19:30). This apocalyptic text does not imagine the first and the last walking side by side. Instead, it imagines an overturning: the top will be at the bottom and the bottom will be at the top. Is this really a model that we want for our society? For me, it is not the model. I believe we have much to learn from neo-paganism and First Nations' spiritual traditions. Their paths appear as better, more just, and responsible paths to me because they see humans as part of the web of life and interdependent on all the other parts of the world. They do not see humans as above other creatures. They see themselves as dependent on the land and they respect all creatures and nature. Yes, they ought to teach the rest of us. Not grounded in a hierarchical model, their spirituality is much more equitable than the Western ones. A sense of balance and harmony, two key concepts, permeate these religious traditions.

S2: As a secular scholar of religion, why do you think people are so resistant to these ideas of secularism?

PM: I am not sure people are resistant to secular ideas. I observe that religion is becoming less relevant, in our parts of the world at least. I think many people are *de facto* secularists even if they do not think of themselves that way. Many people only nominally identify as part of a religious group. Religious pluralism is becoming a fact of life. For instance, with the spread of Islam we have to start thinking about the privileged position Christianity has been given in our societies. What would happen if Islam were to become the dominant religion in Canada or the United States? Would conservative Christians still insist that the dominant religion occupy a privileged position in society? Would they be happy to function as a minority in an Islamic nation under god? Or would it not be better for everyone to have a society that is completely secular?

S2: I would disagree a little bit that people are less and less interested in religion in Western countries. For instance, there are many new-age kind of spiritualities. I see a lot of the same problems happening there as in established religious life. It is an individualized, sentimentalized, privatized, and superficial approach to religion and faith. I find some of these forms of spiritual practices that claim to be detached from politics and society irritating, but they are quite popular in Western societies in Europe and North America today.

PM: This may well be true but there are many pagan and neo-pagan practitioners such as Starhawk, for whom spirituality and social activism are integrally related.[23] Their advantage is that they are not burdened by an ancient canonical text against which they struggle to link their spirituality and their understanding of social justice. The key thing, in my view, is what you do in the world. I do not really care what motivates you. If you are a progressive Christian and that motivates you to donate money to a women's shelter, to pressure governments to extend equality to gays and lesbians, or to make sure people are fed and clothed, that is fine with me. To me, action is the important thing. Just so long as you do not make adopting your particular brand of religion the criterion for receiving the benefits of your social action. What motivates you to do social justice work is less important to me. The spiritual values you choose are your decisions, decisions you make about how you lead your life. I just think the majority of people in North America are not very formally attached to Christianity and Judaism. Islam may still be different, although as mosque culture becomes more regressive, many Muslim women are becoming "unmosqued."[24] And there is undoubtedly more religious attachment among Americans than among Canadians. Certainly, within Christianity, many people are nominally Christian but not really practicing their faith. I do not think they know what secularism means.

But they want a government that is competent, fair, and accountable. If a prime minister or president is a Roman Catholic, most people would find it unacceptable to make canon law or many of the teachings of that church the laws of the nations. People get that part quite well: they generally buy into the notion of "church-state separation." But do they understand what constitutes a secular approach? They do not think much about it or spend a lot of time thinking about whether or not a deity exists. It is a comfortable position to believe there is a deity and a place called heaven to go to when you die. Religion as a social construct helps us deal with the uncomfortable things in life, and the most uncomfortable thing about life is that it ends in death. So, all religions give us some way of thinking that death is not death. For Christianity, it is resurrection. For Judaism, it is your offspring and future generations, and for Hindu traditions, it is the idea of reincarnation. Yet many religions, including the Western ones, expect an end time when a judgment day will right the wrongs in the world. To some extent this idea detracts from dealing with the world today.

S2: Of course, there are many Christians in non-Western countries. Christianity is flourishing in Asia and Africa. For instance, there are more than eighty million Chinese Christians. One can hardly say that Christianity is merely a Western religion at this point.

PM: It is categorized as one of the three Western religions in contrast with Eastern religions like Hinduism or Buddhism and I was using the term "Western" in that sense, not as an indicator of where it is practiced today. Because it is evangelical by nature, Christianity is obviously a world religion. The same is true for Islam. I mean "Western" in the sense that these religions derive from the same roots in the ancient Near East. You are right: Christianity is flourishing in Africa and Asia while to some extent it is disintegrating in Europe and North America. Religions evolve over time. Because they are social constructs, they have a beginning, they develop and change over time, and sometimes they have an end, not just the apocalyptic end they may be looking for. But when they have a canonical foundational text such as the Bible, this text remains frozen in the past and does not evolve over time. Some people ignore the problematic parts of the text and they remain comfortably within the religion. Other people, seeing the limitations of the canonical text that cannot be expanded, abandon their religion. Christianity may be flourishing precisely in areas where human rights are not as advanced as they are in Europe or North America. Hence, Christian teachings may look like a step forward in their context whereas, in other contexts, Christian textual traditions appear outdated because they promote unacceptable human rights standards.

Secular law, on the other hand, can be developed to protect the rights of everybody, whether female, male, gay, straight, black, brown, or white. It has been a struggle to get to where we are in secularized societies. This is why everything goes back to power, in my view. Democracy is so fragile. One of the most alarming things for me is to see how few people exercise their democratic rights and participate in the process. It especially alarms me that women are not more active in exercising their political rights. In Canada, women became persons under the law only in 1929. The right to vote is a very recent phenomenon. I feel frustrated that some of my younger friends and my students believe there are no problems for women anymore. They do not realize they could lose many of the rights won for them over the last century. They could lose them in a blink of an eye.

One of the big debates still on the table in both of our countries relates to women's reproductive rights. There are strong roots in religious discourse relating to this area, and there are many on the religious right who do not think women have the right to control their own bodies. Because of his leanings toward the religious right, our current prime minister would like to recriminalize abortion in Canada. Yet he is aware that almost 80 percent of Canadians support the right of a woman to choose. Therefore, he does not touch this issue. But the religious right would like to see him move in this direction. He has partly placated them by cutting financial support to Canadian organizations like MATCH that support women's rights, including reproductive rights, in the developing world. We must vigilantly protect the rights guaranteed in a democracy because democracy itself is very thin and very fragile.

S2: Yes, and not all institutions practice a democratic ethos. For instance, how about academic institutions?

PM: Exactly. There has been an interesting debate recently in the Society of Biblical Literature (SBL) over who should be allowed to participate in that organization and what constitutes an academic approach to the study of the Bible. Some argue that only those organizations (e.g., colleges, universities, religious groups) that recognize and respect academic freedom should be included. Many religious institutions require faculty to sign faith statements and to teach only what is consonant with the beliefs of the particular tradition. This is about power and control. These hierarchical institutions do not operate on democratic principles. Or we could think about secular corporations, such as Wal-Mart, with a questionable record for hiring and promoting women.[25] Wal-Mart works very hard to prevent unionization that would give employees some protections and legal rights. The rights of women to equitable employment access and the rights of workers to unionize were only established in my country after long struggles for justice and equity. Pay equity laws and employment equity laws, as they exist in Canada, may not work perfectly because not everyone tries to make them work perfectly. But at least they are tools assisting us. The principles on which these laws are based and the laws themselves are not enshrined in mainstream religions or their scriptural texts. They are developments of the modern world typical of secular democracies. The resistance to them often comes from religious organizations. This is precisely what happened to the Equal Rights Amendment in the United States.

S2: So, as a secular thinker, you believe that for diversity and justice to become meaningful practices, they need to be grounded in democratic processes. And through these processes we can implement more and more justice and diversity in society.

PM: Yes, because, in theory, democracy allows everyone to participate. The problem with religions and political parties is that they demarcate "in-groups" and "out-groups." When the "in-group" becomes dominant and powerful, the rights of the respective outsiders are endangered. The biblical tradition is okay for you as long as you are an Israelite/Jew or a Jesus follower/Christian. It is the same for Islam. Throughout history, it has mattered a lot whether you belonged to the group with or without the power at any given time. God never seems to love the outsider as much as the insider.

Hence, checks and balances are important. Undoubtedly the insider/outsider problem exists even in secular societies. For instance, in Canada it seems that if you belong to the political party in power, you have a better chance of getting a political appointment or a government contract, and if your region votes for that party, it seems that more government money flows into your direction. But when the bias becomes too great, we can vote this party out of office and try another. In a democracy, people have the right to organize political opposition and work for change. They have no authoritative text telling them that god loves the in-group and things should stay the way they are.

S2: Of course, currently the United States is actively engaged in bringing so-called democracy to the rest of the world and particularly the Middle East.

PM: It is just that the American system does not seem to work so well. Ours is a parliamentary system which has flaws too, but the system in the United States seems not to be very functional. It is gridlocked. Nowadays, you can hardly make any legislative change in the political system in the United States. For instance, Obama came in with great ideas but he seems totally mired down in the Congress, where the Senate and House seem to be able to block each other and prevent much legislative development. It seems impossible to make progressive change. It comes back to power again. Alas, the multinational corporations seem to be much more powerful than government at this point. That is why we have to empower our government by being politically active. But when less than 50 percent of those eligible to vote bother to vote, the entire system is weakened. That is where education is crucial. Then there is, of course, the money problem. It has become so expensive for people to be involved in the political system. Being a politician is something only the wealthy or those connected to the wealthy can afford. It is not surprising that so many politicians have become corrupted by money interests. But again, we could decide to limit how much money politicians are allowed to spend. The money issue is a big concern in the United States, as well as the limited number of parties. The United States has only two parties to choose from! That is not really diversity.

S2: Yes, that is true, it is not really diversity. I want to push you back a little bit with my earlier comment that the United States wants to bring democracy to the Arab world. Meanwhile, is it not the capitalist, free-market ideology that drives all of these efforts, trying to get cheaper access to oil and getting rid of resistant leaders?

PM: I think this is absolutely correct. Again, it comes back to power. The United States is the power in the world at the moment. So the United States wants to arrange the world in ways that benefit itself, or at least its wealthy elite, and not someone else. This is not surprising. The notion of democracy is a very limited notion. All the rhetoric about going into Afghanistan and making things better for women—well, none of that has happened. Iraq is a mess, and certainly the invasion of Iraq was all about the Bush legacy and just exerting power because you could. The United States can take military action against other countries because it has the military might to do so. But the cost of exercising that military power may well bring financial collapse to the world.[26] The American debt is staggering. And at some point, people within the country may begin to ask what that it is going to do to their way of life. Like most empires, the American one may well undermine itself. The United States may be more in danger from its own internal policies and practices than from any external force. My colleagues in the economics department, where my office is located, made me read *The Coming Generational Storm: What You Need to Know about America's Economic Future*,[27] a book that raises some very serious concerns about the economic challenges that are arising in the United States and threaten the country's economic stability.

S2: Well, I am also Foucauldian in this sense. I think it is scary because ultimately it comes down to power.

PM: Yes, but power shifts and can change over time. If we come back to the notion of diversity and justice, I would say that the goal is to achieve a more equitable distribution of power and that means a more equitable distribution of wealth. We cannot do without our social institutions, but we can change them. Currently, our political systems work against the involvement of women or poor people because they are so connected to money. In our Canadian system, we have one of the lowest percentages of women in political office in any of the developed countries in the world. In large part, this is because the whole system is based on men's lives. For women who want to participate in it, it helps if they are not married, do not have children, have no other domestic responsibilities, and are independently very wealthy. It is really hard for a woman to run for political office, leave home, and go to Toronto or move to Ottawa, or wherever they have to move in order to participate in the government.

Universities are also based on men's lives. Today, in Canada, women make up the majority of undergraduate students but not at the graduate level. Most universities want graduate students to be full time, not part time, and most want PhD students who do two years of residency at a time when women watch their biological clocks. The situation is even worse for young women faculty who must publish or perish to get tenure at a time when they may be raising infants or small children. We have to rethink institutions from the ground up and find ways to make them more inclusive. Diversity is one thing but equitable inclusivity is another matter. Until we find a mechanism to redesign our social institutions, women and other marginalized groups will be discriminated against because our lives are differently ordered.

S2: So as a secular thinker, you are a real revolutionary.

PM: (laughs) Well, I think our institutions have been designed by elite men, for the use of elite men and for the benefit of elite men. Therefore, they reflect elite men's understanding of the world. If diversity and inclusivity are to become realities, you have to rethink the model. What would the model look like if 51 percent of the participants were women? Does the model take into consideration the demands of women's lives? Much of my activism has been in the context of my workplace. My goal has been to change the model and to bring people from underrepresented groups into teaching and administrative positions. People transform institutions, but without a critical mass interested in such transformation, it is hard to achieve.

During my twenty-seven years at the University of Windsor, I have seen some progress. For example, we have tripled the percentage of women faculty but the percentage still remains far below 50 percent. Through our union processes, we have made some changes to make hiring, tenure, and promotion processes fairer to everyone. All appointment processes are monitored by equity assessors. Women in tenure-track appointments can delay the tenure decision beyond the normal five years if they have very young children. Criteria for tenure and promotion must not systemically discriminate against women, visible minority, aboriginal, or disabled academics, nor undervalue work done primarily by such academics. We have access to paid maternity, parental and adoption leaves. Things are somewhat better than when I first came. But much more change is needed.

Making this kind of change would be much easier if the institutional leadership reflected the diversity of the wider institution. My institution suffers from the "old white boys" syndrome which has a systemic impact on what is valued and what is prioritized. Lip service is always paid to equity but when opportunities to diverse leadership arise, they are more often thwarted than embraced.[28] Minority women academics have been paying the price for such hypocrisy more than any other group.

S2: So in other words, even if you do not include God in the discussion and focus on the democratic process as the way to institutionalize and advance issues of diversity, equity, and social justice, it can get very depressing when you look at what is going on.

PM: Yes but, as a woman, I am still happy to be living in this century rather than any previous century even though women have a long way to go before we will realize full social equality in a country like Canada. In looking at the social inequalities that continue to plague society, I do not see religious institutions as leading the way to overcome them. I see some religious people working on social justice issues because there is this split in many religions between the regressives and the progressives. The regressives would like to turn the clock back, or at the very least, ensure that it does not move forward. The Promise Keepers and similar groups are regressive in this sense: they want women at home, subservient and obedient to their husbands, who take the leadership roles in the domestic sphere. Many religious groups have splintered over issues such as the ordination of openly gay and lesbian people. Within any given religious institution there may be voices and counter-voices. This division often leads to power struggles to determine which side will control the organization. The losers often leave or are forced out. In some countries, fundamentalist or regressive voices of a religious tradition hold sway. In those places, the respect for the equality of everyone in society is not evident and human rights are not respected. So it is good to have progressives try to use their religious tradition to promote matters of justice and diversity but, as a secularist, I would not want to rely on their religions to guarantee my rights and freedoms.

S2: What do you think about religious progressives and secularists cooperating with each other? Could we not form an alliance to move toward what both groups want, fostering more rational discourse and seeking equity, diversity, and justice for all creatures on planet earth?

PM: Those alliances already exist. Often, whether you are on the liberal or conservative (progressive/regressive) end of the spectrum is more significant than whether you are secular or religious or even whether you are Christian, Jew, Muslim, Hindu, or pagan. It has to do with the question of what motivates you to do something. For me, the motivation does not come from anything external, such as a deity. The motivation is completely within this world. I am grounded in the idea that we have a social responsibility as human beings. But if your motivation comes from some other source, that is okay as long as the focus is on the goal, which is to make the world more humane, more inclusive, more respectful, and less harmful. We have to reduce harm.

S2: So when religious progressives talk about issues of diversity and justice, secularists would appreciate to talk less about God and more about how to get to our common goals.

PM: If theists are motivated because of the way they understand their divinity and this understanding leads them to work on social justice issues, it is really their own personal choice. It does not have to be the motivation for secularists. And as a secularist, I would not say that there is a deity out there wanting or pushing us to do something. But if that motivates you to make the ideals of the Universal Declaration of Human Rights a reality, then we can work together to get the job done. There are so many people suffering. There is so much bloodshed. There is so much work that needs to be done. We should not fight over why we are doing it. Let's just get on with it and do it.

S2: Well, thank you. It will be good to work together again soon.

PM: Thank you, too.

NOTES

1. Mary Daly, *Beyond God the Father: Toward a Philosophy of Women's Liberation* (Boston: Beacon Press, 1973), 19.
2. See, for example, Mary McClintock Fulkerton's discussion, "Contesting Feminist Canons: Discourse and the Problem of Sexist Texts," *JFSR* 7, no. 2 (1991): 53–73. Fulkerton was critical of my structural analysis of Genesis 2–3, "The Patriarchal Stamp of Scripture: The Implications of Structuralist Analyses for Feminist Hermeneutics," *JFSR* 5, no. 1 (1989): 17–34, in which I argued that the text itself embedded patriarchal ideology and promoted patriarchal interpretations. She mistakenly took the argument in my article to imply that meaning was only in the text to be discovered by readers.
3. See my response to Fulkerton in the "Afterword" to the reprint of my article in A. Brenner, ed., *A Feminist Companion to Genesis* (Sheffield: Sheffield Academic Press, 1993), 167–72.
4. See Pamela Milne, "Doing Feminist Biblical Criticism in a Women's Studies Context," *Atlantis: A Women's Studies Journal* 35, no. 2 (2011): 128–38.

5. David Clines, *What Does Eve Do to Help? And Other Readerly Questions to the Old Testament* (Sheffield: Sheffield Academic Press, 1990), 45–48.

6. Clines is faced with this very issue. He acknowledges that the Bible has "misled people and promoted patriarchy." For him, though, the fact that the Bible has impacted some people for good leads him to remain connected to the Bible, not as an "authoritative" text but as a "resource for living." For me, this position does not solve the problem of the harm the biblical tradition had done to so many.

7. See, for example, Nancy T. Ammerman, "North American Protestant Fundamentalism," in *Fundamentalism Observed*, ed. M. E. Marty and R. S. Appleby (Chicago: The University of Chicago Press, 1991), 1–65; Karen Armstrong, *The Battle for God* (New York: Alfred A. Knopf, 2000).

8. Armstrong, *Battle for God*, xi.

9. Between 1991 and 1995, Martin Marty and Scott Appleby published five large volumes on fundamentalism and offered seventy-five case studies from which they abstracted nine characteristics of fundamentalism.

10. See Gabriel A. Almond, R. Scott Appleby, and Emmanuel Sivan, *Strong Religion: The Rise of Fundamentalisms around the World* (Chicago: University of Chicago Press, 2003), 1–2.

11. See M. Marty and S. Appleby, *Fundamentalisms and Society* (Chicago: University of Chicago Press, 1993), 7. In the same volume, see also Helen Hardacre, "The Impact of Fundamentalisms on Women, the Family and Interpersonal Relations," 129–50, esp. 139–40.

12. See, for example, Ethan Bronner, "Israelis Facing a Seismic Shift Over Role of Women," *New York Times* (January 14, 2012), www.nytimes.com/2012/01/15/world/middleeast/israel-faces-crisis-over-role-of-ultra-orthodox-in-society.html?pagewanted=2&ref=general&src=me [accessed January 16, 2012].

13. Ammerman, "North American Protestant Fundamentalism," in *Fundamentalism Observed*, 1–65.

14. Marieme Hélie Lucas, "The Enemy of My Enemy Is Not my Friend: Fundamentalists, Democracy and Human Rights," *off our backs* 36, no. 3 (2006): 14–17.

15. See, for example, Letty M. Russell, *Human Liberation in a Feminist Perspective: A Theology* (Philadelphia: The Westminster Press, 1974).

16. See, for example, Rosemary Radford Ruether, *Sexism and God-Talk: Toward a Feminist Theology* (Boston: Beacon Press, 1983).

17. See, for example, Karen Engle, "International Human Rights and Feminisms: When Discourses Keep Meeting," in *International Law: Modern Feminist Approaches*, ed. Doris Buss and Ambreena S. Manji (Oxford/Portland, OR: Hart, 2005), 47–66.

18. See, for example, http://www.canada.com/vancouversun/news/story.html?id=80f6fdff-cc0e-4a08-9b96-76f3db32808e [accessed January 17, 2012]. For a more extensive discussion see Marci McDonald, *The Armageddon Factor: The Rise of Christian Nationalism in Canada* (Toronto: Vintage Canada, 2011).

19. For more information, see http://en.wikipedia.org/wiki/%C3%89cole_Polytechnique_massacre [accessed January 17, 2012].

20. See http://www.weforum.org/issues/global-gender-gap.

21. Douglas was one of the founders of the Cooperative Commonwealth Party, Canada's first national socialist party and predecessor to the New Democratic Party of Canada of which he became leader. He was instrumental in the development of our medicare system, our central banking system, old age pensions and unemployment insurance. For a short biography, see http://www.thecanadianencyclopedia.com/articles/tommy-douglas [accessed January 4, 2012]. See also the National Film Board of Canada film produced by Elsie Swerhone, *Tommy Douglas: Keeper of the Flame* (1980).

22. Joseph E. Stiglitz, "Of the 1%, by the 1%, for the 1%," *Vanity Fair* (May 2011), http://www.vanityfair.com/society/features/2011/05/top-one-percent-201105 [accessed January 17, 2012].

23. See, for example, Starhawk, *The Empowerment Manual: A Guide for Collaborative Groups* (Gabriola Island, BC: New Society Publishers, 2011).

24. *Me and the Mosque* (2005), a film written by Zarqua Nawaz, offers an interesting exploration of the growing tendency to physically exclude women from participating in public worship in North American mosques. She links this trend to the arrival of Muslims from countries in which women's human rights are minimal or nonexistent.

25. See, for example, Andrew Martin, "Female Wal-Mart Employees File New Bias Case," *New York Times* (October 27, 2011), http://www.nytimes.com/2011/10/28/business/women-file-new-class-action-bias-case-against-wal-mart.html [accessed January 17, 2012].

26. See, for example, Joseph E. Stiglitz and Linda J. Bilmes, *The Three Trillion Dollar War: The True Cost of the Iraq Conflict* (New York: Norton, 2008).

27. Laurence J. Kotlikoff and Scott Burns, *The Coming Generational Storm: What You Need to Know about America's Economic Future* (Cambridge, MA: MIT Press, 2004).

28. Although the problem might be particularly acute at the University of Windsor, it is widespread. See Stacey Patton, "'Like Flies in Buttermilk': Black Deans Talk Candidly about Diversity in Graduate Studies," *Chronicle of Higher Education* (December 13, 2011), http://chronicle.com/article/Like-Flies-in-Buttermilk-/130092/ [accessed on January 12, 2012].

THREE

I AM, Who Loves the Prophets, Loves You

Meditations on the Progressive/Prophetic at the End of Jewish History

Marc H. Ellis

Titles are fascinating—for what they express and what they hide. It is like our names, first ones especially, which call us and protect us from further probing. As well, there are so many takes on titles, ways to twist and turn them in our desire to be original or to stand out, or at least not to be instantly forgotten, which is so easy today in our virtual culture. Like information, takes on titles can be swept up and away in the cascade of endless information. When ours is one among many in the understandings of issues of importance, we prepare in advance, which makes sense, since we have to have something organized to say. When previously organized, though, we also miss parts of the discussion that may be new to us, the preparation of others that could impact our own understandings.

So I share with you some of my already prepared remarks and leave my last minutes to pick up on the themes that are new to me or that are so old they are like recurring dreams that sometimes go places and more often do not go anywhere at all. Like the discussions of progressive scholars. Have we not heard it all before? I organize my thoughts under two headings. The first heading, "What I (Really) Believe," is followed by the second, "What I (Also) Believe." The third and final part is titled "Thinking (Against) Pessimism (Really)." As will become clear, I believe what I write under these headings, because, in truth, all three are necessary to divine heads from tails in the discussion of God, diversity, and justice. The terms "God," "diversity," and "justice" are far from obvious in what is to be said about them and what they mean individually or collectively. This is also true with the terms "progressive," "faith," the "world," and "politics." All of these terms are loaded; they can be defined in many ways and taken in different directions. I will take all of them in two directions which exist independently of each other and may in the end be dependent as well. As I write of each direction, remember their possible dependence. As I write of their dependence, remember their possible independence.

WHAT I (REALLY) BELIEVE

We are at the end of Jewish history as we have known and inherited it. That this end is hardly noticed or named does not preclude its reality, just the opposite. For me, the lack of discussion confirms the ending itself. When the actions of Jews denote the end and there is no discussion of it, the indicator of the end of Jewish history meter becomes unglued. It is off the charts.

In my reading and listening, I find few references to this end, how this ending came about, who is responsible for it and what the end of Jewish history means for Jews and others. At the end of Jewish history, there is a gap, a silence. This does not mean that everyone is unaware of this end. It simply means that no one is talking about it. Perhaps those who know we are at the end do not want others to know they know. Perhaps the end that is known is too deep a trauma to be named. The fear then is a world without Jewish history. What would such a world be like?

Since everyone knows what is not talked about, a simple series of statements will bring the end of Jewish history as we have known and inherited it to clarity. Here they are, bundled into one elongated sentence: When a people that carries the indigenous prophetic as its baseline and eschatological essence violates a people like Jews have violated the Palestinians, and continues to do so and seeks to make that domination permanent, as the state of Israel with the support of worldwide Jewry has done, when Jews do almost everything to another people that has been done to them, then we are the end of a history that held ethics as its center. Though Judaism and Jewishness continues, it does so with a fatal wound of the heart. Violence becomes the covenant touchstone.

Once you understand that the end has arrived, the silence becomes palpable. You become aware of a void that is unremitting, a dark hole in the universe from which there is no return. You begin to see that what is called "progressive" in the wider movements of non-Jews is the prophetic, only watered down. The prophetic without Jewish content, the expropriation of the prophetic, attempts at the prophetic without Jews—Jews are used to this. While the remaining remnant of prophetic Jews is appalled by this, most Jews are glad to participate in a prophetic without real Jewish content. Thus Progressive Jews abound. They are involved in the watered-down prophetic as a celebratory act of Jewishness without the sacrifice and a relief that the ultimate questions are for the future. Progressives then assert the inclusion of non-Jews and Jews, a diversity that is also watered down.

For the remnant of prophetic Jews, their exclusion elicits the rage of Jewish history. It sets them off in a seemingly irrational rage against the universe. For Jews who want to distance themselves from the prophetic, it allows them to pose under the prophetic spotlight without doing the hard work the prophetic demands. They heave a sigh of relief as if contentment and destiny are one. In a sense, they are saved by the progressive movements, which they often lead.

Let me explain. The people Israel gave the prophetic to the world. It is the greatest gift to the world that has been given or can be. Without the prophetic there is no meaning in the world. There may be no meaning in the world. The prophet is one who embodies the possibility of meaning in the world. Obviously, this does not mean that all Jews carry the prophetic as action in the world. Not in the least. In fact, Jews are also the great strugglers against the prophetic, as we know from history, and as we certainly know today. Ask any university administrator at any of the universities represented here in these essays if Jews are the great strugglers against the prophetic. I mean especially when it comes to what the Jewish establishment wants and needs: the state of Israel. Any critical discussion of Israel is met with a barrage of pressure, usually featuring the charges of anti-Semitism and threats of funding curtailment. In short, shutting up Jews of Conscience who embody the Jewish prophetic is the Jewish community's vocation in our time.

This means that the Jewish support of every progressive issue in the universe is suspect. It means that the Jewish support of every progressive issue in the universe is a form of deflection. It also indicts the progressive movement itself, as it too vacillates on the question of Palestine. The indictment is about this specific issue at hand but should be seen as part of the superficiality and deflection of progressives themselves. Palestine in relation to Jews and progressives is like the virus that keeps moving through the body's system.

Administrators will not tell anyone the truth about this. No way. Nor will the various constituencies represented here tell you the truth about this direct assault on the prophetic. The reason is they participate in it as well through their silence and who they ask to speak and teach at their universities and seminaries. The readings they assign and do not assign. Why should the end of Jewish history rain on their parade?

Sorry to say, on this issue feminism and progressives of every other stripe have sad histories. There is only one feminist who has spoken boldly on this issue of issues, Rosemary Radford Ruether, and many feminists I talk to want her to fade away, be escorted from the stage, or else slip off into the proverbial old-age night. African Americans will not touch the Jewish issue with a ten-foot pole. And when we get to surplus Christianity, well, that surplus is empty of prophetic Jews, and conveniently so.

Progressive Jews like this silence. It allows them to keep placing forward the idea of prophetic Jewishness without the prophetic bite which only makes sense in the Jewish backyard, which is where the prophetic came into being and from which the prophetic spread to other yards in the first place. But then again, everyone likes the Jewish prophetic without the bite. If the Jewish prophetic does not have a bite, others are then emboldened to think of the prophetic in a similar fashion. The prophetic goes down easier without the bite. Believe it. Thus my definition of "progressive": the prophetic without the prophet; the prophetic without the bite; Jewish backyard oratory used to fight the conservatives to a draw. Or so they like to think.

We live in the Golden Age of Constantinian Judaism. Progressive Jews are the left-wing of Constantinian Judaism. Jewish studies/Holocaust studies/scholars in ancient and medieval Judaism—the list is endless. They guard against the Jewish prophetic. Their discourse is well armed by the empire.

I confess that I do not know what God loves, if God loves, or if it matters whether God loves anything, including diversity and justice. I love diversity and justice, or at least prefer it, and no doubt we all do. What meaning diversity has when injustice is the norm is up in the air. Where and how justice comes is debatable. I do know that without Jews who understand that the end of Jewish history has arrived, the entire question of diversity and its relation to justice is weakened. It loses its force. It becomes a charade. The whole movement of justice becomes an add-on—without a center. As in God loves—without the bite. Without a center with a bite, an expression such as "God's love" becomes a proverb without a culture, a free-floater, as in "today is the first day of the rest of your life."

Now I ask your forgiveness in advance for committing the probably unpardonable sin of assuming a center that is not originated by all or shared by all in the same way. This certainly runs against the grain of diversity discourse, God's love, and the whole nine yards of what we all recite as a creed, or should. And it would take more than my allotted space to explain this position. But since Jews of Conscience are not often allowed a real and substantial platform at our great liberal universities and seminaries or in the print media, I have to function as a hit-and-run driver. I have to deliver the blow and leave the scene.

So if you consider that I have left the scene, we can begin again. I can continue on a more hopeful note.

You see just when the Jewish prophetic is on the ropes, pummeled by the Constantinian Jewish establishment and enabled by Progressive Jews and progressive scholars in all their diverse stripes who absent prophetic Jews then curiously employ the Jewish prophetic as their own without the bite, the Jewish prophetic returns. Without an invitation. The Jewish prophetic returns as a wild card, upsetting the conservative and progressive scholars' attempt to proclaim the prophetic without Jews.

Of course, I do understand why progressives, including Progressive Jews, would rather speak and write about the prophetic without prophetic Jews being around. Who in the world wants to see Jewish prophets, up close and personal?

Prophetic Jews are the ultimate party crashers. But please, they are not to be confused with wedding singers who mouth words that others have written with their own blood, sweat, and tears. When employing the Jewish prophetic *sans* Jews, progressives are free to use the prophetic they want and leave the other parts that are too difficult behind. The images that the Jewish prophets throw around are way too bleak and violent for our sensitivities and besides, for the most part, their threats, especially of self- and God-enabled destruction, are directed at the people Israel, at real, live Jews. Who in God's name wants to be party to that?

For progressives, the Jewish prophetic is like a venerated ghost returning from the dead. Better for all if the ghost of the prophets haunts our houses, if they must, even better if the Ghostbusters can get rid of the ghosts completely. Any solution is welcome as long as it provides distance. Then the present claimants of what used to be the House of the Prophets can do their thing. Indeed, this is understandable from every angle, even for the Jewish wedding singers, the well-paid and upwardly mobile stand-ins that fill our universities. I almost wrote, "and seminaries," but prophetic Jews are conspicuously absent there, even the one that is claimed as their one and only Jew.

If we continue with this wedding singer analogy, especially from an age long since past, it is like having a giant life-sized wedding cake where the expected naked lady is ready to pop out but, at the last moment, a Jewish prophet does instead. Female or male, clothed or not, we are reminded of Isaiah wandering naked, Eli being fed by the crows, the young Hannah Arendt with hands on her hips, or what Emmanuel Levinas thought of the Jewish atheists and rebels of the nineteenth and early twentieth centuries. They were all to be stripped of their clothing in one way or another. Embodying the prophetic, they were naked in the world.

Levinas writes that by allying themselves with justice, Jewish atheists and rebels expiated blasphemy in advance. This reminds me of Gandhi's admonition to his people that when they burned their foreign clothes, they burned their own shame. What "foreign" clothes do the prophets ask Jews to burn, and will the Jewish and non-Jewish progressives demand the obvious?

Ask Jewish atheists and rebels of any time and place about God's love. They will not entertain the question of God even for the sake of the wedding party!

Yes, true, I agree, their refusal is too simple, but at least the question of God for them is not conceptual. It is visceral. They cannot reconcile injustice and God, however intelligently argued. They are not going there. Is that what advanced seminary training is for, reconciling God and injustice? I suppose it is obvious why these Jewish prophets are not invited in. It is the fear of the Jewish empire. But it is also a fear of their Christian faithlessness, at least the deep probing of it.

I cannot say I disagree with these Jewish atheists and rebels, though I could not remain there. You see, when I was moving deeper into exile, when I began to experience viscerally the end of Jewish history, when I was being pursued by Constantinian and Progressive Jews and with their enablers, the diversity coalition, who have their survival and their empires to attend to, I had to ask the question of whether I could survive exile without God.

My own response is personal. I would not recommend it to anyone. Simply put, I understood that exile without God was not possible for me. So, taking an unexpected tack, I entered into a prolonged conversation with the God of Israel—yes, that specific God, a God I likewise would not recommend to anyone.

I cannot recommend the prophetic either, especially in the Jewish backyard, which is indigenous of the people Israel. Our backyard, Jewishly speaking, is the prophetic. It is the only backyard of its kind anywhere. It is also our front yard. This means that Jews are surrounded by the prophetic, haunted by it, hemmed in, imprisoned if you will, with no exit from its force or its command.

As for God's love, I would say it has come to this for me. Again, this is strictly personal and not recommended as a be-all and end-all of God language. But in playing around with the always Jewishly impossible naming of God, I have come to this formulation as a name for God: *I AM, WHO LOVES THE PROPHETS*. Or, as in my now-revealed mantra, *I AM, WHO LOVES THE PROPHETS*, loves you.

What this says about diversity, I do not pretend to know. Nor do I know what it says about politics, at least as we think about politics. The world seems to go its own way regardless. There does not seem to be an obvious force behind this formulation. It might just be a soothing appellation to deal with a profoundly unstable existence in the modern world. Or perhaps it is simply a prop to help me survive the world where Jewish history has come to an end. But since the prophetic is wholly unstable and the God of Israel is as well, and since instability seems to be endemic to Jews no matter how much stability Jews want and deserve, my name for God is as good as any in my estimation and, no doubt, as limited.

No matter, at the end of Jewish history, we need to plumb the depths to find the essence of what it means to be Jewish. If there is an essence, it is the prophetic. If the prophetic is the essence and according to our title referring to God's love, the prophets have to come before diversity and, only the prophets, with the formation of the prophetic community, can provide the foundation for justice. Therefore my personal mantra may be, I stress may be, extended to others. Could the *I AM, WHO LOVES THE PROPHETS*, also love non-Jewish prophets?

WHAT I (ALSO) BELIEVE

Of course, the prophetic is Jewish; it is indigenous to the people Israel. It has accompanied Jews; Jews have embodied it. Jews also struggled against it. The prophetic is the essence of what it means to be Jewish. Without the prophetic, Judaism, Jewishness, and Jewish history are curious artifacts and experiences. Like the Gregorian chant, something to marvel over, not to die for. You cannot make sense of Jews or the negation of Jews without the prophetic. Nor can you understand much about Christian history without the Jewish prophetic.

On the negative side, without acknowledging the attempt to stabilize Jesus and the mainstream anti-Semitism Christianity embraced, it would be difficult to understand Christian history. Without the Jewish prophetic as the prime foundation of Christianity, why bother to try to work through its prodigious hypocrisy? Though more distant, Islam is also a puzzle without factoring in the Jewish prophetic.

Inside and out, the prophetic is the center of Jewishness. Nonetheless, the prophetic has radiated outward, to other religions and those who embody those religions, mostly in dissent. The prophetic has also been secularized so that it can animate diverse groups and sometimes be the core of communities that have no religious affiliation. Clearly, the prophetic is alive in the world, with and without Jews.

In fact, today the prime carriers of the Jewish prophetic are outside the Jewish community, including Jews in exile from the Constantinian and Progressive Jewish establishments and non-Jews who carry no Jewish identity at all. One thinks here of liberation theologies and communities around the world. Especially Christian liberation theologies claim the indigenous prophetic of the people Israel as their own, sometimes consciously, and at other times simply as an expression of their Christianity. Like the Jewish prophetic that Jews of Conscience carry, however, Christian liberationists have their own distance from Progressive Christians. Though they often bond together, their main social, economic, and political arena is different. In essence, Christian liberation theologies speak for the dispossessed while Progressive Christians are well entrenched within elite classes, whether they recognize it or not.

For Christian liberation movements whose members live on the edge of modern history, one wonders what diversity means for their lives and future. Certainly, whatever it means, diversity is not and cannot be first and foremost among their concerns. And justice, whether loved by God or not, seems distant, if not impossible. Scholars visit and leave those on the margins, write about their lives and what it means to theology. Scholars may be like God to those on the margins, coming and going without any real change in the lives of the people or, if there is a change, it is often for the worse.

What does the Jewish prophetic look like when it arrives in someone else's backyard? Especially when the hoped for prophetic rescue is far away and the promise of a plague on the houses of injustice seems like pipe dreams, another wedding cake where dictators and other rogues pop out with alarming regularity? Obviously, much of the Jewish prophetic comes packaged and camouflaged in Christian empire, starting as a form of oppression, then doubling back to incite against those who came in the name of the Empire Lord. Yet even when reversed, the Jewish prophetic is itself an imperial layer, trying to strip the deeper imperialism away, but nonetheless being essentially foreign. Here the Jewish prophetic is caught in a cycle of imperialism that it cannot escape. Mostly well-intentioned Progressive Christian visitors arrive and gather their visions, adding yet another layer of truth telling in the still imperial adventure.

The alternative? Not much of one, to be honest. As Simone Weil wrote in her book, *The Need for Roots*, "Those who are uprooted are destined to uproot others." The Jewish prophetic in someone else's backyard is part of that uprooting. Still, where their indigenous has been thoroughly routed, the Jewish prophetic uprooting is to be honored. Honoring, however, means little without telling the truth. The question of questions remains whether someone else's prophetic can liberate those whose indigenous has almost vanished from the world.

Can the prophetic, the people Israel's indigenous, become foundational for another people, religion, or group? The most obvious and closest possibility would be Christianity since it was born in the bosom of Judaism and Jewish life. Clearly, the prophetic has never become indigenous to Christianity. In fact, most of Christian history has been spent struggling against Jews who embody the prophetic. Can this help explain Christianity's traditional animus against Jews and Judaism as its struggle against the prophetic?

In this struggle against the prophetic, Christianity takes the side of Constantinian Judaism. Or, looked at another way, is Constantinian Christianity and Constantinian Judaism the same religion? If the latter is the case, this would mean that Christians who embrace the prophetic are returning to their Jewish roots or adopting them while Christians who struggle against the prophetic are more or less like the Pharisees as they are conveniently portrayed in the Gospels.

It could be that the prophetic once given to the world by the people Israel is, in that giving, free to roam the world, landing where it lands and becoming embodied where it is embodied. The roaming prophetic would mirror the covenant which, once given, exists in the world, at times with the people Israel and then, when forfeited through disobedience and injustice, leaves Israel for the world.

Clearly in our time, the prophetic is outside the people Israel as a whole. Could it be, then, that my earlier God formulation—*I AM, WHO LOVES THE PROPHETS*, loves you—is also universal, therefore applying to any and all who embrace the prophetic in their lives, under whatever banner, named and unnamed?

Here, peoples, communities, and religions pick and choose within their heritage, adding the Jewish prophetic where it applies while discarding aspects that do not. In some ways, this is what prophetic Jews do, though picking and choosing through the indigenous is different than picking and choosing through an add-on. In real life, though, Jews have add-ons as well; the Jewish prophetic was not created wholesale by the people Israel and certainly interactions with other cultures in history have added aspects to Jewish life that now seem wholly Jewish.

Indeed, contemporary Jewish contact with other indigenous realities can help reawaken Jews to their own indigenous. The back and forth of Jews and others, others and Jews, is endemic, beneficial, and enlightening. Can this interaction also embolden these communities to forge ahead, being aware of historical boundaries while also being unconcerned with them?

Obviously the Constantinian establishments of all peoples, groups, and religions warn against these borrowings, even as they have borrowed to confirm their established position. Recognizing the similarities of Constantinian establishments and as well recognizing the similarities of the communities that dissent, it might be more accurate to redraw the boundaries that establish our identity—a Jew being a Jew, a Christian being a Christian, a Muslim being a Muslim, and so forth—and rather find our identities in shared borrowings and commitments toward justice and diversity. The prophetic, that in this community of dissent is received and turned around, then becomes defining of both the broader Constantinian establishment and the broader dissenting community. No longer do religion or geography define the boundary. The prophetic evolves as it travels.

This again differentiates the prophetic from the progressives. The progressive coalition is one made up of those who struggle with their various Constantinian establishments. In this struggle, they try to right a misguided interpretation of the groups, peoples, and religions they come from. So for Progressive Christians, it means regaining what it "really" means to be Christian. For Jews—what it "really" means to be Jewish. For Muslims—what it "really" means to be Muslim. Then the call is to the community to return to the "real."

As if any of these efforts can succeed in even ascertaining what "real" means. As if there is an essence to any of the religions or identities. As if that "real" essence was established, they would actually want to return there.

In general, progressives are renewal people with little or nothing to renew, especially if the renewal is within an empire religion like Christianity or Islam. Carrying empire for a thousand years or more, Christianity and Islam, for example, are empire religions from which, if we are honest, there is no return. The civil war within each of these religions is an illusion. Progressives actually help the empire religion to remain, adjust for time and context, and bide time for another assault. In the end, progressives are empire enablers.

Can progressives align themselves with those embodying the prophetic from different communities? Can those embodying the prophetic benefit from such an alliance? Or is such an alliance an illusion, with the rhetorical flourish of progressives usurping and ultimately diminishing the untidy force of prophetic demands?

My own experience with Jewish and Christian progressives cautions against a shared platform or agenda. This is not because of ill will or even the desire to co-opt a more radical agenda. It is just that progressives are in a different social, economic, and political location, they have different class interests and also a different sense of life's order. Even those refugees from other cultures and geographic locations that seek to subvert the hegemonic discourse of white/Christian/Jewish/male theologies are, in their university/seminary positions, already part of that discourse. Whatever their original motives, they become part of the renewal/survival project. In fact, they are venerated for their critical interventions.

This is true of feminism as well. Of course, the Jewish progressives are in the same empire boat and glad to be. They simply paved the way for others to join in the inclusion/diversity parade, though, if truth be known, these Jewish progressives are about to be overwhelmed by the new subversive voices coming from all over the world. Those voices will also be tamed, but, then, when they become the new progressive dissenting voice, will they also welcome Jews? My experience says no. Even Progressive Jews are subversive if only because beneath and around them is the remnant of the haunting Jewish prophetic.

THINKING (AGAINST) PESSIMISM (REALLY)

Diversity is about inclusion, which is ultimately about assimilation, which is what progressives are about, which is a good thing for sure—as far as it goes. Translated in the progressive religious mind, inclusion/ assimilation is about God's love for diversity and justice. On the God angle, progressives believe that God loves us for wanting and working toward diversity and justice. Since progressives are all about inclusion/ assimilation, why should we not also include/assimilate God to those views? Especially since conservatives who do not want inclusion/assimilation include/assimilate God to their view?

A wonderful civil war we have, and no doubt a necessary one, which I am glad to include/assimilate to, for the sheer delight/rightness of the cause. After all, our social, economic, and political location demands that we fight for those outside the system who do not have a voice that is heard by the powers that be. I am simply arguing that progressives should recognize their limits on what we "really" want, what they are "really" arguing for, and what they "really" assume about God and themselves. Of course, when I include/assimilate myself to this righteous progressive cause I have to use the word "we."

None of us "really" know about God, if God is, what God is, or what God wants. Nor can we operate as if we know. Yet in our civil war with the Constantinians of every stripe—who always know—can we afford to speak and write as if we do not know?

As progressives—notice my inclusion and assimilation into this descriptor—we adopt strategies. If the truth be known, so do liberation theologians. The traditions claimed by the Constantinians as their own have too much power, a power that is probably independent of the Constantinians themselves even though the Constantinians have lots of power. Progressives need to have a strategy and not only complain about the veracity of the "real" claims to be made. What God wants, intends, and demands is too fraught to be left to a right-wing claimant. If they claim ownership to truth and justice, we have to as well.

Why introduce skepticism into the equation when the masses want and respond to certainty? Why continue the historic problems of the Left, debating and splitting over the fine points while power moves on its appointed course? And, to be truthful, what do our arguments mean if there is no constituency for them, a constituency that can also understand what is being said and respond in the way we think right? If progressives give up on the "real" God, we are left floundering, looking weak, without a center or an anchor of truth that rests outside our subjective suggestions.

But actually, if we are truthful, we are destined to fail, progressive or prophetic, anyway, as the Constantinians will fail in due time. What we can do and what is worth doing is to carve out more space for those on the outside, although we know they will, more or less, remain there. If context is not everything, it is an awful lot and the challenge is to see how the context can be moved incrementally without thinking that we are going to alter the larger picture of our time and place. That picture, again more or less, is set. At least for the time being.

I realized this in my struggles within the Jewish world, living as I do, as we all do, in the Golden Age of Constantinian Judaism. This age requires that we define Jewishness, as I do asserting that we have come to the end of Jewish history. Again, as we have known and inherited it, that history being the one that can be seen or recalled as ethical, justice seeking, suffering, and embracing.

When you attend your next Holocaust remembrance, even against your will, just to show up and make sure that you are right with the powers that be, know that your mourning is for the victims of the Holocaust, yes, but also for what has been done in their name *after* the Holocaust and to Palestinians and for your own silence. Know that you have become a bystander in the abuse of Holocaust memory and that your progressive understandings will not allow you to break out of your own imprisonment, which you, muttering under your breath, lay at the feet of the Constantinian Jewish establishment. It should be so placed. And also at your own feet. At your own cowardice.

Not that I blame you. The consequences are real. I know them firsthand. Leave it to the Jews to rain on your parade when they are accused of killing Jesus, when they will not join the Christian or Muslim parade, when they have power after such abuse, and when they dissent about their own abuse of power against another people. Jews are so assertive, insistent, unstable, so in-your-face when they suffer, when they have power and in their disobedience! The Jews!

Yet if we are honest, we are all imprisoned in our contexts. More or less, the historical forces of this or any moment in history are in place. They will not be moved, at least in the immediate sense. Our context imprisons us. Yet context is not everything. Even the context that imprisons us is relative to time and place. The sun that rises on empire also sets on empire. And though the actual sunrise and sunset are ecologically predictable, and the sunrise and sunset on empire seems to mirror that predictability, knowing that the sun will one day set on any particular empire without rising again gives us hope. What is, is not inscribed as inevitable. Though, just to complicate things, we know that the setting of one empire does not mean that empires are history. Just like at every moment of the day and night it is raining somewhere in the world, know that at every moment of history there has been an empire somewhere.

This is where the depth of the prophetic comes in play. The prophetic is hope within the failure to eliminate empire in the world. Once again, this is the opposite view that progressives have. In general, progressive understandings have, as their underpinnings, the same success story as those who pursue progress at any cost. Progress will continue, even as the costs of progress remain steady or escalate. Since progressives participate in and benefit from progress, it is useless to call down the wrath of God on the constituent parts of progress.

Rather, siding with those outside and realizing that success will be marginal at best, a deeper view of success and failure is needed. That depth is found in the prophetic and the God of the prophetic. The God of the prophets is not a God of rescue. Belief in that God is far starker than any celebratory understanding of God siding with diversity and justice. The God of the prophets is a God that demands atheism at the very core of faith. As such, it demands the willingness to suffer without the possibility of rescue.

Like many of our received concepts, the prophets have been dumbed down when they are discussed only in terms of arguing for justice. Certainly justice is central to the prophets and the prophetic. However, justice is only part of the prophetic or, rather, the key that unlocks that which surrounds the prophets and deepens the prophetic plea beyond mere complaint or issue activism.

The depth of the prophetic argument for justice is found in the polyvalent understanding of justice itself—the dignity of the person, the very reason for a social order, the political as a vocation, religion as a purveyor of a destiny beyond the immediate. Justice is ultimately about embrace, reconciliation, forgiveness, and the ultimate meaning of life. The prophet is the one who embodies the possibility of meaning in life and history. The prophetic community devotes its existence to such a possibility.

After all of this we are left only with possibility? The clarion call of the prophet ends only with the gamble that there is meaning in life and history? Moreover, such an (un)clarion outcome is the stuff to render the progressive view of humanity and history questionable, weak, ultimately illusionary, and more about addressing the needs of progressives than those on the margins?

Is that the ultimate pessimism, offering an alternative that is bleaker than the failure you outline?

Indeed, we must end on this note. One need not rely only on Walter Benjamin to see that what we call progress is a storm from paradise. The debris is all around us. The prophet is like Benjamin's Angel, who looks backward and sees the debris piling up. The prophet does not pretend that the debris will be made whole. Rather, the prophet scours the debris for light, keeps moving as darkness reclaims the light, and keeps his eyes wide open. But all of this is another chapter, way beyond the God of the progressives who loves the diversity and justice that might never arrive.

Part II

About Love

FOUR

A World without Tags

A Progressive Palestinian Muslim Scholar Speaks

Isam Shihada

Many important questions and concerns emerge when one observes what is going on in the world today.[1] Some scholars even speak of a clash of civilization and have little hope for peace and justice across different cultures, religions, and societies. They describe our world as if people were not born free, as if God did not create all of us equally, and as if God created people so that we would hate and kill each other instead of learn from each other and coexist in peace. Why are the concepts of justice, diversity, reconciliation, and forgiveness, which I consider the principal teachings of God, absent from our discourse today? I will examine the concept of social and gender justice and diversity in Islam and its importance in a world torn apart by war, radical religious forces, and blind nationalism. I will also shed light on the obstacles and challenges we face and the strategies we must adopt to create a world without tags, a world where people coexist in a just and diverse world without boundaries, a world based on love, respect, and tolerance regardless of color, sex, religion, and ethnicity. Only such a world fulfills the true spirit of God, which is justice and peace.

RELIGION AND RADICAL FORCES

The essence of every religion on earth is justice, peace, and tolerance. Within this context, Nawal El Saadawi points out that "[i]n essence, the messages that were carried to their peoples by the prophets Moses, Jesus

73

and Muhammad were a call to revolt against the injustices of the slave system."[2] The purpose behind these divine messages is to humanize us in order to live a free life based on tolerance, understanding, real engagement, and mutual coexistence.

The danger is that religions are often misused by radical religious forces coming from all religious traditions, including Islam, Christianity, and Judaism. They misread, distort, and misinterpret religions and adapt them to their narrow political and economic agendas. They falsely claim that their misinterpretations represent the true spirit of Islam, Christianity, or Judaism. In my view, reactionary religious forces try to divide us, to create barriers among us, and to shape our lives and futures according to their ambitions and goals. Hence, I agree with the assessment of El Saadawi, who writes that all fundamentalists, whether they are Muslim, Christian, or Jewish, "are partners in the attempt to breed division, strife, racism and sexism."[3] They pose a danger that we as progressive scholars, intellectuals, and communities must recognize for its destructive impact on our present and future. There are many unfortunate examples for this dynamic, and I will refer to only a few cases from the three monotheistic religious traditions of my culture.

All of them illustrate in various ways the impetus of fundamentalist groups toward violence and intolerance. The decree of a *fatwa* against Salman Rushdie in 1989 made by Islamic fundamentalists from Iran is a case in point.[4] The misogynist rule of the Taliban in Afghanistan in the 1990s is another severe instance of Muslim radicalism gone awry.[5] A culminating and world-changing event was undeniably the attack on the United States by another group of Muslim fundamentalists on 9/11, during which about three thousand American civilians lost their lives.[6] All of these offensive acts were committed by radical religious groups in the name of Islam. Yet in Bosnia, Christian radical forces murdered Muslim women, men, and children, and sometimes even buried them alive, between 1992 and 1994.[7] Then, in Lebanon, radical Christian and nationalist forces attacked civilians during the civil war from 1975 to 1990.[8] Finally, in my native country, Palestine, the Jewish state of Israel committed ethnic cleansing of the Palestinian population in 1948,[9] which drove millions of women, men, and children into refugee camps and out of their country. Radical nationalist Jewish religious forces perpetrated such injustice, often justifying the ethnic cleansing as a holy biblical command. As a Palestinian, I feel strongly about this grave harm done to my people. Since 1948, the Palestinian people have had to live their lives as miserable refugees, and those of us who remain steadfastly on our land today—the Gaza Strip, the West Bank, and Jerusalem—continue to suffer under a brutal military occupation. We are often imprisoned, even killed. Our houses are bombed, our children deeply wounded, and our dreams for a peaceful future shattered.

There are numerous other examples throughout history when radical religious forces claimed God's authority, without divine permission, to serve their narrow political, sectarian, national, and economic agendas. An important one played out in Europe at the end of the Middle Ages, when countries and their populations moved through painful periods of reformation and counterreformation, slowly transitioning into modernity and democracy after centuries of brutal and bloody political and religious persecutions and battles. The formation of democratic societies in Europe was a reaction to the injustices meted out against the people in the name of Christianity, and even in the twentieth century ordinary European people suffered greatly to build the peaceful and inclusive countries of today. Political scientist Nader Hashemi makes this point when he states that "the West took several hundred years to develop its secular and democratic institutions through the process of trial and error."[10] A similar process toward secularization and democratization is taking place in the Muslim Arab world today, the so-called Arab Spring, where a process of change and transformation is taking place, with far-reaching effects all around the world.[11]

From a historical perspective, it is clear that violence and religious radicalism have always defined the transition process from traditional and "premodern" forms of social order to modernity and democratic society. Radical groups believe that their faith and culture are under attack and the very existence of their world is seriously threatened, often not an incorrect assessment. In a discussion on Muslim fundamentalism, Karen Armstrong comments on the psychology of radical religious groups in general. She observes that "every fundamentalist movement I have studied in Judaism, Christianity and Islam is rooted in a profound fear of annihilation."[12] Put differently, when societies go through transition from traditional and premodern to modern ways of life, radical religious groups emerge, feeling concerned for their world's survival and hence attacking perceived threats violently and ferociously.

Do these radical religious forces represent us? Do they have the right to act and speak on our behalf? Do they have the right to kidnap our peaceful religions? One may answer "no" for the following reasons: First, radical religious groups violate the basic principles of teachings of God which are based on justice and diversity. Second, they render a reductive version of religion based on exclusion and nullification of the "Other."[13] Third, they neither believe in diversity nor accept difference. Fourth, they think that they are always right and have the absolute truth, a truth which belongs only to God since whatever knowledge we have is little compared to the knowledge and wisdom of God. Finally, fundamentalists are against the idea of pluralism in matters of faith due to their unshakable belief that there is only "one correct school of interpretation of scripture, religion and law."[14] In short, radical religious forces, regardless of the particularities of their religious affiliation, denigrate the core messages of justice, peace, and tolerance found in all religious traditions. They misuse, distort, and misinterpret their religious traditions, and progressive scholars and intellectuals ought to stand up firmly against their attempts to grab political, social, and economic power anywhere.

ISLAM AND THE CONCEPT OF DIVERSITY

Although in the West Islam is often misunderstood, the Muslim religion values diversity greatly. Our main religious text, the Qur'an, is littered with calls for diversity and peaceful coexistence among all people. For instance, Sura 49:13 refers to God as saying, "O humankind, surely, We have created you from a male and a female, and made you tribes and families that you may know each other. Surely the noblest of you with Allah is the most dutiful of you. Surely Allah is Knowing, Aware."[15] In this verse God addresses humanity and not exclusively Muslims. The verse also indicates that God intentionally created humanity as different groups with different colors, habits, cultures, and languages so that we may learn from each other. The verse explains that, to God, difference is a learning experience and only through dialogue do humans learn about themselves, others, and the greatness of God. The passage likewise asserts that the best people are those who are aware and mindful of God's teachings.

Moreover, the Qur'an is clear that God could have created humans without any differences among them, but God chose not to do so. Sura 11:118 addresses this point, stating, "And if thy Lord had pleased, He would have made people a single nation. And they cease not to differ." This verse indirectly demonstrates that, according to the Qur'an, God loves and encourages diversity because Allah graces different people with different ways and rituals to shape and regulate their daily lives.

Yet the Qur'an is not the only witness for the Muslim appreciation of diversity among different peoples. Muslim history gives ample evidence of the long tradition of positive and peaceful life together among Muslims, Jews, and Christians, and the value of intellectual exchange among the different religious groups living together in Muslim countries, as for instance during the centuries of the Abbasid Empire and the *Al-Andalus* civilization.[16] This fact is often observed and emphasized, as Amir Hussain, a professor of theological studies at Loyola Marymount University, explains:

> Pluralism that we see in the modern world has ancient roots. From the eight to the fifteenth centuries, much of Spain was Muslims, and Al-Andalus was a high point of Islamic civilizations. Cordoba in Muslim Spain became one of the most important cities in the history of the world. Christians and Jews were involved in the Royal Court and in the intellectual life of the city.[17]

This was a proud moment in Muslim European history that illustrates the deep inclination toward acceptance and appreciation of Islam toward people of other faith traditions. Islam encourages us to celebrate our common humanity in spite of our various religious and other differences. This sentiment is widely shared by Muslim scholars.

One of them is Omid Safi, a professor of Islamic studies, who wonders if humanity is able to become mature enough to not identify with "exclusive groups [anymore] but [with] the totality of humanity as the Quran calls us the offspring of Adam. Can we envision each other as members of one body, to feel the pain of another as our own? Only then will we be worthy of the name 'human being.'" [18] In my view, Safi's question has become perhaps more urgent now than in past centuries when modern transportation and forms of communication were less readily available and when perhaps less was at stake than today. After all, today not only do many people live under military occupation and political domination, but all of humanity lives under the constant nuclear threat of planetary annihilation. Islam has much to contribute to nurturing peaceful coexistence and love for diversity, as the Qur'an and Muslim history in Spain exemplify.

JUSTICE AND DIVERSITY IN THE PALESTINIAN CONTEXT OF MILITARY OCCUPATION

The importance of justice and diversity in daily life urges me to reflect on the miserable situation of Palestinians, living in the Gaza Strip in particular and in the Occupied Territories in general. I want to ponder deeply whether the main principles of justice and diversity are applied in Palestine, also called the Holy Land. My personal experience serves this attempt to find a solution to the challenges we as Palestinians face today.

I was born as a refugee in a camp in Gaza and know personally what it *means* to live under harsh and constant occupation, what it *means* to live in utter poverty, and what it *means* to share a small bedroom with my eight siblings when my parents and brothers and sisters were hardly covered by a zinc roof protecting us from neither the simmering summer heat nor the harshness of cold winter nights. I remember clearly and as if it happened yesterday when my father told us in a whisper that to survive this cruel and unjust world in which God's principles of justice and diversity are seriously violated, we must become educated. He told us again and again that nobody would be able to take our education and hope from us. He also reminded us persistently that those sowing love will reap love and those sowing hatred will only reap hatred.

Supported with these principles and ideals instilled in me, I pursued my educational journey of hope. In 1986, I went to study at Al Najah University in the West Bank but, unfortunately, in 1987 the university

was closed by the Israeli military due to the first Palestinian Uprising
from 1987 to 1994.[19] I had to leave school, go to Israel, and work in a
restaurant to save some money to continue my education elsewhere later.
My educational journey of hope continued in 1990 when I went abroad
and completed my education with a PhD in English literature and gender
studies. In 2000, I returned to Gaza, where I worked at a local university.
There I taught my occupied Palestinian people, who have been desperate
for justice and peace. I also helped our female students, who are victimized and persecuted by long years of occupation, by educating them
about the sinister reactionary forces trying to stifle women's voices, restricting their freedom, and blurring their identities. I taught them about
their own legitimate rights as women and human beings.[20]

It has been very clear to me that, as a scholar and a public intellectual,[21] I represent the mind of my people. I need to speak truth to power
and replace injustice with justice in an attempt to save my community
and my people from threatening forces in the guise of unjust occupation
and blind nationalism. I have also promoted awareness among my students and explained to them the value of multicultural experiences, as I
have lived them, with the goal of effecting positive changes in them and
giving them hope.

My educational journey has certainly not been easy. It was a hard and
painful path because of the Second Palestinian Uprising, the Intifada
from 2000 until today, during which Gaza has been besieged.[22] For instance, Israeli checkpoints that divide Gaza into three parts have made it
impossible not only for me to reach my students but also for ordinary
people to move freely. The siege imposed on Gaza in late 2000 severely
intensified after Hamas came into power in 2007.[23] The constant siege
imposed on Gaza has had a disastrous impact on Palestinians living in
Gaza. It has meant that we cannot travel or trade freely. Our sick people
cannot be treated in hospitals outside Gaza. Students cannot attend universities in the West Bank or abroad, and academics cannot attend conferences or do research abroad. For many years, I, too, was unable to
leave Gaza to attend conferences in the United States, South Africa, or the
United Kingdom to advance my academic career and to help my students
build a better educational future for themselves. In other words, the siege
has been a collective punishment for all human beings living in the Gaza
Strip. Finally, the most recent Israeli war on the Gaza Strip was in
2008–2009, and my family and I almost lost our lives during it. Tanks and
shells bombed our house indiscriminately from every direction for almost two days.

I remember this time clearly when our house was under constant
shelling and we were hiding in the bathroom. We were cut off from the
world, without telephone, electricity, food, water, not even milk for my
baby daughter and medicine for my pregnant wife. The only thing for me
to do was put them behind my back, expecting to die first and hoping

they would survive. At that moment, I felt helpless and could only wait for God's mercy. Miraculously, we were saved by the Red Cross while thousands of innocent civilians were killed, injured, and houses bombed and erased.[24] The Red Cross sheltered people like us in schools. Until the end of the war in mid-January 2009, they gave us food, water, and medicine. I am haunted by the scene when my family and I came out of our destroyed home, holding a white flag as a sign that we are innocent human beings who deserve to live in peace and dignity. I remember the scene with my tearful eyes, touching my wife and daughter to make sure their bodies were really uninjured after the bombs had fallen for so long in Gaza.

My traumatic experience is only one of the countless untold stories that my fellow Palestinians endured, especially those who still live under the harsh military occupation in Gaza and the Occupied Territories. The Israeli military has created inhumane geographical boundaries by erecting the cruel separation wall in the West Bank.[25] Israel keeps punishing innocent human beings collectively and persecuting Palestinians under the endless pretexts of security. All of it means that Israelis keep betraying the principles of God's justice and diversity because the ongoing Israeli occupation of Palestinian land contradicts the principles of God's justice. There can be no peace without justice. There can be no peace without diversity and the acceptance of the "other." When these statements are applied to the case of Palestine it means that those of us who live in Israel and Palestine do not have peace because God's principles of justice and diversity are not respected and not practiced. This must change.

Today, we are living in a global village where boundaries are coming down, walls have fallen,[26] and people from different nationalities communicate easily with each other and live together thanks to innovative technologies. These changes lead me to think of the importance of diversity and pluralism in our fast-changing world. For example, countries such as South Africa and the United States are reconciling with their own histories, fostering internal peace, coexistence, tolerance, and democracy.[27] Religious studies scholar Diana Eck is correct when she maintains that "the goal of pluralism is not simply 'tolerance' of the other, but rather an active attempt to arrive at understanding."[28] Likewise, in my view, all people living in Palestine and Israel ought to reconcile with their own various histories, lick their wounds, so to speak, and move toward one pluralistic and diverse state, without walls, and respectful of human rights and all religions.[29]

All people of all faiths living in one state together, whether this is in Israel/Palestine or elsewhere, should approach God peacefully and practice their faith without any form of persecution because, as Sura 2:256 in the Qur'an states, "There is no compulsion in religion." All of us, including Palestinians, ought to be free to choose and to elect our own democratic government. It is the only option we have because we know from history and experience: violence begets violence and hatred breeds more hatred. American civil rights leader Martin Luther King Jr. said it well: "Through violence you may murder the hater, but you do not murder hate. In fact, violence merely increases hate. . . . Returning violence for violence multiplies violence, adding deeper darkness to a night already devoid of stars. Darkness cannot drive out hate; only love can do that."[30]

I believe that we must create a pluralistic and diverse just society in Palestine to create a better future for our children without fear, demonization, bloodshed, and nullification of the "other." There is no such thing as a "lesser" person. We must relentlessly strive toward "a universal notion of justice in which no single community's prosperity, righteousness and dignity comes at the expense of another."[31] It does not suffice that people from different religious and ethnic backgrounds live together. We must actively engage with one another. Pluralism without active engagement of the "other" is not good enough because, as Amir Hussain proposes, a diverse and pluralistic society ought to be committed "to engaging the very differences we have to gain a deeper sense of each other's commitments. Pluralism is not and cannot be a non-participant sport."[32] We should therefore promote a culture of justice, diversity, tolerance, and peace because we know there is no peace without justice and diversity, as peace is the natural conclusion of justice and diversity. Without justice and diversity, there will be no peace at all. Peace is only achievable when all people have equal human rights and everybody can live in dignity and freedom. The Dalai Lama knows about this simple-sounding observation when he writes, "Peace, in the sense of the absence of war, is of little value to someone who is dying of hunger or cold. Peace can only last where human rights are respected, where the people are fed, and where individuals and nations are free."[33] For sure, the Dalai Lama's insight also applies to Palestine.

GENDER JUSTICE IN ISLAM

Islam emphasizes justice and, in fact, it is the duty of Muslims to do justice. This advice is a Qur'anic teaching. For instance, Sura 5:8 states, "O you who believe, be upright for Allah, bearers of witness with justice; and let not hatred of a people incite you not to act equitably. Be just; that is nearer to observance of duty. And keep your duty to Allah. Surely Allah is Aware of what you do." A similar recommendation appears in Sura 4:135, according to which God states:

> O you who believe, be maintainers of justice, bearers of witness for Allah, even though it be against your own selves or (your) parents or near relatives—whether he be rich or poor, Allah has a better right over them both. So follow not (your) low desires, lest you deviate. And if

you distort or turn away from (truth), surely Allah is ever Aware of what you do.

The Muslim religion promotes equality for women.[34] The Qur'an mandates that women have the right to choose their own mates, pursue education, work, possess and inherit. For instance, Sura 4:15 states, "For men is the benefit of what they earn. And for women is the benefit of what they earn." Moreover, in pre-Islamic Arabia, female infanticide was a common practice, but it was completely forbidden by Islam. As Sura 16:58–59 states, "And when the birth of a daughter is announced to one of them, his face becomes black and he is full of wrath. He hides himself from the people because of the evil of what is announced to him. Shall he keep it with disgrace or bury it (alive) in the dust? Now surely evil is what they judge!"

Islam teaches against slavery. It also asserts the sanctity of human life,[35] as, for instance, in Sura 5:35: "And whoever saves a life, it is as though he had saved the lives of all men." The same notion is also articulated in Sura 6:151: "Kill not the soul which Allah has made sacred." The Qur'an contains numerous calls for helping poor people, caring about one's neighbor and practicing charity. The Qur'an, especially a section called "The Women," calls for gender justice. This section stresses women's equal rights for education, work, and ownership of property. Hence, Muslims know that it is impossible to imagine a democratic society which does not guarantee women's equal rights. Omid Safi makes this point when he writes that "there can be no progressive interpretation of Islam without gender justice. When we talk about gender, it is not only an issue of women but human beings too. Gender injustice debases and dehumanizes the Muslim males who participate in the system."[36]

Hence, the Qu'ran articulates unambiguously that women and men are equal.[37] Allah created men and women so that there could be love, mercy, and compassion, as stated in Sura 30:21: "And of His signs is this that, He created mates for you from yourselves that you might find quiet of mind in them, and He put between you love and compassion. Surely there are signs in this for a people who reflect." The Qur'an also emphasizes that God views both men and women as equal with full rights and anticipated rewards:

> Surely the men who submit and the women who submit, and the believing men and the believing women, and the obeying men and the obeying women, and the truthful men and the truthful women, and the patient men and the patient women, and the humble men and the humble women, and the charitable men and the charitable women, and the fasting men and the fasting women, and the men who guard their chastity and the women who guard, and the men who remember Allah much and women who remember—Allah has prepared for them forgiveness and a mighty reward. (Sura 33:35)

The Qu'ran also advises men to live with their wives in harmony and treat them well. Sura 4:19 urges men to treat women well, warning them that their potential disdain for women is their own bias not shared by God: "And treat them kindly. Then if you hate them, it may be that you dislike a thing while Allah has placed abundant good in it."

Despite the Qur'an's clear support for women's rights, many Muslim societies neglect to follow these teachings. Within this context, the Muslim activist Isalm-Husain holds "the oppression of women within Muslim countries betrays Islam's principle of gender equality."[38] It is sad to acknowledge that Muslim women have been systematically excluded from the intellectual religious production throughout history. The denial of women's contributions to Muslim history has prevented women from directly contributing to the religiously dominant discourse even today. This exclusion relegated them to oppressive patriarchal, androcentric interpretations of religious texts such as the Qur'an, which characterized women as passive, evil, shameful, and weak and as in need of supervision by the males of their immediate families.[39]

In Muslim societies, the oppression of Muslim women clearly violates the teachings of the Qur'an that call for women's equality.[40] And yet it is widely known that much malpractice is done to women in the name of Islam. The practices of veiling and polygamy are among them. Discussions on the veil abound,[41] with attempts to explain who should wear it, why, when, what its shape should be, and whether the veil is a religious or political marker. Put differently, the Qur'an recommends viewing women not as a source of seduction. Rather, and like men, they ought to live as models for morality and chastity. According to feminist scholar Nawal El Saadawi, both women and men are "ordered to show sexual restraint and respectability through the proper Qur'anic legislations."[42] Yet, in contrast to these teachings found in the sacred text of Islam, there are many places in which women are forced, and sometimes they themselves choose, to wear the veil in the attempt to conform to social, religious, and political standards of patriarchal society.[43]

Then there is the problem of polygamy in Islam. In the Qur'an, polygamy is only allowed as "the protection of the orphans and widows." During war, women and children lose their husbands and fathers, respectively. The Qur'an recognizes that it is impossible for a husband to do justice to more than one woman even if he tries. As Sura 4:3 states, "And if you fear that you cannot do justice to orphans, marry such women as seem good to you, two, or three, or four; but if you fear that you will not do justice, then (marry) only one." In Sura 4:129, the phrase "you cannot do justice between wives, even though you wish (it)" reaffirms this belief that a man cannot treat several women equally even if he intends to. Another argument speaks against polygamous practice among Muslim men. Common sense tells us that a man marrying several women surely prefers the newest wife over the earlier ones, but such a preference contradicts the principle of equality and justice articulated in the Qur'an. Yet despite this Qur'anic insight, unfortunately, polygamy is widespread among Muslim men, even though it is "a dreadful and dehumanizing instrument for the brutalizing of women's sensibilities."[44]

To put an end to these malpractices, feminist Muslim scholars, among them Fatima Mernissi, Leila Ahmed, and Amina Wadud, reject the reductive patriarchal interpretations of Islam and unveil the underlying economic and political forces of such practices.[45] Their work has also shown that all religions, including Islam, are progressive and liable for critical deconstruction to find answers to meet our human and peaceful needs. American feminist scholar, Elizabeth Fernea, explains:

> Islamic women begin with the assumption that the possibility for equality already exists in the Quran itself. The problem as they see it is malpractice, or misunderstanding of the sacred text. For these Muslim women, the first goal of a feminist movement is to re-understand and evaluate the sacred text and for women to be involved in the process, which historically has been reserved for men.[46]

Muslim feminists, labeled by Miriam Cooke as supporters of "Islamic Feminism,"[47] have much to gain from new Qur'anic interpretations. Their goal of establishing justice and citizenship for Muslim women will surely make a huge difference in the future. Part of the intellectual and religious battle concerns the practice of polygamy, which, after all, is also a demeaning practice for men.

Islamic feminists shed light on women's roles within religious communities. By deconstructing the dominant androcentric religious theories and practices, they show how mainstream Muslim society still excludes women. Islamic feminists have thus worked hard to keep their religious, political and gender identities in place while they resisted the pernicious alliance of patriarchy, nationalism, and Islamic fundamentalism controlling so many Muslim women, and also men today.[48] They have demonstrated what is at stake when feminists critique Muslim history and reassign women to their rightful place next to men, so that Muslim society and religion emerge as just communities in which women flourish after centuries of unjust marginalization and sexist oppression.

SOCIETIES WITHOUT TAGS: TOWARD A CONCLUSION

Democratic societies—whether Muslim or not—ought to be built on justice, gender justice, and diversity. Gender justice is the measuring scale for how successful we as human beings, including Palestinians who want to live in a democratic society of their own, are in creating democratic, just, diverse, and pluralistic societies that do not classify people with tags and turn them into "second-class citizens."

The question is, how we can achieve peace? Is it possible to have peace without diversity, without accepting "the other" as a fully human being? What are the obstacles and challenges we face which prevent us from ensuring justice, diversity, and peace in our world? My answer is that we have to ensure acceptance of "the other," remove boundaries, live and engage with one another, isolate the radical forces, and ensure justice for women. We have peace today in South Africa only after applying the principles of diversity and justice, and the same is also true in the United States. We do not have peace in Palestine today because Palestinians are not treated as full human beings and citizens with full rights. Hence, I propose the one-state solution to both Palestinians and Israelis, grounded in the principles of diversity and justice. Only then can people live together, engage with one another, and practice their own faiths freely by taking into account that there are Muslims, Jews, and Christians in Palestine. It is not only a national or political issue for Palestinians and Israelis. It is a human issue for all people living there, without any kind of exclusion. As long as we, Palestinians and Israelis, do not embrace the principles of justice and diversity, we will continue betraying God's principles of justice and diversity. It is my deep conviction that there will be no peace anywhere in the world without diversity and justice. It is not only an issue for Palestine. It is applicable to every place in the world. Only then will we realize and ensure that there will be a world without tags. The conviction that God is a symbol of justice and diversity may serve to unite us as human beings to work against all forms of injustice in our world. As a Palestinian and a Muslim scholar of English literature and gender studies, I would like to be part of this effort.

NOTES

1. For more information on discourses of clash of civilizations, see Samuel P. Huntington, *The Clash of Civilizations: Remaking of World Order* (New York: Touchstone Press, 1996); Bernard Lewis, *The Crisis of Islam: Holy War and Unholy Terror* (New York: Random House, 2003); Rohan Gunaratna, *Inside al-Qaeda: Global Network of Terror* (New York: Columbia University Press, 2002); Steven Emerson, *Jihad in America: The Terrorists Living among Us* (New York: Free Press, 2002); Emran Qureshi and Michael Sells (eds.), *The New Crusade: Constructing the Muslim Enemy* (New York: Columbia University Press, 2003); John Esposito, *The Islamic Threat: Myth or Reality?* (New York: Oxford University Press, 1992).
2. Nawal El Saadawi, *The Nawal El Saadawi Reader* (London/New York: Zed Books, 1997), 74.
3. Ibid., 93.
4. For more information, see Kenan Malik, *From Fatwa to Jihad: The Rushdie Affair and Its Aftermath* (Brooklyn: Melville House Publishing, 2010).
5. For more discussions on Taliban's rule, see Ahmed Rashid, *Taliban: Militant Islam, Oil & Fundamentalism in Central Asia* (New Haven, CT: Yale University Press, 2000); James Ferguson, *Taliban: The Unknown Enemy* (New York: Da Capo Press, 2011).
6. For more details on the September 11 attacks on the United States, see Joseph B. Lambert, *9-11 America under Attack* (Bloomington: Author House, 2002); Rohan Guna-

ratna, *Inside al-Qaeda: Global Network of Terror* (New York: Columbia University Press, 2002).

7. For more information on the war in Bosnia, see Paul Mojzes (ed.), *Religion and the War in Bosnia* (Atlanta, GA: Scholars Press, 1998); Edgar O'Balance, *Civil War in Bosnia, 1992–94* (New York: St. Martin's Press, 1995); Eric Markusen and Martin Mennecke, "Genocide in Bosnia and Herzegovina," *Human Rights Review* 5, no. 4 (2004): 72–85; Michael Sells, *The Bridge Betrayed: Religion and Genocide in Bosnia* (Berkeley: University of California Press, 1996).

8. For a discussion on the Lebanese civil war, see Robert Fisk, *Pity the Nation of Lebanon* (New York: Athenaeum, 1990); Tabitha Petran, *The Struggle over Lebanon* (New York: Monthly Review Press, 1987).

9. See, for example, Ilan Pappe, *The Ethnic Cleansing of Palestine* (Oxford: Oneworld, 2006); Noam Chomsky, *The Fateful Triangle: The United States, Israel and the Palestinians* (Boston: South End Press, 1983); Efraim Karsh, *Palestine Betrayed* (New Haven, CT: Yale University Press, 2010); Norman Finkelstein, *Image and Reality of the Israel-Palestine Conflict* (New York: Verso, 1995).

10. Nader Hashemi, *Islam, Secularism and Liberal Democracy* (New York: Oxford University Press, 2009), 44.

11. For more information on the Arab Spring, see Robert Fisk, "Why the Middle East Will Never Be the Same Again," *The Independent* (September 20, 2011). The article is available online: www.independent.co.uk/opinion/commentators/fisk/robert-fisk-why-the-middle-east-will-never-be-the-same-again-2357514.html [accessed on December 6, 2012].

12. Karen Armstrong, "Is a Holy War Inevitable?" *GQ* (January 2002): 98. See also Karen Armstrong, *The Battle for God* (New York: Knopf, 2001).

13. For more on representation of the "Other," see Stuart Hall, *Representation: Cultural Representations and Signifying Practices* (London: Sage Publications, 1997).

14. Hashemi, *Islam, Secularism and Liberal Democracy*, 42.

15. All quotations are taken from Maulana Muhammad Ali, *The Holy Quran: Arabic Text, English Translation and Commentary* (Lahore: Ahmadiyya Anjuman Ishaat Islam, 1991).

16. For more information on the coexistence among Muslims, Jews, and Christians throughout history, see Maria Menocal, *The Ornament of the World: How Muslims, Jews, and Christians Created a Culture of Tolerance in Medieval Spain* (Boston: Brown, 2002); Abdul Aziz Said and Meena Sharify-Funk (eds.), *Cultural Diversity and Islam* (New York: University Press of America, 2003).

17. Amir Hussain, "Muslims, Pluralism, and Interfaith Dialogue," in *Progressive Muslims: On Justice, Gender and Pluralism*, ed. Omid Safi (Oxford: Oneworld, 2003), 257.

18. Omid Safi (ed.), *Progressive Muslims: On Justice, Gender and Pluralism* (Oxford: Oneworld, 2003), 12.

19. For more information on the first Palestinian uprising, see Jamal Nassar and Roger Heacock (eds.), *Intifada: Palestine at the Crossroads* (New York: Praeger, 1990).

20. For more information on the sufferings of Palestinian women living under Israeli occupation, see A. Cheryl Rubenberg, *Palestinian Women: Patriarchy and Resistance in the West Bank* (Boulder, CO: Lynne Rienner, 2001). For a discussion on Palestinian Islamic groups, see Ziad Abu-Amr, *Islamic Fundamentalism in the West Bank and Gaza: Muslim Brotherhood and Islamic Jihad* (Bloomington: Indiana University Press, 1994).

21. For more information on the public intellectual, see Edward W. Said, *Representations of the Intellectual: The 1993 Reith Lectures* (New York: Pantheon Books, 1994).

22. For more information on the impact of the Second Intifada on the lives of people living in the Gaza Strip, see Toine van Teeffelen and Ronald de Hommel (eds.), *Caged In: Life in Gaza during the Second Intifada* (Bethlehem, Palestine: Arab Educational Institute, 2004).

23. For more discussion on the structure and ideology of Hamas and its conflict with Fatah, see Beverley Milton-Edwards and Stephen Farrell, *Hamas: The Islamic Re-*

sistance Movement (Cambridge: Polity, 2010); Frederic P. Miller, *Fatah-Hamas Conflict* (Germany: VDM Publishing House, 2009).

24. For more information on the Israeli war on Gaza from 2008 to 2009, see Norman Finkelstein, *This Time We Went Too Far: Truth and Consequences of the Gaza Invasion* (New York: OR Books, 2010).

25. For a discussion on the wall around the West Bank built between 2002 and 2003, see Ray Dolphin, *The West Bank Wall: Unmaking Palestine* (London: Pluto Press, 2006). Two documentary movies, *Miral* (2010) and *Budrus* (2009), record the impact of the West Bank wall on the lives of the Palestinians.

26. On the fall of the Berlin Wall and its impact on the lives of the German people, see Michael Burgan, *The Berlin Wall: Barrier to Freedom* (Minneapolis, MN: Compass Point Books, 2008).

27. For information on the experiences of South Africa after the apartheid system, see Farid Esack, *Quran, Liberation and Pluralism: An Islamic Perspective of Interreligious Solidarity against Oppression* (Oxford: Oneworld, 1997); Nancy L. Clark and William H. Worger, *South Africa: The Rise and Fall of Apartheid* (New York: Longman, 2004). For a study on American slavery, see Eric Foner, *The Fiery Trial: Abraham Lincoln and American Slavery* (New York: Norton, 2010); Aaron Sheehan-Dean, *Concise Historical Atlas of the U.S. Civil War* (New York: Oxford University Press, 2008).

28. Diana Eck, *A New Religious America: How a Christian Country Has Now Become the World's Most Religiously Diverse Nation* (San Francisco: Harper San Francisco, 2001), 70–71.

29. For information on the one-state proposal as the solution to the Israeli-Palestinian conflict, see Virginia Tilley, *The One-State Solution: A Breakthrough for Peace in the Israeli-Palestinian Deadlock* (Ann Arbor: University of Michigan Press, 2005); Ali Abunimah, *One Country: A Bold Proposal to End the Israeli-Palestinian Impasse* (New York: Metropolitan, 2006); Leila Farsakh, "The One-State Solution and the Palestinian Conflict: Palestinian Challenges and Prospects," *Middle East Journal* 65, no. 1 (Winter 2011): 55–71.

30. Martin Luther King, "Where Do We Go From Here: Chaos or Community," in *A Testament of Hope: The Essential Writings and Speeches of Martin Luther King, Jr.*, ed. James M. Washington (San Francisco: Harper San Francisco, 1991), 633.

31. Safi, *Progressive Muslims*, 4.

32. Hussain, "Muslims, Pluralism, and Interfaith Dialogue," 252.

33. Dalai Lama, *A Policy of Kindness* (Sidney: Snow Lion, 1990), 17.

34. For extensive information on Islam, see Mahajabeen Isalm-Husain, "The Qur'an Does Not Discriminate on the Basis of Gender," in *Islam: Opposing Viewpoints*, ed. Jennifer A. Hurely (San Diego: Greenhaven Press, 2001), 76–83; John Esposito (ed.), *The Oxford History of Islam* (New York: Oxford University Press, 2000); Karen Armstrong, *Islam* (London: Modern Library, 2000); John Esposito and Azzam Tamimi (eds.), *Islam and Secularism in the Middle East* (New York: New York University Press, 2000); John Esposito and Dalia Mogahed, *Who Speaks for Islam? What a Billion Muslims Really Think* (New York: Gallup Press, 2007); Hashemi, *Islam, Secularism and Liberal Democracy*; and Wilfred Smith, *Islam in Modern History* (Princeton, NJ: Princeton University Press, 1957).

35. For more information on human rights in the Qur'an, see Muhammad Sharif Chaudhry, *Human Rights in Islam* (Lahore: Pakistan Islamic Education Congress, 1993); Riffat Hassan, "On Human Rights and the Qur'anic Perspective," *Journal of Ecumenical Studies* 19, no. 3 (1982): 51; and Shaheen Sardar Ali, *Gender and Human Rights in Islam and International Law: Equal Before Allah, Unequal Before Man?* (The Hague/Boston: Kluwer Law International, 2000).

36. Safi, *Progressive Muslims*, 10–11.

37. For more information on the ambiguous portrayal of women in the Hadith, see Fatima Mernissi, *The Veil and the Male Elite: A Feminist Interpretation of Women's Rights in Islam* (New York: Basic Books, 1991).

38. Isalm-Husain, "The Qur'an Does Not Discriminate on the Basis of Gender," 76.

39. For information on the Wahhabis and Salafis's obsession of excluding women, see Khaled Abou El Fadl, *Speaking in God's Name: Islamic Law, Authority and Women* (Oxford: Oneworld, 2001); Natana J. DeLong-Bas, *Wahhabi Islam: From Revival and Reform to Global Jihad* (New York: Oxford University Press, 2004); Roel Meijer (ed.), *Global Salafism: Islam's New Religious Movement* (New York: Columbia University Press, 2009); Michael Cooke, "On the Origins of Wahhabism," *Journal of the Royal Asiatic Society* 3, no. 2 (1992): 191–202; Mohammed Ayoob, *The Many Faces of Political Islam: Religion and Politics in the Muslim World* (Ann Arbor: University of Michigan Press, 2008); and Azza Karam, *Women, Islamism and the State* (New York/Basingstoke: St. Martin's Press/MacMillan, 1998).

40. For an extensive and detailed discussion on the rights of women in Islam, see Asgharali Engineer, *The Rights of Women in Islam* (London: Hurst, 1992); Ahmed Khairat, *The Status of Women in Islam* (Egypt: Dar El-Ma'arif, 1975); Ziba Mir-Hosseni, *Islam and Gender: The Religious Debate in Contemporary Iran* (Princeton, NJ: Princeton University Press, 1999); Ali Mohammad Syed, *The Position of Women in Islam: A Progressive View* (Albany: State University of New York Press, 2004); Lamia Shehadeh, *The Idea of Women in Fundamentalist Islam* (Gainesville: University Press of Florida, 2003); Lila Abu-Lughod, *Veiled Sentiments: Honor and Poetry in a Bedouin Society* (Berkeley: University of California Press, 1986); Lila Abu-Lughod (ed.), *Remaking Women: Feminism and Modernity in the Middle East* (Princeton, NJ: Princeton University Press, 1998); Gisela Webb, *Windows of Faith: Muslim Women Scholar-Activists in North America* (New York: Syracuse University Press, 2000); Fatima Mernissi, *The Forgotten Queens of Islam* (Minneapolis: University of Minnesota Press, 1993); Elizabeth Fernea and Basima Bezirgan (eds.), *Middle Eastern Muslim Women Speak* (Austin: University of Texas, 1977); Elizabeth Fernea, *In Search of Islamic Feminism: One Woman's Global Journey* (New York: Doubleday, 1998); Mashood A. Baderin, *Islam and Human Rights: Advocacy for Social Change in Local Contexts* (New Delhi: Global Media Publications, 2006); and Amina Wadud, *Quran and Woman: Rereading the Sacred Text from a Woman's Perspective* (New York: Oxford University Press, 1999).

41. For the debates on the veil, see Mernissi, *The Veil and the Male Elite*; Ali Mohammad Syed, *The Position of Women in Islam: A Progressive View* (Albany: State University of New York Press, 2004); Saadawi, *The Nawal El Saadawi Reader*; Leila Ahmed, *Women, Gender and Islam* (New Haven, CT: Yale University Press, 1992); Anwar Hekmat, *Women and the Koran: The Status of Women in Islam* (Amherst: Prometheus, 1997); and Elizabeth Fernea, *In Search of Islamic Feminism: One Woman's Global Journey* (New York: Doubleday, 1998).

42. Saadawi, *The Nawal El Saadawi Reader*, 85.

43. For a discussion on women being forced to veil, see Zahra Kamalkhani, *Women's Islam: Religious Practice among Women in Today's Iran* (New York: Kegan Paul International, 1998); Allison M. Jaggar and Iris M. Young (eds.), *A Companion to Feminist Philosophy* (Oxford: Blackwell, 1998); Ahmed Rashid, *Taliban: Militant Islam, Oil & Fundamentalism in Central Asia* (New Haven, CT: Yale University Press, 2000); and Khaled Abou El Fadl, *Speaking in God's Name: Islamic Law, Authority and Women* (Oxford: Oneworld, 2001).

44. Riffat Hassan, "On Human Rights and the Qur'anic Perspective," *Journal of Ecumenical Studies* 19, no. 3 (1982): 51.

45. For more information on Islamic feminist scholars, see Miriam Cooke, *Women Claim Islam* (New York: Routledge, 2001); Amina Wadud, *Quran and Woman: Rereading the Sacred Text from a Woman's Perspective* (New York: Oxford University Press, 1999); Margot Badran, *Feminists, Islam and the Nation* (Princeton, NJ: Princeton University Press, 1995); and Margot Badran, *Feminism in Islam: Secular and Religious Convergences* (Oxford: Oneworld, 2009).

46. Elizabeth Fernea, *In Search of Islamic Feminism: One Woman's Global Journey* (New York: Doubleday, 1998), 416.

47. Miriam Cooke, *Women Claim Islam* (New York: Routledge, 2001), 59.

48. For information on the dangerous alliance between nationalism and Islamic fundamentalism, see Bruce Lawrence, *Shattering the Myth: Islam Beyond Violence* (Princeton, NJ: Princeton University Press, 1998); Octavia Paz, *One Earth, Four or Five Worlds: Reflections on Contemporary History* (New York: Harcourt, 1985).

FIVE

Class Matters in an Age of Empire

A White Feminist Working-Class American Speaks

Susanne Johnson

In his classic book written one century ago (1912), German theologian Ernst Troeltsch posed a question that begs attention yet today: "[What is] the significance of Christianity for the solution of the social problem of the present day?" Writing in the context of the German Empire, Troeltsch observed:

> [T]his social problem is vast and complicated. It includes the problem of the capitalist economic period and of the industrial proletariat created by it; and of the growth of militaristic and bureaucratic giant states; of the enormous increase in population, which affects colonial and world policy, of the mechanical technique, which produces enormous masses of material and links up and mobilizes the whole world for purposes of trade, but which also treats men and labor like machines. [1]

A century later, these words are even *more* apt—certainly not less. They foreshadow the ever more "vast and complicated" reality we now name as the "American Empire," which many scholars agree is *the* defining social problem of our present era. [2] By its very nature and dynamics, the reality of Empire confounds and contradicts our claim to be a nation that secures "liberty and justice for *all*" and belies our affirmation that "God loves diversity and justice." In order for Empire to "work," diverse identity groups must somehow be led to fear one another as outsiders and threats, or potential terrorists, or competitors for scarce resources and jobs. "Misrecognized" groups are kept narrowly focused on gaining recognition and respect. That way, the masses of working-class laborers (the "proletariat") are kept segmented, thereby unable or unwilling to unite and resist being treated "like machines."

The matter of Empire is urgent, insists theologian David Griffin, because "the nation that is seeking to become the world's first borderless empire, the United States of America, — is also the nation that, precisely through its imperialist policies, is the primary threat to the survival of the human species (along with that of many other species as well)."[3] We must end the American Empire before it ends us, Chalmers Johnson declares.[4] This imperative is no less important for the church than for the nation as a whole, given the church's mission to stand in solidarity with people and places abandoned by Empire and to resist Empire itself and to reduce its injustices.

Richard Horsley argues that while biblical writers are not unanimously and unambiguously anti-imperial or pro-imperial, but rather speak with different and sometimes ambivalent voices, nevertheless we can reclaim scripture as "a history of faithful resistance against Empire."[5] A broad range of contemporary scholars essentially concur with this point, such as Walter Brueggemann, who insists that biblically grounded faith compels the disruption of Empire. Scripture, he contends, is narrative witness to a God who is allied against Empire, who intervenes for the lowly ones, and who invites us to a future shaped like the *basileia* of God.[6] The theological symbol *basileia*, Elisabeth Schüssler Fiorenza reminds us, connotes a political vision that appealed to the oppositional imagination of people victimized by the Roman imperial system. It envisions an alternative world free of hunger, poverty, and domination of the most vulnerable, especially immigrants, widows, orphans, and the poor.[7]

One of the significant challenges we face in resisting Empire lies in how difficult it is to see what is going on in the first place, for it is the very nature of Empire to secure hegemony — the consent of those being dominated — by supplying the symbols, representations, and practices of socio-political and economic life in such a way that the basis of unequal relations of power and privilege remains hidden, normalized, and taken for granted.[8] In this chapter, I seek to make visible at least one of the lynchpins of Empire and one of its significant forms of injustice — that of *class exploitation* — and to situate the reality of class within the multiple, interlocking oppressions — that is, the "matrix of domination," which is part and parcel of Empire. My thesis is that by having a better conceptual grasp of what class actually is and the hidden ways it operates, we obtain a more adequate understanding of the "vast and complicated" nature of Empire and, more particularly, "the significance of Christianity for the solution of the social problem of the present day"[9] — namely, Empire, and collective grassroots resistance against it.

Inasmuch as class exploitation is a reality that cuts across gender, race, ethnicity, immigrant status, sexual orientation, age, and religious identity, insight into its dynamics provide a basis on which Christians may link arms with persons of diverse faith traditions and work collectively to reduce its injustice and seek the common good in our society and in the global commons. A vision of God as the "Utterly Just One" resonates across many faith traditions. Deeper grounding in this conviction can help people of faith provide more compelling and consequential witness to God's own mission of inclusive love and justice in and for the sake of the world and its full flourishing.

AN AUTOBIOGRAPHICAL EXCURSUS

Like many academics, I refer to the triumvirate of race, class, and gender. But frankly, in my teaching I have given far more attention to race and gender than to class, probably because I used to have only vague notions of how to conceptualize class in the first place. Aside from scholarly interest, about a decade ago I discovered the redemptive power of using class as a conceptual lens through which to understand my own upbringing in a poor, working-class family, and especially to gain insight into my parents and their impact on my life, and even to reclaim working-class people as "my people." This was a significant turn for me, for I had worked so long and hard to escape my working-class roots, and to make the professional middle class my home, especially by earning a doctoral degree—I was the first person ever to do so in my extended family—and by joining the faculty of a highly respected private university in the Southwest. And yet, like many working-class people who move into the professional middle class, for many years life in this new world seemed out of sync. Something was always a little off, "like an engine with imprecise timing." [10]

My turning point to reclaim "a usable past" was prompted when I read *Worlds of Pain*, an ethnographic inquiry into the lives of white working-class "intact" families (i.e., no single-parent homes) by sociologist Lillian Rubin. [11] Her subjects recalled parents who worked hard, yet never quite made it, in homes that were overcrowded, stressed, and so preoccupied with the daily struggle for survival that it precluded long-range planning for the future. These issues were true of my upbringing, although my conservative, churchgoing family was much more stable than many of Rubin's subjects, 40 percent of whom were children of divorce or desertion. What grabbed my attention most was her observation that emotional deprivation often follows on the heels of material deprivation. Parents distracted by financial worry often have little energy left to give emotional support and approving praises to their children. I yearned for this but received so little. Strained, distant, or damaged child-parent relationships can leave children and youth feeling alienated or isolated, and render them vulnerable to being exploited by predators who shower them with attention. Rubin helped me see my parents in a new light and to empathize with their own "world of pain."

I was one of six children and the only girl in my family. We lived in a small town in rural southeast Missouri. Though very bright, my parents did not attend college. Not only did they lack financial capital, they also lacked what French sociologist Pierre Bourdieu calls *social capital*, a network of connections to help them navigate the system and track down help. My mother was intellectually gifted enough that she skipped an entire year of high school and graduated early, at the top of her class. A college scholarship that should have gone to her went instead to a much less accomplished student—precisely because the girl had the benefit of social and cultural capital that my mother lacked, coming from an abjectly poor, rural farm family.

My father was a blue-collar, low-wage worker who did menial labor for the local public utility company. Outfitted in a green uniform, he walked neighborhoods all day, rain or shine, reading meters on houses. Then the company trained him to climb wooden poles that carried electric lines and to install wires or fix broken ones. There were times during my childhood when I was terrified for him. In the middle of the night, during horrible thunderstorms, the phone would ring, and he would have to go out on emergency calls in the midst of lightning and pounding rain to repair broken electric wires. While corporate elites are astronomically rewarded for assuming financial risk, working-class laborers are seldom given any recognition or reward for assuming physical risk to life and limb.

As it turns out, many of the things I criticized my parents for and presumed to be their individual idiosyncrasies and personal flaws were actually structural effects of class status, and of what Bourdieu calls a "class habitus." This is akin to the feminist notion that the personal is political. In essence, a habitus is the set of subjective dispositions—the habits of thought, feeling, and action—that persons interiorize early in life as they interact with the objective, structural conditions or constraints of their social space.[12] Bourdieu emphasizes that, in complex ways, self-agency and social structures are mutually constitutive, dialectical realities. Unconsciously, working-class people accept inequitable structural arrangements and asymmetrical power relations as the self-evident way things are supposed to be. Thereby, they learn not to aspire to what seems unthinkable, unattainable, and inaccessible. Instead, they learn to desire and want what seems realistically within reach.[13] They still exercise self-agency and choice, but within a severely diminished range of perceived options. The notion of class habitus helps to explain why, among other things, my parents did not push me and my brothers toward college, while parents of middle- and upper-middle-class friends did so.

WORKING CLASS IN ACADEMIA

When I gained insight into the impact that working-class status exerted on my parents, I recognized how much of my resentment toward them was unfounded. I learned not only to forgive them but also to reclaim disowned parts of myself and my life journey. Today I consider my working-class background to be an asset, especially as a resource for classroom teaching and for scholarship, rather than a source of embarrassment. This has been redemptive. For me, it has been a "God thing," not a purely academic enterprise.

An additional source of support and insight—and impetus for telling my story—is a small body of literature written by academics who, like me, have experienced the journey from working-class roots into the professional middle class as sometimes confusing, lonely, and terribly difficult to articulate to persons whose background and assumptive world is the professional middle class. Even as other marginalized identity groups have articulated their stories, working-class academics are also beginning to tell theirs. Given that in the United States there is so little public discourse about class, most people do not realize how culturally foreign the societal institutions dominated by the professional middle class are at first to persons who assimilate into them from working-class backgrounds. Only those of us who have made this journey really know and appreciate the psychological and emotional toll this process can extract.

As Alfred Lubrano vividly depicts in his book, *Limbo: Blue Collar Roots, White-Collar Dreams*, persons who grow up working class and later move into the world of the middle class find themselves straddling two worlds—often not feeling completely at home in either one, living in a kind of "American limbo." Lubrano calls such persons "Straddlers" and he includes himself, writing, "Most of us Straddlers hold within ourselves worlds that can never be brought together. I often feel inhabited by two people who can't speak to each other."[14]

Through numerous interviews, Lubrano found that professors "are the most self-conscious Straddlers, many of them working with middle-class colleagues who don't understand them."[15] Indeed, in the volume *Working Class Women in the Academy*, female academics raised in blue-collar homes write poignantly about the sense of living in two worlds, not feeling completely at home in the professional world of academia, but also no longer feeling at home with their working-class upbringing.[16] In a similar book, *This Fine Place So Far from Home: Voices of Academics from the Working Class*, Laurel Johnson Black confesses, "I feel suspended, dangling."[17] One of the most poignant lamentations on the disjuncture between working-class upbringing and middle-class life is from bell hooks. In *Where We Stand: Class Matters*, she intimates:

I have written many books about injustice, about ending race, gender, and class exploitation, but this is the only book I have written that focuses directly on the issue of class. More than any other book I have written, writing it aroused in me intensities of pain that often left me doubled over my writing table, hurting to my heart, weeping. For no matter the class privilege I hold today, for most of my life I have lived as one with the poor and working classes. The class connection and unity I felt in my family of origin and with other poor and struggling folks as I made my way through graduate school and up the economic ladder affords me a constant awareness of class pain, of class yearning, and of the deep grief that is caused by a pervasive sense of class failure many poor and working-class people feel because they do not manage to earn enough, to earn more, to effectively change their economic lives so that they can know well-being.[18]

Similarly, Donna Langston reveals that "because of my education and job, I often have little control over the worlds I enter socially. So I continue to live in two worlds, aware of the violence between them. Academe is a new place of loneliness for me. Most academics from working-class backgrounds end up on the bottom of the academic heap."[19] Even in the academy, as in other societal institutions, there is invisible class oppression and domination. But as Barbara Jensen points out, this domination happens in genteel practices and settings,

by way of what Bourdieu calls "cultural capital." Professional middle class social style, language, and knowledge constitute a kind of social currency. People who have learned these things can use it for entrance into, and access to some amount of power in the academy (as in business and government). Cultural barriers may be as effective in shutting out working class people as are the (significant) economic ones, perhaps more so.[20]

Whether in universities, corporations, or other workplaces, the head start that accrues to middle- and upper-middle-class people is essentially invisible. In popular language, Annette Lareau comments, middle-class people have been born on third base but truly believe they hit a triple.[21] As white people are carefully taught not to recognize white privilege, males are taught not to acknowledge male privilege, and elites and professionals in our society are "taught" not to acknowledge class privilege. Most professional people do not realize the sheer extent to which they work from a base of unacknowledged class privilege and power, combined with other forms, such as white privilege or male privilege.

THE INTERSECTIONALITY OF CLASS, RACE, AND GENDER

In terms of daily lived experience, whether or not persons are consciously aware of it, classism is operating in their lives in three distinct but interrelated spheres: economic, political, and cultural. These spheres, in turn, exert influence at three levels: personal biography; community or identity group (gender, race, ethnicity, etc.), including inter-group relations; and the systemic level of societal institutions. These are all structured in ways that maintain and reproduce the capitalist mode of production and distribution, including church and para-church agencies, such as publishing houses.[22] My own narrative focuses on class habitus as an explanatory concept for understanding how subjectivities are shaped in family upbringing and how class is subjectively experienced by people raised in working-class families. Nevertheless, there is a dynamic tension, which must not be collapsed, between the reality of class as a dimension of individual identity and self-agency and class as a structured set of asymmetrical relations of power, position, and privilege between broad social groupings in our society.

Only for heuristic purposes can class be explored as an analytically distinct category. Scholars recognize that in actual lived experience, class does not act independently from other socially constructed, ascriptive dimensions of identity, especially gender, race, ethnicity, and sexual orientation. Actually, these should not even be seen first and foremost as aspects of individual or group identity, but rather as socio-political and cultural constructs that intersect in highly complex ways and operate simultaneously to structure and maintain relations and practices of social, economic, and political inequality, domination, and subordination among persons and groups. Conceptually, this is known as intersectionality, which Leslie McCall summarizes as a method of exploring "the relationships among multiple dimensions and modalities of social relationships and subject formations."[23] Feminist scholars have long been at the vanguard of exploring this notion. In fact, McCall states that "intersectionality is the most important theoretical contribution that the field of women's studies, in conjunction with related fields, has made so far."[24] Although any of the constructs among gender, class, race, ethnicity, and sexual orientation can be foregrounded for purposes of analysis, feminists refuse to give primacy to any single one of them, instead focusing on their complex, matrix-like interactions.

FOUR SCHOOLS OF THOUGHT ABOUT CLASS

Michael Zweig contends that "[t]he long silence about class in the United States is finally coming to an end."[25] For one thing, over the past couple of decades the field of working-class studies has emerged and begun to bourgeon as a new academic discipline. It updates a tradition of scholarship on labor history, and now includes critical attention to intersectionality as well as ways the working class is represented in literature and popular culture.[26] The recent flurry of interest notwithstanding, as Erik

Wright states, there are few concepts in sociological theory more hotly contested than that of "class."[27] No clear-cut, universally agreed-upon definitions, no agreed-upon enumeration of classes, and no fixed formulas exist which determine who belongs to which class. The point of this chapter is not to propose a precise definition, since even expert sociologists have not achieved this feat. It is, rather, to paint in broad strokes what some of the basic conceptual issues are, and to suggest a few basic heuristic concepts by which social justice strategies can be successful. Four broad schools of thought about class stand out.

The Subjective Classification Approach

A first school of thought approaches class as a matter of subjective identification around such things as cultural lifestyle, taste, preference, or occupation, or as subjective ascriptions of status and standing, such as "the respectable class" or "white trailer trash." Cultural and discursive approaches to class underscore the importance of images. They emphasize that "the language and images available in the culture construct people's experiences of and attitudes about class as much as (if not more so than) their work or lifestyle."[28] The contribution of this approach lies in the critical analysis of depictions and representations of class in literature and popular media, with a particular focus on demeaning and stereotypical images of the working class. Yet the emphasis on cultural and symbolic dimensions of class, critics say, often results in a lack of attention to economic structures and other elements of material existence.[29]

The Objective, Gradational Approach

A second school of thought uses the word "class" to capture objective properties of economic inequality and to identify an objective position on a distributional scale, indexed by income and other assets, such as education. In this approach, class is a *gradational* concept. The standard image, as illustrated in Dennis Gilbert's model, is of rungs on a ladder, with the rungs corresponding, for example, to upper class, upper middle class, middle class, lower middle class, lower class, and underclass.[30] A popular series, "Class Matters," published in the *New York Times* in 2005 and later published as a book, reflects such an understanding. Class is objectively based on the combination of occupation, education, income, and wealth.[31]

This concept of class figures most prominently in popular discourse, coupled with the myth of meritocracy. Most Americans believe that we are an extremely economically mobile society, and that if individuals are simply willing to get an education, work hard, and stay honest, they can "move on up" and join the Jeffersons. However, in sharp contrast to the view of America as the land of opportunity, the Economic Mobility Project, along with many other empirical studies, demonstrates that class mobility in the United States is *minimal*, actually much less than in most other industrialized nations.[32]

The Weberian Approach

A third school of thought is grounded in the Weberian tradition that conceptualizes class in relational terms, in contrast to the objective gradational model.[33] In Weber's framework, a person's class position is seen in terms of her or his relation to the market, while in the Marxian tradition (see below) the focus is on the relation to the means of production. Weber generated a three-component framework for explaining what he saw as the socioeconomic stratification of society, and for comprehending a person's "life chances." This involves a complex interplay between class, status group, and power. For Weber, class is based on a person's economic position, while status group is based on a combination of education, occupation, and income. Status group membership is a matter of social prestige, influence, position, and distinctive lifestyle—operating as a source of power apart from class.

The Marxist Approach

A fourth school of thought is based in the Marxist conception that capitalist development leads to the formation and polarization of two classes with fundamentally opposing interests, the capitalists (bourgeoisie) and the laborers (proletariat), as well as a third class (the petit bourgeoisie), whose interests straddle the other two classes.[34] These classes are not defined by differences in income or cultural taste and lifestyle but rather by their relation to the means of production. Capitalists own the factories, businesses, corporations, machinery, and all other materials necessary for the production of goods and services. Workers and laborers have only their own bodies and labor power, which they sell to owners for a fixed wage. Owners and employers use various means to ensure that labor creates much more value than what workers are compensated for, and they then appropriate the "surplus value" of labor for their own exclusive advantage. Given the great degree to which capitalists "live off the labor of others while at the same time enjoying the social and political power that accrues by controlling the surplus product," Marx explained that relations between the two classes of capitalists and laborers are inherently based on exploitation.[35]

Economist Michael Zweig maintains that in order to comprehend and address class-related conflicts today, we would be better served if we changed the understanding of class in the United States from the division of "rich and poor" to the division of "worker and capitalist."[36] In contrast to popularized notions of class which emphasize vast differences in wealth and income, in Zweig's neo-Marxist perspective class relates to vast differentials in power accrued precisely through eye-popping differentials in wealth. In this vein Zweig declares, "When I talk about class, I am talking about power. Power at work, and power in the larger society. Economic power, and also political and cultural power."[37] This power operates to the tremendous benefit of an elite few and the tremendous burden of many others, especially the working class.

As a group, the working class is comprised of people over whom much power is exercised while they lack opportunity to exercise any significant degree of power. They are situated in their workplaces and in society such that they must constantly take orders, rarely with the right to give orders. They have little or no work autonomy, are seldom encouraged to exercise creativity and personal judgment in their work, have no officially recognized authority and expertise, and are given few opportunities to develop their capabilities or to pursue work-enhancing opportunities. They are also seldom recognized for work well done and they are often given jobs that are dirty, dangerous, and demeaning (but with no financial reward for such) and are exposed to denigration and disrespect on account of their class status.

Asymmetrical power arrangements in the workplace do not stay confined there. They leap out and shape all other institutions and practices of society. The asymmetries—of power and privilege, of social deference and respect, of voice and authority, of access to choices and options—get transferred from institution to institution, from one setting to another, until all of society is pervaded and colonized by classist relations, mostly operating in barely noticeable ways. Class oppression is all pervasive, and no zone of society is left neutral or untouched. It transcends work relations and extends into the realms of culture, popular media, economic transactions, education, politics, and even religious and symbolic arenas.

THE 36 PERCENT OR THE "NEW CLASS"

In contrast to the assumption that the United States is mostly a middle-class society, in *The Working Class Majority: America's Best Kept Secret*, Zweig demonstrates that the U.S. labor force is actually 62 percent working class, 36 percent middle class, and 2 percent corporate elite or capitalist class.[38] Today's middle class consists primarily of a "new class" of noncapitalist professionals—sometimes called the professional managerial class (PMC)—that is situated between the capitalists and the working class. It shares interests with each but is not fully identifiable with either.[39] The PMC enjoys class-related power derived from "ownership" of special knowledge.[40] In this view, capital, labor, and knowledge are seen as basic and essential to the production of goods and services. Production entails the coordination of capital, knowledge, and labor, and each component is associated with a distinctive class, based on ownership of one of these resources. Capitalism is structured so that it produces three basic classes, not simply two. Scholars often neglect this point, and it is essentially obscured by the Occupy movement. As economist Chuck Barone explains, these three classes "are structurally opposed to each other, creating a class system of power and authority, social domination and subordination, and economic exploitation."[41]

Some scholars maintain that the professional class today serves to reproduce the capitalist class and its exploitative relations with the working class. Political theorist Sheldon Wolin holds that universities have become co-partners with superpower capitalism, providing a feeder system into it, and subcontracting for it. Other scholars, however, favor the exact opposite, contending that professionals are largely antagonistic to capitalist interests.[42] But this latter argument, maintains David Croteau, overlooks the fact that even as capitalists "can exist and profit only through the exploitation of workers,"[43] and by the same token "a professional knowledge class can exist only if there is a relation of exploitation between it and the working class. That is, the value of their knowledge and skill comes from the fact that others do not have it."[44] Through producing, owning, and deploying knowledge and skills that working-class people do not have, scholars gain power, position, and privilege over others, not only in the academy but also in broader society.[45]

Scholars in various disciplines who claim to be neo-Marxist in their orientation are thus in an ambiguous and self-contradictory position. Croteau points out that "factions of the professional class have an interest in excluding working-class participation in their knowledge specialties. The socialization of knowledge would undermine the basis for professional-class power just as the socialization of capital would undermine the basis for capitalist power."[46] This tension highlights the highly contradictory location that the professional intellectual class occupies within contemporary class relations.[47]

In its emphasis on the dichotomy between the 99 percent and the 1 percent, the Occupy movement not only eclipses the conceptual distinctiveness of the "new class" but also obscures the fact that in terms of daily lived experience, working-class people (especially the working poor, people of color, and immigrants) are exploited and excluded by both capitalists (the 1 percent) and by the professional managerial and knowledge class (the 36 percent).[48] In terms of the Occupy movement, it is more than off-putting to hear elite scholars and professionals say or imply that they are in the same boat as working-poor people in our society. It is especially troubling when rhetoric of "deep solidarity" comes from elite scholars whose children are in expensive private schools, having abandoned poor, working-class children to the plight of crumbling public schools. It seems disingenuous of them not at least to acknowledge the ambiguity and contradictions built into their own class position in society. Deep, authentic solidarity between the professional-managerial class and the working class is possible only if and when members of the former are self-aware of their own relative class privilege and of the contradictions inherent in their class vis-à-vis other classes.

An essential point here is that working-class people experience exploitation and oppression at the hands of not only the 1 percent but also the 36 percent. The danger exists that scholars who do not invest in being scholar *activists* and have little interest in acknowledging and ending their own class-based privilege will simply seek to parlay and capitalize on the OWS movement to enhance their positions in the academy. This, too, is a form of class exploitation and domination.

CLASS, CAPITALISM, AND PATRIARCHY

Feminist theorists with a neo-Marxist orientation contend that we cannot address class exploitation within capitalism without also addressing patriarchy, for these issues are so deeply entwined. Though in his classic work, *Origins of the Family, Private Property, and the State* (1884), Engels expressed optimism that women's participation in the labor force would be the key to their emancipation; obviously, such a hope has not worked out. In all spheres of the labor market and public domain today women are still in an inferior position to men. This fact is best explained, insists Heidi Hartman, by the mutual reinforcement and accommodation between patriarchy and capitalism, which ensnares women in a vicious cycle.[49] Prior to the emergence of capitalism in the fifteenth through eighteenth centuries, patriarchy already existed as an indirect, impersonal system of control of women by men, mediated by society-wide institutions. For Hartman, patriarchy means

> a set of social relations between men, which have a material base, and which, though hierarchical, establish or create interdependence and solidarity among men that enable them to dominate women. Though patriarchy is hierarchical and men of different classes, races, or ethnic groups have different places in patriarchy, they also are united in their shared relationship of dominance over women; they are dependent on one another to maintain that domination. Hierarchies "work" at least in part because they create vested interests in the status quo. Those at the higher levels can "buy off" those at the lower levels by offering them power over those still lower. In the hierarchy of patriarchy, all men, whatever their rank in the patriarchy, are bought off by being able to control at least some women.[50]

The material base on which patriarchy fundamentally rests lies in men's control over women's labor power, which is maintained by excluding women from access to economically productive resources, and by restricting women's sexuality. In the contemporary capitalist society, job segregation by gender is the primary mechanism that maintains the domination of men over women through according "women's work" lower status. Further, the gendered services that women render to men exonerate the men from having to perform time-consuming tasks, and often unpleasant ones, both inside and outside the family setting. Men subsequently benefit both from higher wages and from gender-driven domestic division of labor. This, in turn, operates to weaken women's position in the labor market and to perpetuate the vicious patriarchal cycle.[51]

In capitalist societies, there is a strong partnership between patriarchy, capitalism, and classism. Capitalist development creates places for a hierarchy of workers, and then gender and racial hierarchies determine who fills those places. "Patriarchy is not simply hierarchical organization, but hierarchy in which particular people fill particular places."[52] Workers end up positioned on a gradient determined by particular intersections of gender, class, race, ethnicity, sexual orientation, immigrant status, and age. Patriarchy thus shapes the form that modern capitalism takes, just as the emergence of capitalism transformed patriarchal institutions. Such a view "emphasizes the role of men as capitalists in creating hierarchies in the production process in order to maintain their power. Capitalists do this by segmenting the labor market (along race, sex, and ethnic lines, among others), and playing workers against one another."[53] This fractures the possibility of forming working-class consciousness and political solidarity, while it also ensures an ongoing, unending supply of cheap labor and easily exploitable workers. In this system, based on their class, race, nationality, marital status, sexual orientation, and age, men have differential access to patriarchal benefits and power over women—even as women are subordinated and subjected to differing degrees of patriarchal power, also depending on intersections of their race, ethnicity, nationality, class, marital status, age, and sexual orientation. But ultimately, patriarchal capitalism boomerangs on men, inasmuch as capitalists use women as unskilled, underpaid labor to undercut male workers.

Oppression is full of such contradictions, Patricia Hill Collins declares in a classic essay titled "Toward a New Vision: Race, Class, and Gender as Categories of Analysis and Connection."[54] She writes that "once we realize that there are few pure victims or oppressors and that each one of us derives varying amounts of penalty and privilege from the multiple systems of oppression that frame our lives, then we will be in a position to see the need for new ways of thought and action."[55] Collins is among the first feminist scholars to posit and explore how race, class, and gender are analytically distinct systems that nevertheless intersect in highly complex ways to produce asymmetrical relations of power and privilege, what she calls a "matrix of domination," and which some scholars refer to as "vectors of oppression and privilege."[56]

Although the intersectional point of view does not deny that specific groups experience oppression more harshly than others, or that in certain contexts one specific vector may be more visible and salient than others, such acknowledgement does not minimize the contention that race, class, gender, and other categories are simultaneously operative in structuring socioeconomic and power relations in any and all societal settings. For example, while we traditionally approach the institution of slavery through the analytical lens of racism, slavery also structured class and gender relations in complex, interlocking ways.

Collins asserts that even today the antebellum plantation can be used as a compelling metaphor for comprehending a variety of American social institutions and their interlocking dynamics of oppression. Slavery was profoundly patriarchal as an institution, resting on white male authority and property rights, joining the political and economic within the institution of the family.[57] Control over white women's sexuality was important because heirs were needed to inherit plantation property and wealth, even as control over black women's sexuality ensured an ongoing supply of slaves. While under slavery blacks certainly experienced the harshest treatment—as mere chattel, race, class, and gender interlocked to structure systemic relations of domination and subordination. Collins states:

> So we have a very interesting chain of command on the plantation—the affluent White master as the reigning patriarch, his White wife helpmate to serve him, help him manage his property and bring up his heirs, his faithful servants whose production and reproduction were tied to the requirements of the capitalist political economy, and largely propertyless, working-class White men and women watching from afar.[58]

While it is important not to denigrate the achievements of those who struggled for social change before us, the basic patterns of class, race, and gender relations which formed the "matrix of domination" in slavery essentially remain intact today. It is simply that actual conditions are not as visible and starkly severe. Collins, therefore, wonders whether many of us who are employed by American colleges and universities actually work on modern plantations. She invites us to reflect on her queries:

> Who controls your university's political economy? Are elite White men overrepresented among the upper administrators and trustees controlling your university's finances and policies? Are elite White men being joined by growing numbers of elite White women helpmates? What kinds of people are in your classrooms grooming the next generation who will occupy these and other decision-making positions? Who are the support staff that produce the mass mailings, order the supplies, fix the leaky pipes? Do African Americans, Hispanics, or other people of color form the majority of the invisible workers who feed you, wash

your dishes, and clean up your offices and libraries after everyone else has gone home?[59]

One key difference between the actual antebellum slave plantations and plantation-like social institutions today lies in the power of the ruling class—the patriarchal corporate capitalists—to keep its hegemony invisible. It relies on the more diffuse and unconscious ways that oppression is enacted today. In contrast to repressive regimes such as North Korea, in a society such as ours the operation of oppression and domination is largely unconscious, tacit, and hidden by design. This happens through the manipulation of value and symbol systems whereby status quo social, cultural, economic, and political arrangements are made to seem desirable, natural, and beneficial to every social class. They are not seen clearly as obviously artificial constructs designed simply and solely for the benefit of the elite ruling class.

A significant challenge we face is our own cooptation and complicity in reproducing classist and other relations of domination and subordination. Iris Young explains that the status quo is kept intact "as a consequence of often unconscious assumptions and reactions of well-meaning people in ordinary interactions, media and cultural stereotypes, and structural features of bureaucratic hierarchies and market mechanisms— in short, the normal processes of everyday life."[60] In other words, as we go about our daily lives and engage in ordinary social, economic, and religious practices and transactions, all of us are implicated in reproducing relations of domination, oppression, and exploitation—even when we are not their willful agents.[61]

JUSTICE AS REDISTRIBUTION, RECOGNITION, REPRESENTATION

Given that classism operates in three interrelated spheres—economic, cultural, and political—and also intersects in distinct ways with gender, race, ethnicity, or sexual orientation, our conception of justice must help us address this very complex interplay. I find the model proposed by feminist critical theorist Nancy Fraser to be particularly helpful in this regard. Within a single, comprehensive framework, her approach to justice integrates concern for *redistribution* in the economic sphere, *recognition* in the socio-cultural sphere, and parity of *representation* in the political sphere.[62] The reduction of injustice depends on balanced attention to all three areas, but today, unfortunately, concern for recognition tends to outweigh and eclipse the rest.

Fraser observes that the struggle for recognition and respect of difference has become the paradigmatic form of public conflict in the United States and around the world. Ever since the 1980s, diverse identity groups in the United States have increasingly mobilized around religion, nationality, ethnicity, race, gender, sexual orientation, and physical ability. Further, around the globe today, cultural, ethnic, racial, and religious conflicts fuel violent struggles between diverse groups, inciting wars and ethnic cleansings. In his award-winning book *Exclusion and Embrace*, theologian Miroslav Volf contends that hatred and exclusion of diverse others is among the most intractable problems in the contemporary world. It has reached such a crisis that, in his view, the very future of our world depends on how we deal with identity and difference.[63]

The deep dilemma is that theological and political attention centered on identity, otherness, difference, recognition, and respect stands in tension with politics and theology centered on socioeconomic injustice, poverty, class exploitation, and disempowerment. These two sets of issues, Fraser explains, focus on two broadly conceived, analytically distinct forms of injustice. One is cultural and symbolic injustice rooted in cultural imperialism, misrecognition, and disrespect of diverse others. The other is socioeconomic injustice, rooted in economic-political systems and structures, and in vast differentials of power and wealth. Fraser is not alone in her concern that a focus on the "politics of recognition" threatens to displace concern for the "politics of redistribution." She seeks to resolve the tension and integrate these concerns by demonstrating that although cultural imperialism and economic deprivation are analytically distinct realities, they nevertheless are intertwined and mutually reinforcing. Both are forms of injustice rooted in policies and practices that systematically disadvantage and oppress some groups vis-à-vis others, resulting in a vicious cycle of cultural (including religious), economic, and political subordination and exclusion. Further, she proposes a shift in what we mean by the notion of "misrecognition" in the first place. To be misrecognized, she suggests, is to be denied the status of a full and equal partner in the public sphere, as well as to be denied parity of participation in the decision-making of societal institutions, including the political sphere. Overcoming misrecognition, accordingly, requires challenging and changing institutions and social practices instead of valorizing, essentializing, and reifying group identity, and inadvertently pressuring people to conform to a given group culture.[64]

BEYOND MAINSTREAM MULTICULTURALISM

The conventional response to addressing the contested "politics of recognition" has been mainstream multiculturalism. This approach treats class, race, ethnicity, gender, and sexual orientation as dimensions of personal and group identity to be recognized and affirmed. But E. San Juan and certain other scholars worry that the specifically Marxist insight into class as structured relations of exploitation, domination, and subordination are rendered superfluous when class is subsumed into a matrix of race, gender, and class seen and celebrated as personal and group identity.[65]

A multicultural approach to diversity overlooks the fact that these categories are best understood as socio-political constructs which structure and institutionalize relations of domination and subordination, and which compound class exploitation.

In his book *The Trouble with Diversity: How We Learned to Love Identity and Ignore Inequality*, Walter Benn Michaels similarly decries the fact that in our celebration of diversity as a value in American cultural imagination we have displaced an urgently needed emphasis on reducing economic inequality.[66] The narrow focus on identity politics siphons off energies needed to cultivate working-class solidarity. Today we need a strategy whose starting point is class exploitation seen as an injustice to be remedied and that is also attuned to suffering imposed by racism, ethnocentrism, sexism, and the like. Only on this basis will working-class people be able to find common ground and organize across the divides of diverse identity groups. This is their only hope of amassing the collective power needed to restrain the ever-intensifying exploitation of labor by capital. Disrespect for difference is not the fundamental problem besetting poor working-class people in our nation and around the globe. The problem at stake is exploitation and relations of domination and subordination. We must go beyond affirmative responses and develop transformative strategies that address underlying structural conditions.

A HOPEFUL WAY FORWARD: NOT OCCUPY—BUT *ORGANIZE!*

In his monumental *Ethics*, published posthumously, Dietrich Bonhoeffer insisted that Christian life is public, to be lived out in reference to the basic sectors of society, which he calls "mandates," including labor, economics, politics, government, family, and the church. These sectors are to be conjoined, he explained, in relations of mutual collaboration, mutual limitation, and mutual accountability, so that no single institution is absolute, but each is fully accountable to the others. In short, they are to be held in creative tension "with, for, and against one another."[67] But today, the balance of power necessary for ensuring mutual limitation and accountability is frighteningly skewed. There is so much power and wealth concentrated in the hands of so few elites that we grope for adequate terminology to depict what is actually going on. Among the terms employed are Empire, Superpower, plutocracy, corporatocracy, kleptocracy, oligarchy, Second Gilded Age, hereditary aristocracy, and plantation. Transnational mega-corporations and elite capitalists have amassed such inordinate power and wealth they are now able to circumvent the control of the state, while their interests have also been fused with it. Political theorist Sheldon Wolin suggests that the United States has morphed into a new and strange kind of political hybrid, where economic power and state power are conjoined and virtually unbridled in their wielding of unaccountable power.[68]

What some people call Empire, Wolin calls Superpower "bent upon reconstituting the existing system so as to permanently favor a ruling class of the wealthy, the well-connected and the corporate, while leaving the poorer citizens with a sense of helplessness and political despair."[69] Superpower eviscerates the ideal of democracy, which Wolin argues is not a static form of government or set of bureaucratic apparatuses run by the state, but rather a set of processes and practices at the local level. After a bleak account of what is going on, Wolin wonders "whether there are countervailing forces that . . . may stake out a political place in which to develop a counter-paradigm."[70] For him, the answer is yes; it lies in an emphasis on the local. Our best hope for reviving democracy and over-coming class domination, he believes, lies in ordinary working folks coming together locally to deliberate and to learn how to exercise their own power and to restrain Superpower. Wolin insists that authentic participatory democracy is "fugitive democracy" because it is something that breaks out in unexpected places among unexpected people—beyond the control of the state. It happens when ordinary people collectively resist injustices imposed by the regime of Superpower. Democratic citizens are fugitives for justice, not from justice. By the same token, if there is ever going to be consequential, public practice of Christian faith, it is going to have to be "fugitive Christianity," the praxis of faith that explodes beyond the grip of the status quo bureaucracy of the institutional church, which tends to domesticate everything in sight, as it is more concerned about shoring up sagging membership rolls than with the transformation of society, or with the situation of the working-class majority.

It is precisely such a vision of locally engaged politics and "fugitive faith" that Jeffrey Stout explores in *Blessed Are the Organized: Grassroots Democracy in America*.[71] He amply illustrates that something much more stunning, effective, transformative, and long-standing than the Occupy Wall Street (OWS) movement is currently taking place, but it is unfortunately under the public radar screen: faith-based community organizing. This tradition descends from the work of Saul Alinsky in the mid-1930s in the Chicago area, where the meatpacking industry notoriously exploited ethnic working-class immigrants. Known as "Back of the Yards," this area of abject squalor, poverty, danger, and oppression was immortalized in Upton Sinclair's *The Jungle*.

Alinsky, whose Jewish mother instilled in him a passion for justice, enlisted the help of Roman Catholic bishops in bringing together dozens of neighborhood associations, unions, congregations, and schools—what sociologists refer to as mediating institutions—into a coalition called Back of the Yards Neighborhood Council (BYNC). He realized that only by recruiting and organizing institutional members rather than individual members and only by forming stable ongoing organizations would exploited workers and their families ever be able to generate collective power sufficient enough to offset and restrain the over-amassed power of corporate capitalists and the military-industrial-congressional complex. The BYNC became the model for what is now called *broad-based* organizing (instead of community organizing). This phrase signals that efforts are rooted in, but also transcend, local neighborhoods and local communities, bringing people together across lines of class, gender, race, ethnicity, nationality, geography, immigrant status, and religion.

The foremost purpose of these grassroots organizations is to provide working-class people and their allies a vehicle through which they can generate collective political power and use it to hold elected officials and the most powerful elites of society accountable to the common good.[72] Broad-based organizing groups see themselves as "universities of hope" that teach working-class people the arts of public engagement, grounded in their respective faith commitments. Today, broad-based organizations are one of the rare places in society that bridge divisions between identity groups and create solidarity of effort for the common good.

An empirical evaluation of eight years of work on the part of broad-based organizing groups in a variety of locations reached five conclusions. First, broad-based organizing groups are effective in holding government and corporate sectors accountable, and in winning concrete policy changes for working-class people, predominantly of color, that improve their communities. Second, they alter the relations of power at the most basic level of influencing resource allocation. Third, they recruit, train, and develop strong citizen leaders through mentoring, and through processes that are highly relational, participatory, and deliberative. Fourth, they increase civic participation at the local level and sometimes regional level, especially through holding public accountability sessions with elected officials. Fifth, they build stable and financially viable organizations which are accountable to the communities in which they are located.[73]

Given our contemporary plight, Nancy Fraser insists that it is not enough that we scholars simply have a good analytic perspective on what is going on, for this alone is not capable of overcoming vast asymmetries of power, or reducing class exploitation and other deep injustices. These ills can be overcome only by active political struggle in solidarity across lines of class, race, gender, and other differences. I agree with Stout's claim that the ever-escalating exploitation and imbalance of power "can be set straight only if broad-based [interfaith] organizing is scaled up significantly, only if it extends its reach much more widely throughout American society than it has to date."[74] The good news is that beyond the limelight of Occupy, promising signs of effective resistance against Empire are bubbling up from the grassroots. As a result of interfaith broad-based organizing, stunning transformations and reversals of injustice are happening in urban, suburban, and rural areas across the nation.

It is time that we not only occupy places where working-class people are being exploited but also add our solidarity to their efforts in organizing, reaching toward *basileia*, the community of Shalom promised by God.

NOTES

1. Ernst Troeltsch, *The Social Teaching of the Christian Churches*, volume II (Louisville, KY: Westminster John Knox, 1992), 1010.
2. I use "Empire" as an extended metaphor to refer to the facts of how ruling class elites in the United States, comprised of capitalists along with elites in the military-industrial-congressional complex, use over-accumulated power and wealth to exercise hegemony over the masses of ordinary people in the United States and around the globe, doing so through military, political, economic, intellectual, cultural, and symbolic means, seen and unseen, direct and indirect, formal and informal. The "pistons" that drive contemporary Empire include unrestrained neoliberal corporate capitalism, economic globalization, imperialism (including cultural and religious imperialism), and militarism (which has become the handmaiden to U.S.-capitalist interests around the globe).
3. David Ray Griffin, John B. Cobb, Jr., Richard A. Falk, and Catherine Keller, eds., *The American Empire and the Commonwealth of God: A Political, Economic, Religious Statement* (Louisville: Westminster John Knox, 2006), v.
4. Chalmers Johnson, "Can We End the American Empire Before It Ends Us?" *TomDispatch.com* (May 17, 2007), http://www.alternet.org/story/51975 [accessed December 6, 2012].
5. Richard A. Horsley, ed., *In the Shadow of Empire: Reclaiming the Bible as a History of Faithful Resistance* (Louisville: Westminster John Knox, 2008), 7.
6. Walter Brueggemann, *Hope within History* (Louisville: Westminster John Knox, 1988).
7. Elisabeth Schüssler Fiorenza, "Critical Feminist Biblical Studies: Remembering the Struggles, Envisioning the Future," in *New Feminist Christianity: Many Voices, Many Views*, ed. Mary E. Hunt (Woodstock, VT: Skylight Paths, 2010), 96.
8. Peter McLaren, "Critical Pedagogy: A Look at the Major Concepts," in *The Critical Pedagogy Reader*, eds. Antonia Darder, Mara Baltodano, and Rodolfo D. Torres (New York: Routledge, 2002), 69.
9. Troeltsch, *The Social Teaching of the Christian Churches*, 1010.
10. I borrow this image from Alfred Lubrano, *Limbo: Blue Collar Roots, White-Collar Dreams* (Hoboken, NJ: John Wiley & Sons, 2004), 9.
11. Lillian Rubin, *Worlds of Pain: Life in the Working Class* (New York: Basic Books, 1992).
12. Pierre Bourdieu, *The Logic of Practice* (Stanford, CA: Stanford University Press, 1990), 53.
13. While each individual's habitus may have unique autobiographical elements, Bourdieu conceptualized habitus as a shared, class phenomenon, not simply an individual reality, although there are many individual variations within the class habitus; see Bourdieu, *Logic of Practice*, 60.
14. Lubrano, *Limbo*, 194.
15. Ibid., 2.
16. Michelle M. Tokarczyk, and Elizabeth A. Fay, eds., *Working Class Women in the Academy: Laborers in the Knowledge Factory* (Amherst: University of Massachusetts Press, 1993).
17. Laurel Johnson Black, "Stupid Rich Bastards," in *This Fine Place So Far from Home: Voices of Academics from the Working Class*, eds. C. L. Barney Dews and Carolyn Lesty Law (Philadelphia: Temple University Press, 1995), 25. See also, for example, Alan Shepard, John McMillan, and Gary Tate, eds., *Coming to Class: Pedagogy and the*

Social Class of Teachers (Portsmouth, NH: Boynton/Cook Publishers, 1998); Jake Ryan and Charles Sackrey, eds., *Strangers in Paradise: Academics from the Working Class* (Lanham, MD: University Press of America, 1996); and Janet Zandy, ed., *Liberating Memory: Our Work and Our Working-Class Consciousness* (New Brunswick, NJ: Rutgers University Press, 1995).

18. bell hooks, *Where We Stand: Class Matters* (New York: Routledge, 2000), 157.

19. Donna Langston, "Who Am I Now? The Politics of Class Identity," in *Working Class Women in the Academy: Laborers in the Knowledge Factory*, ed. Michelle M. Tokarczyk and Elizabeth A. Fay (Amherst: University of Massachusetts Press, 1993), 68.

20. Barbara Jensen, "Across the Great Divide: Crossing Classers and Clashing Cultures," in *What's Class Got to Do with It? American Society in the Twenty-First Century*, ed. Michael Zweig (Ithaca, NY: Cornell University Press, 2004), 177.

21. Annette Lareau, *Unequal Childhoods: Class, Race, and Family Life* (Berkeley: University of California Press, 2003), 13.

22. Chuck Barone, "Extending Our Analysis of Class Oppression: Bringing Classism More Fully into the Race and Gender Picture," http://users.dickinson.edu/~barone/ExtendClassRGC.PDF [accessed December 6, 2012].

23. Leslie McCall, "The Complexity of Intersectionality," *Signs: Journal of Women in Culture and Society* 30, no. 3 (2005), http://www.journals.uchicago.edu/doi/pdf/10.1086/426800 [accessed December 6, 2012].

24. Ibid.

25. Michael Zweig, ed., *What's Class Got to Do with It? American Society in the Twenty-First Century* (Ithaca, NY: Cornell University Press, 2004), 1.

26. See Pepi Leistyna, *Television and Working Class Identity: Intersecting Differences* (New York: Palgrave Macmillan, 2012); John Russo and Sherry Lee Linkon, eds., *New Working-Class Studies* (Ithaca, NY: ILR Press, 2005); David R. Reodiger, ed., *The Wages of Whiteness: Race and the Making of the American Working Class* (Brooklyn: Verso, 2007); and Sherry Lee Linkon, ed., *Teaching Working Class* (Amherst: University of Massachusetts Press, 1999).

27. Erik Olin Wright, "Social Class," in *Encyclopedia of Society Theory*, ed. George Ritzer (Sage Publications Online), www.ssc.wisc.edu/~wright/Social%20Class%20--%20Sage.pdf [accessed December 6, 2012].

28. Linkon, *Teaching Working Class*, 4.

29. Ibid.

30. Dennis Gilbert, *The American Class Structure in an Age of Growing Inequality* (Los Angeles: Pine Forge Press, 2008), 231.

31. Bill Keller, "Introduction," in *Class Matters*, ed. *New York Times* and Bill Keller (New York: Times Books, 2005).

32. See, for example, http://www.economicmobility.org/reports_and_research/Economic%20Mobility%20Project%20Fact%20Sheet.pdf [accessed December 6, 2012].

33. Wright, "Social Class," 2.

34. David Croteau, *Politics and the Class Divide: Working People and the Middle Class Left* (Philadelphia: Temple University Press, 1995), 225.

35. Croteau, *Politics*, 224.

36. Michael Zweig, "Six Points on Class," *Monthly Review* 58, no. 3 (July–August 2006), http://monthlyreview.org/2006/07/01/six-points-on-class [accessed December 6, 2010].

37. Michael Zweig, *The Working Class Majority: America's Best Kept Secret* (Ithaca, NY: Cornell University Press, 2000), 1.

38. Ibid., 29.

39. Croteau, *Politics*, 230. The name "Professional-Managerial Class" was first articulated by Barbara and John Ehrenreich, "The Professional-Managerial Class," in *Between Labor and Capital*, ed. Pat Walker (Boston: South End Press, 1979), 5–45. Other names include "new middle class" and "new petty bourgeoisie." While scholars agree that a non-capitalist class exists, there is an extensive debate on how to conceptualize its nature and significance within a Marxian framework. See Val Burris, "Class Struc-

ture and Political Ideology," *Critical Sociology* 25, no. 2 (1999), http://pages.uoregon.edu/vburris/class.pdf [accessed December 6, 2012].

40. Croteau, *Politics*, 232.

41. Barone, "Extending Our Analysis of Class Oppression," 13.

42. Croteau, *Politics*, 229.

43. Ibid.

44. Ibid., 230.

45. Croteau explains that this form of exploitation is different from a "pure" exploitation model based on the appropriation of surplus value of labor. The notion of exploitative and antagonistic relations between professionals and the working class is recognized by many sociologists, but not yet fully worked out. Barbara and John Ehrenreich explain it best; see Ehrenreich, "The Professional-Managerial Class," 230.

46. Ibid., 234.

47. See Erik Olin Wright, "Intellectuals and the Class Structure of Capitalist Society," in *Between Labor and Capital*, ed. Pat Walker (Montreal: Black Rose, 1978), 191–211.

48. It is important to note that the neo-Marxist three-class framework is different from the class stratification or gradational model that supporters of OWS repudiate in favor of the binary model of the 99 versus the 1 percent. As the economist Chuck Barone emphasizes, there are actually two primary structural bases of class oppression. Besides "capital ownership," there are "command positions" within organizational hierarchies filled by managers, administrators, and educationally credentialed professionals who serve the interests of the capitalist owners of production; see Barone, "Extending Our Analysis of Class Oppression," 39.

49. Heidi Hartman, "Capitalism, Patriarchy, and the Subordination of Women," in *Social Class and Stratification: Classic Statements and Theoretical Debates*, ed. Rhonda F. Levine (Lanham, MD: Rowman & Littlefield, 2006), 185.

50. Ibid., 185–86.

51. Ibid., 185.

52. Ibid., 188.

53. Ibid., 185.

54. Patricia Hill Collins, "Toward a New Vision: Race, Class, and Gender as Categories of Analysis and Connection," in *Social Class and Stratification: Classic Statements and Theoretical Debates*, ed. Rhonda F. Levine (Lanham, MD: Rowman & Littlefield, 2006), 244.

55. Ibid.

56. George Ritzer, *Contemporary Sociological Theory and Its Classical Roots: The Basics* (Boston: McGraw-Hill, 2007), 204.

57. Collins, "Toward a New Vision," 247.

58. Ibid., 248.

59. Ibid.

60. Iris Marion Young, *Justice and the Politics of Difference* (Princeton, NJ: Princeton University Press, 1990), 41.

61. Even so, Young explains that this diffuse, systemic view of oppression does not mean that individual persons or groups do not intentionally set out to harm members of oppressed groups. They do, in fact. A certain category of such acts are called "hate crimes," harm purposefully perpetrated against persons of a despised religion, race, sexual orientation, disability, ethnicity, or nationality.

62. Accordingly, Fraser uses the term "politics of redistribution" to refer to strategies aimed to remedy class exploitation and economic injustice, "politics of recognition" for strategies designed to remedy forms of cultural imperialism and religious injustice, and "politics of representation" to underscore the importance of parity of participation among diverse identity groups in the public sphere and all societal institutions. For a summary of her position, see Martha Palacio Avendaño, "Interview with Nancy Fraser: Justice as Redistribution, Recognition and Representation," *Barcelona Metropolis* (March–June 2009), http://www.barcelonametropolis.cat/en/page.asp?id=21&ui=181 [accessed December 6, 2012].

63. Miroslav Volf, *Exclusion and Embrace: A Theological Exploration of Identity, Otherness, and Reconciliation* (Nashville: Abingdon Press, 1996).

64. See Nancy Fraser, "Social Justice in the Age of Identity Politics: Redistribution, Recognition, and Participation," in *Matters of Culture: Cultural Sociology in Practice*, eds. Roger Friedland and John Mohr (Cambridge: Cambridge University Press, 2004).

65. E. San Juan, Jr. "Marxism and the Race/Class Problematic: A Re-Articulation," http://clogic.eserver.org/2003/sanjuan.html [accessed December 6, 2012].

66. Walter Benn Michaels, *The Trouble with Diversity: How We Learned to Love Identity and Ignore Inequality* (New York: Metropolitan Books, 2006).

67. Dietrich Bonhoeffer, *Ethics* (New York: Touchstone, 1995), 287.

68. Sheldon S. Wolin, *Democracy Incorporated: Managed Democracy and the Specter of Inverted Totalitarianism* (Princeton, NJ: Princeton University Press, 2010).

69. Sheldon S. Wolin, "Inverted Totalitarianism," *The Nation* (May 19, 2003), http://www.thenation.com/article/inverted-totalitarianism [accessed December 6, 2012].

70. Wolin, *Democracy Incorporated*, 595.

71. Jeffrey Stout, *Blessed Are the Organized: Grassroots Democracy in America* (Princeton, NJ: Princeton University Press, 2010).

72. One of the most important contributions of the faith-based organizing tradition is its attention to *power*—what it is, how to generate it, how to exercise it justly. For two books on a Christian theology of power, see Robert C. Linthicum, *Building a People of Power: Equipping Churches to Transform Their Communities* (Waynesboro, GA: Authentic Media, 2005); Linthicum, *Transforming Power: Biblical Strategies for Making a Difference in Your Community* (Downers Grove, IL: IVP Books, 2003).

73. Jeannie Appleman, "Evaluation Study of Institution-Based Organizing for the Discount Foundation," http://comm-org.wisc.edu/papers97/appleman.htm [accessed December 6, 2012].

74. Stout, *Blessed Are the Organized*, 286.

Part III

About Diversity

SIX

Celebrating Diversity Is Not What It's All About

A Progressive White Male German American Theologian Speaks

Joerg Rieger

There can be no doubt that diversity is one of the crucial topics of our time. Uniformity is no longer an option, because the world and the people that live in it are more diverse than we ever imagined. Developing appreciation for diversity is not optional in this context. The ability to appreciate diversity and otherness is such an essential part of life today that the levels of maturity of individuals, communities, and societies may be judged by it.

THE PROBLEM OF CO-OPTING DIVERSITY FOR UNJUST PURPOSES

While diversity is a fact of life, the question is how we address it and what we do with it. Too often, diversity is co-opted by the powers that be, which in our time refer to free-market capitalism as well as mainline religion. For several reasons, free-market capitalism is deeply interested in what is sometimes called "celebrating diversity." Understanding the diversity of consumers and markets is directly linked to increasing the success of businesses, as this will allow adjusting both production of goods and marketing strategies accordingly. Being sensitive to different cultures and subcultures is good for business and also buttresses the

115

economic bottom line, as manifested in advertising campaigns. In Hispanic neighborhoods in the United States, advertising billboards produce
greater success if they convey their message in Spanish rather than English. Furthermore, hiring a diverse workforce is not just a matter of meeting the legal requirements of affirmative action but also of being better
able to adjust to the different markets. For instance, it is believed that
women relate better to other women or that African Americans are more
successful in African American settings.

It is, therefore, not hard to see why postmodern capitalism endorses
diversity and thrives on it. But why would mainline religion be interested
in diversity? After all, it is well known that worship, whether on Sunday
morning or on other days of the week, is still among the most segregated
events in U.S. society. While religion tends to be less in tune with the
demands of diversity than the business world, those religious leaders
who observe demographic trends have argued for years that churches
and other religious organizations need to become more inclusive if they
want to maintain their share of the religious market.

For the past two or three decades, for instance, "Hispanic ministry"
has been promoted in the United States, especially in places with growing Hispanic populations, in view of projections that substantial portions
of the U.S. population will be Hispanic in the near future. In big cities like
Dallas the Caucasian population has already shrunk below the 50 percent
mark, and the change is due in large part to the growth of the Hispanic
population.[1] To put it bluntly, mainline religion is interested in diversity
in order to keep the numbers of churchgoers up and to be able to go on
with business as usual. The 1989 Hymnal of the United Methodist
Church seems to follow this logic. Though concessions are made by including some Spanish-language hymns, business as usual goes on since it
retains even the worst status-quo-affirming hymns, such as "It Is Well
With My Soul" and "The Old Rugged Cross."[2]

What is the problem in these cases? Is not what liberals are calling
"celebrating diversity" a good thing? Who could object to an increase in
diversity in the worlds of economics and religion? Are we not all ultimately *enriched* by this diversity, in the literal and figurative meaning of
this word? What could possibly be wrong with pluralism—for example,
the sort that manifests itself in the food courts at American malls? Is
being able to choose from Chinese, Japanese, Italian, Mexican, and various American foods a sign of progress? Why should we not try to please
everyone if we can?

The problem with celebrating diversity and pluralism in these ways is
that the existing differentials of power are not addressed but bypassed,
perhaps even covered up. In the realm of religion, for instance, there is an
enormous difference between filling the pews with diverse groups of
people and inviting a diverse group of people into positions of leadership
and power. Too much of Hispanic ministry was and still is geared to

maintaining the status quo by adding church members without any effort to understand people with Latin roots and without taking into account that such a shift in membership also demands shifts in leadership, religious culture, and, ultimately, theology.

In these cases, celebrating diversity means celebrating the status quo. When I asked a candidate who interviewed for a professorship in evangelism years ago how evangelism would be different in Hispanic West Dallas than in Anglo East Texas, his response was that all that needed to be changed was the food served after the evangelistic service: barbeque in East Texas, and *cabrito* and *tamales* in West Dallas. It is probably not a coincidence that this candidate later became a prominent leader of the church.

The situation in a capitalist economy is no different. While diversity is celebrated in the workforce and at the customer base, U.S. law implies that a publicly traded company must work for the benefit of the stockholders rather than its workers or customers.[3] I am not aware that diversity is celebrated at the level of the stockholders, especially considering that there is a relatively small group of people who own the majority of stock and thus control the future of the corporations. Female leaders and workers, for instance, are actively pursued because they can increase the profit for stockholders. Aware of this logic, we should not be surprised that in the wake of the recent economic catastrophes more men lost their jobs than women.[4] While this gender discrepancy seems to indicate gains of a traditionally disadvantaged group, the real reason has to do with the fact that women still earn less than men for comparable work, and they are cheaper for the company. Once again, these forms of celebrating diversity mean celebrating the status quo.

For academics, the matter moves uncomfortably close to home when we look at the politics of diversity in higher education. Diversity is easily co-opted when schools pride themselves upon faculty appointments that increase gender, ethnic, and racial diversity without committing to address these issues more deeply. Thus, in academia diversity is often co-opted when, for instance, a newly appointed woman faculty member is expected to address gender in her teaching and research while the rest of the faculty continues with business as usual. In fact, the position of the business-as-usual faction is now stronger than before because it does not have to deal with the challenges of diversity anymore when this duty is delegated to the new hire.

In sum, approaches to diversity that merely celebrate it in pluralistic fashion—where business as usual not only is left unchallenged but also emerges with new strength from beneath the covers—are counterproductive. The inconvenient truth is that celebrating diversity amounts to celebrating the status quo. Diversity makes the status quo more colorful, more powerful, and more attractive than it would otherwise be.

THE NEED FOR DIVERSITY IN THE WORK FOR JUSTICE

The point to be argued in this section is that diversity makes no sense without justice. Likewise, as we shall see shortly, justice makes no sense without diversity. Some of the more prominent differences among us are not mere natural coincidences. Rather, they are tied up with power differentials, and this is precisely why the reference to justice is crucial. Diversity, especially when it comes to human relationships, is often connected to differentials of power that have been constructed over time for the benefit of some and the loss of others. In the history of chattel slavery, for instance, natural differences in skin color that are otherwise fairly meaningless were successfully emphasized for the purpose of enslaving people. Biological and theological arguments supported the practice of enslavement. They were constructed to justify the status quo. However, they were, of course, demonstrably invalid. It is simply not true that there are different human races, for instance, as those who enslaved Africans argued. There is only one human race.[5]

While there are many different definitions of justice, a common definition of justice in the biblical texts is of particular interest here. The Hebrew verb, *ṣdq*, means "to be faithful" to the community established by the covenant.[6] In the biblical tradition, justice is not an abstract concept of fairness; it has to do with relationships and the restoration of relationships when they are broken. In the midst of those broken relationships the power dynamics need to be addressed so that the relationships can be adequately restored.

Some examples from gender and racial discourses may help to clarify what is at stake. The topic of gender justice, for instance, is often understood to be about improving the conditions of women. It is a common assumption in our society that the topics of feminism and women's liberation are women-related topics that are of little immediate concern for men. No wonder undergraduate and graduate courses on these subjects are mostly taken by female students and only a very small number of male students, who usually already consider themselves allies. Feminism thus appears to be a special-interest issue for women. The same is true for ethnic minorities. Concerns of African Americans or Hispanics in the United States are usually seen as special interests as well, and thus white people mostly disregard them. Celebrating diversity appears to be the solution because it allows each group to pursue their own interests while everybody else can relax and go back to business as usual.

If the problem is defined as one of broken relationships, it is no longer possible to use the notion of diversity to keep various interests separate. If gender oppression has to do with broken relationships between men and women rather than with a lack of pluralism, gender is not a special interest for women only. It also pertains to men. Hence, justice is not accomplished by just celebrating the diversity of men and women, but it begins with figuring out how the relationship between men and women was broken and how diversity between the genders has been exploited for the advantage of some and the disadvantage of others. Likewise, if oppression along the lines of ethnicity and race is understood as one of broken relationships, we begin to understand that the problem affects not only those who suffer from oppression but also those who benefit from it. Justice in this context demands not merely a superficial appreciation of diversity but also a deeper understanding of how diversity has been used and misused by the powers that be, and what needs to change in order to be able to truly honor diversity without oppression and exploitation.

In the current context, we are beginning to understand these challenges when it comes to discourses of gender, ethnicity, and race. Projects and conferences on "dismantling racism," for instance, have long argued that racism is not just racial prejudice but "racial prejudice plus power."[7] This is a crucial step in the right direction. Similarly, the notion of class, which has been severely underrepresented in the trinity of race, class, and gender, can help us see even more clearly.

Like gender and race, class is often regarded as the problem of one particular group rather than as a matter of relationships defined by power. Most Americans believe that class is a form of "social stratification," a notion that acknowledges various class levels, starting with the poor and ending with the rich. However, this notion fails to take seriously the relationship of the classes. For instance, when the discourse of class as social stratification displays a concern for the poor, the implication is that such a concern is optional for non-poor people, as if the classes were unconnected. In other words, concern for the poor is a matter of special interest for the non-poor, and, at best, for the rich such a concern is a matter of *noblesse oblige*. Another example of this misunderstanding is the current cry of "class struggle," which is uttered whenever there is an effort to support the poor and working people and a connection is made among the classes—for instance, by reminding the rich of their economic responsibilities.

If class, however, is not a matter of stratification but a matter of relationship like race and gender, the argument will change. Whatever else needs to be said about the notion of class struggle, it becomes clear that such a struggle is never a one-way street. The common assumption that class struggle is waged against the rich whenever there is support for the lower classes covers up the fact that there is already a class struggle waged from the top down, which is much more severe and much more wide ranging. In the relationship between employers and employed, for instance, the still-growing discrepancy of income is increasing not by accident but because ever more severe pressures are being leveled against the workforce. The fact that workers' salaries have remained flat for the past three decades in the United States and are even decreasing, while the income of CEOs and top investors is constantly rising,[8] is rooted in a relationship marked by class struggle. As Warren Buffet, one of the three wealthiest individuals in the world, observed, there *is* class struggle, and *his* class is winning.[9] Justice is clearly violated here as relationships are violated.

To be sure, class is not just about money: the decline of salaries and especially the reduction of benefits for workers is matched by a decline of influence and power, and hence by a distorted relationship. These declines and reductions do not happen by accident, and the economic necessity of these developments needs to be questioned since corporations make more money rather than less. The events in the fall of 2011 in Wisconsin offer another example. State politicians explained that cuts in the state budget were the reason for reducing wages and benefits of government workers. Yet the whole situation was a pretext to weaken the organization of government workers and thus their power. This reduction of power of Wisconsin workers and people brought them together. They fought back and sought to restore justice by being in solidarity, forming cross-class relationships, and reclaiming some of their power from corporate interests.

Hence, the struggle between the classes reflects positions of power and distortion of relationship and justice, whereby the power of workers is under attack in various ways, including severe legal restrictions on forming unions.[10] The firing of traditional workers who are then rehired on temporary contracts is not just a matter of savings in salaries and benefits. Temporary workers are also prevented from organizing their interests and are unable to make their voices heard. The pressures experienced by the American workforce represent an interesting context in which to discuss Gayatri Spivak's famous question of whether the subaltern can speak.[11] Spivak's question was raised in a historical context where the subaltern did not seem to be able to make any difference to the system. Later, Spivak considered other historical contexts and identified some possibilities, but the question remains: How much of a difference can the subaltern as subaltern make? Without denying the subjectivity of the subaltern, we need to keep in mind its tribulations even in the United States.

In a context where classes exist not because of human difference or natural stratification but because of a social system based on relations of power, celebrating diversity supports injustice and thus becomes the ultimate joke. While celebrating diversity makes some sense when it comes to the plurality of gender, ethnicity, and race, celebrating diversity makes no sense when it comes to classes locked in a one-sided struggle. Nevertheless, some approaches point in this direction, which shows how deeply ingrained this view of diversity is. The work of Tex Sample illustrates the problem. While Sample does not endorse a shallow celebration of diversity, his studies of working-class Americans are designed to convince middle-class church people of the value of including workers in their congregations.[12] As a result, classes are brought together without focusing on what it is that creates class differences in the first place. Who will benefit from this move?

A focus on class exposes the broken relationships and the role of power in our time more clearly than some of the other conflicts, which are more familiar to scholars in the United States. As the economy is getting back on track after the most severe economic crash since the 1930s, the number of billionaires is on the rise, but 50 percent of the jobs lost are projected never to return.[13] Unemployment levels are at record highs—in some regions and among some population groups, as high as 23 percent—and employers use this situation to play the employed against the unemployed.[14] In numerous sectors salaries are slashed and benefits are eliminated, as workers are threatened with job loss. To be sure, both blue-collar and white-collar workers are affected, while profit margins rise and top managers and top investors gain.

Another example of broken relationships and the role of power emerges in the paradoxical situation in which the principles of the free market economy are employed only at the lower levels. It locks regular buyers and sellers, as well as small employers and their workers, into a race to the bottom, while the upper classes use their power to escape these vicious circles. If top managers were subject to the market just like middle managers, small business people, and employees, they could not receive astronomical severance packages anymore, especially when they fail, in contrast to today's practice. That they do receive such bonus payouts is due to the severe imbalance of power which enables large banks and corporate entities to rely on government bailouts during the worst moments of the current economic crisis. The bailouts are indicative of a failure in relationship, and so the bailouts were not passed on to the struggling people. In less turbulent times, these imbalances of power find expression in tax reductions for the rich and government programs supporting corporations and the rich, while unemployment benefits and social welfare programs for needy people are steadily reduced.

Accordingly, justice, understood as the restoration of broken relationships, requires that class differences are not merely celebrated but exposed as a struggle between those who lose and those who gain. The common economic argument that extreme gain at the top translates into gain across the population is not valid anymore.[15] Rather, we are confronted with a paradox. Only if we refuse to superficially celebrate oppressive differences will we be able to appreciate human diversity. Superficial celebrations of diversity, built on top of perceived diversities, need to be deconstructed to restore broken relationships and to begin opening the view for the contributions of all.

The Jewish and Christian traditions, based on the Hebrew Bible and the New Testament, have important contributions to make. To be sure, the biblical God of justice does not celebrate superficial diversity grounded in injustice. Rather, in situations in which diversity is grounded in injustice, God takes sides. For instance, when the Israelites are enslaved in Egypt, God does not call for the celebration of diversity but for the liberation of the slaves. God calls Moses, who was raised as an Egyptian prince despite being a Hebrew, not in order to mediate between the different Hebrew and Egyptian cultures, but for the task of leading the Israelite slaves to freedom: "The cry of the Israelites has now come to me; I have also seen how the Egyptians oppress them. So come, I will send you to Pharaoh to bring my people, the Israelites, out of Egypt" (Exod. 3:9–10). This statement is clear: there is no appreciation for diversity without abandoning a superficially defined diversity, one that could endorse enslavement of one people by another.

It is too often overlooked that the God portrayed in the New Testament also takes sides. This God appreciates diversity, as demonstrated, for instance, in the birth narratives of Jesus, a narrative that has always been celebrated among Christians and their religious organizations. Jesus is born in unusual conditions: Jesus is born in unusual conditions: in a stable, welcomed by shepherds, animals, and angels, and to parents who have to travel at the time of Jesus' birth. What is often overlooked in the retellings of Jesus' humble beginnings is that here, too, God takes the side of those on the underside of history. The shepherds are working people, day laborers who tend other people's animals and do not own the animals. Jesus' parents travel not by choice but by the decree of the Roman emperor for the purposes of taxation. Jesus' mother is of humble origin and, as an unmarried woman, in a precarious situation. Appreciation of this sort of diversity is not a harmless support of pluralism, but endorses those who are different from the status quo, marginalized in society.

Importantly, Jesus' humble origins are not a matter of embarrassment but crucial to the story. Similarly, his mother is not shy and silent, as generations of artists have portrayed her, but she speaks out and praises God by "lifting up the lowly" and taking a stand in the midst of the problems that oppressive diversity has created. The God who lifts up the lowly, says Mary,[16] is the one who "has brought down the powerful from their thrones." This is not a shallow celebration of diversity. Likewise, her worship of the God who "filled the hungry with good things" and "sent the rich away empty" (Luke 1:46–44) articulates a theology that takes sides with the oppressed and marginalized in society. If justice requires the restoration of unjust economic relationships, it has to begin with deconstructing a notion of diversity that defines it superficially as a celebration of everybody's differences regardless of the underlying power dynamics.

THE NEED FOR JUSTICE IN THE CELEBRATION OF DIVERSITY

While there can be no true appreciation for diversity without justice, there can be no justice without diversity. Why is this so? Would not a situation where everybody looks the same and is treated exactly the same be the most just situation? In other words, would not a situation where diversity and concern for diversity were eliminated be inherently more just than a situation where diversity exists?

The truth is that the opposite is the case. Diversity is a fact of life, marking communities, people, and myriad ecological niches around the globe. If diversity is part of our world, treating everyone or everything exactly alike does not contribute to justice. The diversity of the abilities of children may provide an example. A wrestling match between a teenager and a five-year-old child would lead to an unsurprising outcome, as there is little chance for the five-year-old to win. Simple bodily differences need to be taken into account, which is why most sports separate men and women. Likewise, in the language sections of standardized tests for college and university applications like the SAT and GRE, native English speakers educated in U.S. schools have significant advantages over non-native speakers educated in other parts of the world. Many institutions of higher education are aware of this problem and make allowances for non-native speakers and international students in the admissions process. Hence, the treatment of different people as the same does not advance the cause of justice.

A similar logic emerges from biblical narratives about the realm of God. It is based on justice, and so nobody has to look alike. Diversity and differences are not only tolerated but respected and valued, especially when it comes to the "least of these." Thus the Jesus of the biblical Gospel narratives is portrayed as placing himself in solidarity with the marginalized and oppressed. He takes great care to respect those who were seen as different and of lesser value in the social networks in the first century CE, such as day laborers, servants, women, children, foreigners, and sick people. The Gospels teach that justice in these contexts is worked out not in the abstract but on the basis of particular concerns. Accordingly, farm workers need their daily wage to survive, regardless of the reaction of people defending the status quo (Matt. 20:1–16), children are taken seriously in a world that dismisses children (Mark 9:33–37; 10:13–16), and women are presented as agents rather than as recipients of patronizing mercy (Luke 18:1–8). The parables of Jesus feature workers, servants, those suffering from life-threatening diseases, shepherds, and others on the margins. These parables speak not only about the worlds and struggles of those who are different but also about their agency and the difference that they can make.

Wherever well-meaning efforts at working for justice fail to respect this kind of diversity, problems are inevitable. One example is the civil rights struggle in the United States, during which African American women experienced oppression by African American men who placed themselves in leadership positions without considering the voices of women. In response, womanist movements have emerged in which African American women have made their voices heard, developing analyses that have brought together the concerns of race, gender, and class.[17] Since then, womanist theology has risen within many churches and Christian groups, and in return some have come to appreciate diversity more deeply.

Another example is the labor movement in the United States. While the U.S. labor movement has occasionally struggled with linking justice concerns with diversity across the lines of race and gender, when they include concerns of women and racial minorities, organized labor has become stronger. More recently, organized labor has begun to take seriously the concerns of undocumented immigrants. In the process, it has become obvious that the community of workers is always strengthened when the "least of these" are included. Organizations such as Jobs with Justice exemplify the importance of the concern for diversity in the struggle for justice.[18]

In short, then, justice cannot be accomplished without taking diversity seriously. In the history of the United States, this lesson was learned only gradually, as women, men without property, and minorities were initially not allowed to vote and excluded from the political process. Broadening the basis of democracy, which occurred only after the excluded groups made their voices heard and challenged the monolithic rule of propertied white men, is a fundamental matter of justice.

Furthermore, justice requires actively engaged respect for diversity when relationships are broken and diversity is used to maintain power differentials among groups. Christian biblical traditions challenge a silent cooptation into broken relationships, as for instance between the downtrodden and the powerful or the hungry and those who are full. Accordingly, justice requires the taking of sides. It objects to the distortions of relationships in favor of new relationships based on justice and equality. This process may entail that the powerful be pushed off their thrones and the rich be sent away empty (Luke 1:52–53).

Often people raise the concern that new injustices are created when God takes the side of those enduring the most pressure in broken relationships. What happens, for instance, when the liberated slaves of the Exodus narrative enter the Promised Land? Will there be a simple role reversal, so that the formerly oppressed will become the oppressors of those already living on the land? The Bible contains numerous conquest fantasies, according to which the Israelites conquer Canaan, break down the walls of its cities, kill the inhabitants, and take over the land.[19] Yet there is also another tradition in the Hebrew Bible, in which the Israelites do not conquer the land but enter into various relationships with the people already living there. Some influential interpretations maintain that the liberated slaves joined forces with the oppressed people in the land and this movement ushered in liberation from an unjust monopoly of city states.[20] Read accordingly, the biblical narratives also promote appreciation of and active engagement with diversity, which leads to an alliance of the oppressed and a challenge to authoritarian city rule over ancient rural Canaan. Justice was served not by a reversal of oppressors and oppressed but by the formation of new relationships. It was marked by a new appreciation of diversity grounded in justice-seeking principles.

In the New Testament, the Pauline discussion of the church as the body of Christ points in a similar direction. The image of the body, according to which all members relate to each other organically, has long been cherished by those who appreciate diversity. It thus illustrates the problems of a shallow celebration of diversity. In Paul's world, the image was used by those who supported the Roman Empire and endorsed its social power differentials. The image of the body enabled them to define the lower classes as servants of the upper classes, just as the feet serve the head. Proponents of this position left little doubt that the feet should be content and not try to exercise the functions of the head or even aim to become the head. Paul turns this image upside down when he emphasizes the particular importance of the lower extremities. He explains:

> The eye cannot say to the hand, "I have no need of you," nor again the head to the feet, "I have no need of you." On the contrary, the members of the body that seem to be weaker are indispensable, and those members of the body that we think less honorable we clothe with greater honor, and our less respectable members are treated with greater respect. . . . But God has so arranged the body, giving the greater honor to the inferior member. . . . If one member suffers, all suffer together with it; if one member is honored, all rejoice together with it. (1 Cor. 12:21–26)

In contrast to the dominant treatment of the feet and the hands as well as working people and slaves, Paul views them as indispensable and to be treated with great respect. Consequently, if their social contributions are indeed as indispensable as Paul proclaims, their contributions should also be valued economically and politically in equal terms.

Yet Paul's position is outrageous in the halls of power to this very day. After all, he writes, "If one member suffers, all suffer together with it" (1 Cor. 12:26). In Pauline theology, then, justice is only served when the diversity of the "least of these" is not only appreciated but also positively recognized and rewarded for the contribution the marginalized and oppressed make to the whole. The prerequisite for this kind of justice is that a superficially defined diversity that merely celebrates the status quo must be rejected.[21] Translated into today's context, Paul's statement implies that the CEO is not superior to the workers. Hence, pay scale differentials need to become more equal, and if Pauline principles were applied, companies would need to listen to workers to get the economy back on track today.

In sum, diversity and justice need each other. Justice is necessary to practice diversity without fear of exploitation and repression. Similarly, justice is required to reject false notions of diversity that, often unwittingly, celebrate differentials of power rather than empower those who bear the brunt of unjust relationships. Diversity is necessary so that justice can help us build relationships in which "the least of us" are the guide toward justice in the world.

BEYOND SUPERFICIAL DIVERSITY AND JUSTICE CLAIMS: CONCLUDING COMMENTS

In postmodern times, justice and diversity have often been played against each other. Where diversity and difference are emphasized, pluralism often seems to take the place of justice. Since, it seems, each group and each person has their own agenda, all should be able to do as they please. This argument overlooks, however, that (distorted) relationships exist even in a pluralistic world, even if only underground. Moreover, these relationships are invariably relationships shaped by unjust power differentials. We need to openly deal with these broken relationships to create more just relations.

Hence, when justice is introduced into the discussion, we become empowered to push beyond shallow celebrations of diversity. We are able to reshape existing broken relationships. Yet as the relationships are reshaped, we need to be careful not to homogenize the various parties. The inclusion of justice is crucial so that we do not treat as alike those who are different, and so we ensure that differences are not glossed over and exploited for the benefit of some over and against others. Justice allows differences to come to fruition and leads to situations in which all can be free to contribute to the whole according to their abilities and all receive what they need. That the first shall be last and the last shall be first (Matt. 20:16) is such an expression of hope, upheld and lived by those who believe in the realm of God on earth.

NOTES

1. In 2010, only 45.3 percent of the population was classified as "white persons not Hispanic"; see http://quickfacts.census.gov/qfd/states/48000.html [accessed December 6, 2012].

2. In these hymns, the status quo is affirmed by focusing on otherworldly topics. Exchanging heaven for earth, earth is left to its own devices.

3. The precedent was created 1919 in the Michigan Supreme Court, in a case against Henry Ford; see Wikipedia, *"Dodge v. Ford Motor Company,"* http://en.wikipedia.org/wiki/Dodge_v._Ford_Motor_Company [accessed December 6, 2012].

4. Heather Boushey, *Equal Pay for Breadwinners: More Men Are Jobless While Women Earn Less for Equal Work* (Washington, DC: Center for American Progress, 2009), 1. Available at http://www.americanprogress.org/issues/2009/01/gender_economy_report.html [accessed December 6, 2012].

5. See, for instance, R. C. Lewontin, "Confusions about Human Races" (June 7, 2006), http://raceandgenomics.ssrc.org/Lewontin/ [accessed December 6, 2012].

6. Klaus Koch, *"ṣdq,* gemeinschaftstreu/heilvoll sein," in *Theologisches Handwörterbuch zum Alten Testament,* vol. 2, ed. Ernst Jenni and Claus Westermann (München and Zürich: Christian Kaiser Verlag, Theologischer Verlag, 1984), 507–30.

7. See http://www.racialequitytools.org/ci-concepts-ra.htm [accessed December 6, 2012].

8. See http://motherjones.com/politics/2011/02/income-inequality-in-america-chart-graph [accessed December 6, 2012].

9. Ben Stein, "In Class Warfare, Guess Which Class Is Winning," *New York Times* (November 26, 2006), http://www.nytimes.com/2006/11/26/business/yourmoney/26every.html [accessed December 6, 2012]. It is for this reason Buffet called for tax increases for the rich in 2011. Buffet's proposal was met with harsh rejections by conservatives, although a poll shows that 68 percent of millionaires (61 percent of those who own investments of $5 million or more) actually support raising taxes on the wealthy. Robert Frank, "Millionaires Support Warren Buffett's Tax on the Rich," *Wall Street Journal* (October 17, 2011), http://blogs.wsj.com/wealth/2011/10/27/most-millionaires-support-warren-buffetts-tax-on-the-rich/ [accessed December 6, 2012].

10. Between 25 and 60 million workers want to organize but only 500,000 are able to do so every year; see Michael Payne, "Unionization: A Private Sector Solution to the Financial Crisis," *Dissent* (Spring 2009): 59. The AFL-CIO estimates that 60 million workers would like to be organized in unions, while opponents of the Employee Free Choice Act reduce this number to a still sizable figure of 25 million workers. According to the United Nations Universal Declaration of Human Rights, article 23, paragraph 4, "Everyone has the right to form and join trade unions for the protection of his interests"; see http://www.un.org/en/documents/udhr/index.shtml#a23 [accessed December 6, 2012].

11. Gayatri Chakravorty Spivak raised her famous question in a 1988 essay titled "Can the Subaltern Speak?" in *Marxism and the Interpretation of Culture,* ed. Cary Nelson and Lawrence Grossberg (Urbana: University of Illinois Press, 1988), 271–313. For Spivak's more recent take on this question, see Gayatri Chakravorty Spivak, *A Critique of Postcolonial Reason: Toward a History of the Vanishing Present* (Cambridge, MA: Harvard University Press, 1999), 308–11.

12. See, for instance, Tex Sample, *Hard Living People and Mainstream Christians* (Nashville, TN: Abingdon Press, 1993).

13. Will Deener notes that, unlike in the previous four recessions, more than half of the layoffs will be permanent; see his piece titled "Working?" in the *Dallas Morning News* (July 13, 2009): 4D.

14. For some of the unemployment statistics that back up these numbers, see http://www.shadowstats.com/alternate_data/unemployment-charts [accessed on December 6, 2012].

15. For an extensive exploration of this argument, see my book titled *No Rising Tide: Theology, Economics, and the Future* (Minneapolis: Fortress Press, 2009).

16. This New Testament hymn is reminiscent of Hannah's prayer in Samuel 2:1–10.

17. The work of Alice Walker is often referenced as one of the inspirations of the womanist movement, but no single person or author should be considered as the origin.

18. See www.jwj.org. The organization was founded to expand the horizons of the labor movement and to include the large number of workers whose jobs are outside of

the confines of organized labor. For a local example of the work of JWJ, see http://wrbdallas.blogspot.com/ [accessed December 6, 2012].

19. For instance, see the book of Joshua in its entirety.

20. Hebrew Bible scholar Norman Gottwald, in *The Hebrew Bible: A Brief Socio-Literary Introduction* (Minneapolis: Fortress Press, 2009), 150–57, distinguishes among accounts that depict the entrance into Canaan as conquest, immigration, and social revolution. The social-revolution account combines some of the insights of the other accounts and views the revolution as proceeding from the bottom up when various oppressed groups joined forces.

21. For a more in-depth interpretation of the apostle Paul in the context of the Roman Empire, see my book *Christ and Empire: From Paul to Postcolonial Times* (Minneapolis: Fortress Press, 2007), especially chapter 1.

SEVEN

Does God Really Love Diversity?

A Chinese American New Testament Scholar Speaks

Sze-kar Wan

"You f--king communist bitch, why don't you go back where you came from," the man screamed at me across the parking lot. "Foreigner" is the new N-word, which can no longer be used in fashionable circles. That is why so many people have tried to prove Barack Obama is a Muslim born in Kenya. He has a foreign-sounding name, just like "Sze-kar Wan," and that is enough to infuriate many who think that a "foreigner" is president of the United States. Change the word "president" to any position of authority and the same sentiments hold true. Modern discourse has made it socially unacceptable to rail against a black man, since that would be racism and racism makes one appear low class. A black American is an African *American*, but a black Muslim is a *foreigner*. The legal or constitutional angle is just a bonus. The real prize is to deal with him the same way we have dealt with all foreigners and undesirables. Violence against foreigners is not only tolerated, it is patriotism. Violence against a communist? That makes you a hero! "Foreigner" is the new N-word, and it rhymes with "illegal immigrant."

Asian Americans are racialized as foreigners. Asian American men are also feminized—hence "bitch"—in a monstrous act of racial castration, but that is another story for another time. Whenever I introduce myself as American, the response is, invariably, "But you don't *look* American!" If people ask me, "Where are you from?" and I say, "I am from Boston," they say, without fail, "No, no, no, I mean, where are you *really* from?" In her rants against her fellow Asian American students that

129

went viral on YouTube in 2011, a UCLA student complains that if the university is letting these foreigners into "our" school, the least they can do is to behave themselves and learn "our" manners.[1]

Does God really love diversity? Many in this "Christian nation" might say "No." After all, the biblical texts do appear to privilege exceptionalism as defined by insiders. When I approach these texts as a Chinese American, which is to say, as a discursive foreigner, I am also forced to answer in the negative. I would add an important qualification, however: the biblical texts, the basis for my response, are products of complex historical circumstances and ideological factors, and that very complexity might provide modern readers a glimmer of hope.

In the following I examine the so-called Servant Songs (Isaiah 40–55)[2] and Third Isaiah (Isaiah 56–66) in what Christians call the "Old Testament" and what Jews call simply "The Bible." I also analyze Luke-Acts, a two-volume work, written in the late first century and found within the Christian canon. The Hebrew texts were written from the perspectives of conquerors, the winners of history who advanced a narrative that, conveniently enough, legitimated their occupation and concomitant displacement of local inhabitants. Architects of this ancient "manifest destiny" installed the new masters as "returnees," putative long-forgotten "rightful" claimants of their ancestral "Promised Land," while designating the aborigines as "foreigners" or "usurpers" who had to be removed before peace could be restored. Luke-Acts was composed at a time when the fledgling Christian movement was becoming self-conscious of its place in the Roman Empire. Its author was anxious to distance the Christians from their Jewish contemporaries while emphasizing the antiquity of Christianity in its Jewish heritage. This schizophrenia can be explained only by a Lukan supersessionism that aims at replacing the chosen people with the Christians.

Occupiers, imperial powers, and their faithful brokers have throughout the history of the biblical West naturally read these biblical texts as unproblematic, objective history. But the displaced, the occupied, and the landless have succeeded in complicating the matter by reading these texts from the bottom up—that is, from the perspectives of those who have their homes taken away from them and who have been branded aliens in their own land. Literary critic and postcolonial theorist Edward Said called this reading strategy "counterpuntal." In contradistinction from mainstream, top-down interpretations, a counterpuntual approach aims at composing an internally cogent *counterpoint* that is independent from the received score but, when juxtaposed with the latter, produces a full, harmonious, polyphonic whole.[3]

UNIVERSALIST ETHNOCENTRISM OF THE SERVANT SONGS IN DEUTERO-ISAIAH

The Servant Songs (Isaiah 40–55) begin with the prophet urging his fellow exiles to prepare for the eventuality of the return to Jerusalem in the sixth century BCE, when Cyrus of Persia, the "victor from the east" (41:2), is inflicting mortal wounds upon the Babylonians (see also 44:28; 45:1). The penalty for violating the sacred covenant with God has been paid, double in fact (40:2); God now opens up highways through the barren infertility of the desert, leading the people back to Zion (40:3–5). The oracle promises that Jerusalem "shall be rebuilt" and the temple's "foundation shall be laid" (44:28c–d).

Whatever joy or pride the prophet feels about the return, however, is tempered by the irony that a foreign king is accomplishing this feat of rebuilding Jerusalem. So here is the paradox: reestablishment of the people and return to self-determination are possible only if the people let go of trying to succeed on their own. They wonder if their God is so enfeebled by the many years of exile that they must rely on an outsider to perform the impossible. Is Yahweh so lost in the landscape that a Persian now paves the return to the temple? The prophet answers, "Our God is the creator of heaven and earth and all its inhabitants" (44:24–28; 45:9–13; 51:12–16).[4] The prevalence of creation terminology and the wide distribution of references to God's creative acts throughout make it unmistakable that creation is the theological foundation of the Servant Songs.[5] These poems stress the universal scope of God's control over all creation, all social and political institutions, nations, empires, and all inhabitants of the earth, especially political and military figures who fulfill the divine plan by letting the people return to Zion:[6]

> Thus says YHWH,
>> your redeemer, the Holy One of Israel:
> For your sake I will send to Babylon
>> and break down all the bars,
>> and the shouting of the Chaldeans will be turned to lamentation.
> I am YHWH, your Holy One,
>> the creator of Israel, your King (Isa. 43:14–15).[7]

Thus, in these Servant Songs, God the redeemer and God the creator become one. But as God's creatorship constitutes the theological basis for the restoration of Israel, redemption is also folded into the creation of the world, especially the creation of Israel.

The prophet relentlessly reminds Israel of the "former things" that happened under God's rule:

> Thus says YHWH,
>> who makes a way in the sea,
>> a path in the mighty waters,

who brings out chariot and horse,
    army and warrior;
they lie down, they cannot rise,
    they are extinguished, quenched like a wick (Isa. 43:16–17).

Yet these "former things," the prophet states, Israel should "forget" —
even though rhetorically he has just reminded Israel of them. God will do
a new thing for the chosen people now:

To make a way in the wilderness
    and rivers in the desert . . .
to give drink to my chosen people,
    the people whom I formed for myself (Isa. 43:19–21).

The prophet also intertwines the theme of chosenness with the theme of
creation:

But now hear, O Jacob my servant,
    Israel whom I have chosen!
Thus says YHWH who made you,
    who formed you in the womb and will help you (Isa. 44:1–2).[8]

The self-understanding and self-perception of Israel are balanced on the
dialectic between the universality of the creator God and the special elec-
tion that God bestows on the chosen people. In other words, the creator
before whom all mortals tremble, who "stirs up the sea so that its waves
roar . . . stretching out the heavens and laying the founds of the earth,"
and whose name is "YHWH of hosts," is the very one who tells Zion,
with climactic tenderness, "You are my people" (51:12–16).[9]

Only within the security of this chosenness, created in the nexus of
universalism and ethnocentricity, does the prophet handle Israel's embarrassment of being saved by Cyrus the Persian. The starting point, here
as before, is the three interrelated complex of ideas: creation, redemption,
and chosenness.

Thus says YHWH, your redeemer,
    who formed you in the womb:
I am YHWH, who made all things,
    who alone stretched out the heavens,
    who by myself spread out the earth (Isa. 44:24).

By fiat, God pronounces the restoration of Jerusalem and Judah:

[Jerusalem] shall be inhabited. . . .
    [The cities of Judah] shall be rebuilt,
and I will raise up their ruins (Isa. 44:26).

The redeemer-creator can just as easily command the river to dry up
(44:27) as God can command Cyrus to "carry out all my purpose" or to
have Jerusalem rebuilt and the foundation of the temple laid (44:28).

From here, it is an easy step for the prophet to proclaim Cyrus as God's "messiah," the anointed one,

> whose right hand I have grasped
>> to subdue nations before him
>> and strip kings of their robes,
> to open doors before him —
>> and the gates shall not be closed:
> I will go before you
>> and level the mountains,
> I will break in pieces the doors of bronze
>> and cut through the bars of iron,
> I will give you the treasures of darkness
>> and riches hidden in secret places,
> so that you may know that it is I, YHWH,
>> the God of Israel, who call you by your name.
> For the sake of my servant Jacob,
>> and Israel my chosen,
> I call you by your name,
>> *I surname you, though you do not know me.*
> I am YHWH, and there is no other;
>> besides me there is no god.
>> *I arm you, though you do not know me,*
> so that they may know, from the rising of the sun
>> and from the west, that there is no one besides me;
>> I am YHWH, and there is no other.
> I form light and create darkness,
>> I make weal and create woe;
>> I YHWH do all these things (Isa. 45:1–7, emphasis added).

In other words, Cyrus the Persian king accomplishes God's purpose. Yet the Persian king is no more than an instrument, an *unwitting* instrument at that: "I surname you, though you do not know me. . . . I arm you, though you do not know me." Ultimately, God acts and the beneficiary of God's actions is Israel. This combination of monotheism ("There is no other God beside me," 45:5, 6; cf. also 45:14) and creation (cf. also 45:9–12) traces a straight path from Israel to God, thereby allowing the path of redemption to lead back to Jerusalem through Cyrus, the "messiah," the only non-Israelite ever so designated in the biblical text. It is an idea about universalism that is grounded in a particular people, Israel. God acts in the world on behalf of Israel. It is a universalism emerging out of the particularity of one people.

At the time of the Servant Songs, this belief in universalism had already been in place for a few centuries. According to Isaiah 10:5–6, God chose the Assyrians to punish the Israelites for their iniquities. God used the Assyrians to a divinely ordained end, even though they were sinful (10:12). They will, of course, receive their just deserts in due course, in the hands of Cyrus, "whose right hand I have grasped to subdue nations before him and strip kings of their robes" (45:1). Choosing similar instruments now, the prophet promises in a triumphal tone, God is directing the way through the infertile wilderness back to the Promised Land, to the benefit of Israel and Judah. God will restore them.

But this is not a "real" universalism, because it assumes Israel is *primus inter pares*. According to the prophet's historiography, world events from the exile onwards always revolve around Israel. Every event and every nation exist merely to help God punish Israel or to restore it. The root cause of its destruction, and therefore the Assyrian victory, is its iniquities, and the imminent Persian victory is likewise part of the divine intention to restore Israel to its former land. Accordingly, the prophet affirms that Israel's special mission initially established in the Abrahamic covenant (Genesis 15 and 17)—to be a light to the nations—has never been made obsolete, and Israel retains its chosenness. Prior to the exile, it was foretold that God would shine a light on all nations in the new kingdom (Isa. 9:1–2), and this prophecy was being fulfilled during the Babylonian exile. Israel is installed as the agent through whom God's salvation will reach the ends of the earth:

> I am YHWH, I have called you in righteousness,
>> I have taken you by the hand and kept you;
> I have given you as a covenant to the people,
>> a light to the nations,
>> to open the eyes that are blind,
> to bring out the prisoners from the dungeon,
>> from the prison those who sit in darkness (Isa. 42:6–7; cf. also 49:6).

Underlying this special mission is the assumption that the moral laws of God are applicable not only to Israel but also to all nations. Israel, allegorized as the Servant of God, will have to instruct the nations about God's law (50:4–11; 32:13–53:12), because God's justice (*mishpat*) and righteousness (*tsedaqah*) are superior to all other forms of justice and righteousness. In fact, "it is through the Torah that the sovereignty of the one God over the whole world is efficacious and discernible."[10] Here we come full circle. As the Torah is elevated as the divine law with which the universal God governs all the nations of the earth, universalism is now made the handmaiden of ethnocentrism.

THIRD ISAIAH'S DESCENT INTO TRIBALISM

Israel's role in God's plan of creation-redemption is seen as unique, and the self-perception of Israel as "a light to the nations" is central to its national consciousness. As Bible scholar Duane Christensen explains, "The nations are the matrix of Israel's life, the *raison d'être* of her existence."[11] While this is undeniably one form of universalism, it is also profoundly ethnocentric and perhaps should be dubbed "universalist binarism." Such binarism might be less destructive than an *exclusivist* binarism that seeks to deny outsiders all benefits that insiders have arrogated to themselves, but it is binarism nonetheless. It might well be more insidious because it is disguised as universalism.

Third Isaiah (56–66), written after the resettlement of the self-styled "exiles" in Israel and presupposing a Palestinian setting, chronicles how this universalist binarism teeters on the brink of tribalism.[12] The prophet begins with a resounding affirmation of the place of "foreigners" in Israel: "Do not let the foreigner joined to YHWH say, 'YHWH will surely separate me from his people'" (56:3), because God will promise them a share of this nation reborn:

> And the foreigners who join themselves to YHWH,
>   to minister to him, to love the name of YHWH,
>   and to be his servants,
> all who keep the Sabbath, and do not profane it,
>   and hold fast my covenant —
> these I will bring to my holy mountain,
>   and make them joyful in my house of prayer;
> their burnt offerings and their sacrifices
>   will be accepted on my altar;
> for my house shall be called a house of prayer
>   for all peoples.
> Thus says YHWH God,
>   who gathers the outcasts of Israel,
> I will gather others to them
>   besides those already gathered (Isa. 56:6–8).

This is a hopeful declaration of universal peace, presided over by God and accompanied by the presence of the glory of YHWH. Light will break through the darkness that has a stranglehold on not just any people but earth itself. It is a universal light visible to all peoples and nations who are in darkness and who are drawn to it.

> Arise, shine, for your light has come,
>   and the glory of YHWH has risen upon you.
> For darkness shall cover the earth,
>   and thick darkness the peoples;
> but YHWH will arise upon you,
>   and his glory will appear over you.
> Nations shall come to your light,
>   and kings to the brightness of your dawn (Isa. 60:1–3).

Israel, of course, has an implicit role to play: "*Your* light" here reminds it of its special mission to be "a light to the nations," to bring God's moral law and salvation to all.

The offer to the foreigners is a generous one on the surface. They have the same rights of abode as the Israelites: "I will gather others to them besides those already gathered" (56:8), for "my house shall be called a house of prayer for all peoples" (56:7). But these rights are contingent on certain conditions, chief among them that the "foreigners" first agree "to minister to [God], to love the name of YHWH, and to be [God's] servants. . . . [K]eep the Sabbath, and do not profane it, and hold fast my covenant" (56:6). In other words, the "foreigners" are none other than proselytes who have "joined" themselves to the Israelite religion, the worship of Yahweh. "These I will bring to my holy mountain" (56:7), proclaims the prophet. To what extent, then, are they still "foreigners"? Are they not converts who have renounced their own religions and hence, in the context of the ancient near east, their own culture and ethnicity? In fact, that they are still called "foreigners" tells us that they are no better than second-class citizens to the returning Israelites.[13]

Whatever Third Isaiah says about Palestine and however much the prophet idealizes Israelite ownership, the historical land is no *terra nullius*. It has been occupied prior to the Return and continues to be occupied when the Israelites occupy the land. "Homeland" is therefore a contested notion, constructed by one side of the debate with prejudice. Local inhabitants see the newcomers as intruders, occupiers, conquerors, emissaries representing a foreign overlord, or colonists in service of an empire.[14] In other words, they are being colonized, and the sure sign for the condition for legal "rights" to live on their own land is the abandonment of their ancestral customs, law, culture, religion, and indeed their own ethnicity. They must abide by codes and laws written from the belly of the empire for the benefit of the emperor and his clients and imposed upon the locals through sanctioned military violence and intimidation.

This pattern of forced assimilation suffuses Third Isaiah and determines the relationship between Israelites and outsiders. When the light of God is revealed to the earth, the sons and daughters of Israel will return from afar. Alongside the returnees are "the wealth of the nations" depicted in detail (60:5–7), to be sent from all corners of the world. Israel will have so ascended the ranks of nations that others will send their tributes to Israel (60:8–9, 11, 14) because, finally, God the redeemer will show the world that "the mighty one of Jacob" is in charge:

> You shall suck the milk of nations,
>   you shall suck the breasts of kings;
> and you shall know that I, YHWH, am your Savior
>   and your redeemer, the Mighty One of Jacob (Isa. 60:16).

One shudders at the jarring image of the invaders as suckling children, draining the life and vitality from the vanquished.

By contrast, woe to those who do not recognize the glory of YHWH or refuse to acknowledge the superiority of the reconstituted Israel: "For the nation and kingdom that will not serve you shall perish; those nations shall be utterly laid waste" (60:12). This is martial language describing a scene of conquest. "The nations shall bring you their wealth," because they have been defeated. "Their kings [are] led in procession" (60:10)—as captives being led to the central sanctuary for slaughter as a thanksgiving offering to God. Moreover, "foreigners"—the same "foreigners" of Isaiah 56—"shall build up your walls, and their kings shall minister to you" (60:10). "Foreigners" in this context cannot refer merely to foreign nations outside Israel. They are the proselytes, the second-class citizens of an earlier oracle, aborigines who have been co-opted into the alien and alienating social and political world of the returnees-colonizers.

Binarism has had a devastating effect on the kingdoms of Judah and Israel when they fell to powerful empires. Death and destruction were visited upon the people, and the kingdoms were razed to the ground. Yet when the exiles are granted a "return" to their land, they idealize a scenario that is no less binary. They announce that "foreigners" will serve "us" for a change, while "we" enjoy "their" fruits and "their" wealth. They proclaim Israel to rule, while the locals, now designated "foreigners," till their soils, harvest their fruits, and repair their ruins, all for their benefit. They imagine a reverse of national fortune, when Israel's miseries turn to joy, poverty becomes prosperity, broken homes are repaired, and their fruit trees bloom again. The problem is, Israel's wealth in this scenario is built on the poverty of the putative foreigners, and Israel's power is exercised on the back of the aborigines. Israel wins only if the others lose. The power construct is reversed, but binarism survives.

According to the binary logic, then, a proclamation of the Jubilee brings up its reverse, "the day of vengeance of our God" (61:2). The Israelites, the mourners, will be comforted, and they will "build up the ancient ruins" and "raise the former devastations" (61:4). But that restoration is paralleled by a malediction pronounced on the foreigners: "Strangers shall stand and feed your flocks, foreigners shall till your land and dress your vines" (61:5), while the formerly dishonored people, Israel, will be priests and ministers of the land, enjoying "the wealth of the nations" (61:6). If the proclamation of Third Isaiah is good news to the newcomers, it assuredly is not good news to the aborigines.[15]

LUKE'S REINSTATEMENT OF ETHNOCENTRISM

The thinly disguised ethnocentrism of Third Isaiah must have been known to the early followers of Jesus, because there is evidence, even within the New Testament canon, that they critiqued and corrected it, but ultimately fell back to the same ethnocentric traps. In a programmatic pericope introducing the two-volume work Luke-Acts, the Lukan Jesus finds himself in a synagogue in his hometown Nazareth, where he preaches from Isa. 61:1–2a:

> The Spirit of the Lord is upon me,
>   because he has anointed me
>   to bring good news to the poor.
> He has sent me to proclaim release to the captives
>   and recovery of sight to the blind,
>   to let the oppressed go free,
> to proclaim the year of the Lord's favor (Luke 4:18–19).[16]

The initial reaction of the synagogue is favorable. When Jesus sits down to preach, all eyes are fixed on him, according to Luke, wondering what this home-grown prophet is about to say (4:20). Jesus does not disappoint. For the first time in Luke's narrative, the adult Jesus speaks publicly: "Today this scripture has come to be fulfilled in your hearing (literally *ears*)" (4:21). Thereupon the congregation is bedazzled by "the words of grace that come out of his mouth" (4:22). As an ultimate sign of approval, they ask, rhetorically but with evident admiration, "Isn't this Joseph's son?" (4:22).[17]

To understand the congregation's reaction requires us to lay bare what exactly the Lukan Jesus is proclaiming. The brevity of the saying is reminiscent of another short public pronouncement, "Repent, the kingdom of God is at hand," recorded in the Gospel of Mark (1:15), as both are epitomes characterizing the tenor of Jesus' preaching. All verbs used in verse 22 are in the imperfect tense, a tense typical for recounting not just an isolated event but a recurring past. They convey a general reception of Jesus by his hometown folk over a period of time. According to Luke, Jesus attends synagogue in his hometown (v. 14), and his audience is already aware of his burgeoning reputation in Capernaum (v. 23). This is, after all, the start of Luke's narrative proper, according to which Jesus' reputation is just beginning to spread, his public ministry is about to take off, and the congregation is anxiously waiting for him to declare his messiahship. This explains the crowd's enthusiastic reception.

Luke's Jesus ends his reading of Isaiah with the line "to proclaim the year of God's favor" (4:19). "The year of God's favor," as most scholars agree, refers to the year of Jubilee, which in spite of its canonical status in Leviticus 25 might never have been put into practice.[18] Nevertheless, the idea of debt forgiveness, the reversion of land to the ancestral owner, the release of slaves, and the general idea of socioeconomic reform to relieve the burden of the people have always enjoyed great appeal. It is no accident that Third Isaiah chooses the Jubilee images to describe how the anointed one of God will restore Israel.[19] Whatever the extent of the jubilary vision of Luke, his Jesus proclaims it here because only a king, the anointed, could ever be in a position to make that declaration. For this reason, high tension follows Jesus' reading of the Torah scroll. It is broken only when he announces, "Today this prophecy is being fulfilled even as you hear it" (4:21; my translation), thereby taking the messianic mantle forcefully with this "Nazareth Manifesto" (Wright). The text of 4:22 does not say, "[The listeners] speak well of him," as the New Revised Standard Version (NRSV) translates, but rather literally reads, "[T]hey were bearing witness to him."[20] They hear Jesus' messianic claim and support him because they eagerly await the royal restoration of Jubilee.

But the intent of Luke's citation of Isaiah 61 has as much to do with what he includes as what he omits. The proclamation of Isa. 61:2 consists of two parts: the first proclaims a jubilary restoration, but the second celebrates "the day of vengeance of our God." In accordance with Third Isaiah's exclusivist binarism, the pronounced Jubilee and the expected divine vengeance are synonymous pairs. While the restoration of Israel is good news to Israel, it means devastation to the locals. Israel's jubilee implies condemnation to the ethnic Other. Exclusivist binarism dictates that there cannot be one without the other. Good news to Israel means devastation to the Other.

Binarism has deep roots in the Jubilee legislation found in Leviticus 25. Land is not to be sold in perpetuity (25:18–24). Any land sold because of hardship returns to the original owner after fifty years (25:25–28) because the land is God's (25:23). All financial debts must likewise be calculated on the basis of the jubilary fifty-year cycle, at the end of which all debts are forgiven (25:13–17). The theological basis for this radically egalitarian vision is the covenant: "I am YHWH your God, who brought you out of the land of Egypt, to give you the land of Canaan, to be your God" (25:38). God is the only permanent landlord whereas all others are mere tenants or stewards who dwell on the land at the pleasure of God. The Jubilee restores Israel to its pristine state when God gave the land to the Israelites.

The prohibition against slavery stands on the same theological foundation. A person cannot be sold into slavery but must be employed as a hired or bondservant to be released in a Jubilee year (25:39–42). The rationale is again the covenant: "For they are my servants, whom I brought out of the land of Egypt; they shall not be sold as slaves" (25:42).

But the Levitical code has an escape clause:

> As for the male and female slaves whom you may have, *it is from the nations around* you that you may acquire male and female slaves. You may also acquire them from among the aliens residing with you, and from their families that are with you, who have been born in your land; and they may be your property. You may keep them as a possession for your children after you, for them to inherit as property. These you may treat as slaves, but *as for your fellow Israelites, no one shall rule over the other with harshness* (Lev. 25:44–46, emphasis added).

This is a massive exception of gigantic proportion. The Jubilee restoration applies only to insiders, since it is *our* God who established *our* covenant with *us*. The egalitarianism does not apply to those outside Israel's ethnic boundaries.

Against this background, Luke's omission of the second line, the malediction of Isa. 61:2b, cannot be accidental. It is a deliberate attempt to sever the link between the equivalency of restoration for "us" and condemnation for the others. Luke's fastidious account of how the scroll is given to Jesus, how he unrolls it himself and finds his own place (Luke 4:17), and how he rolls up the scroll after reading and returns it to the attendant (4:20) is the storyteller's way of noting that the reading ends deliberately and intentionally.[21] Luke rejects the ethnic reasoning behind Third Isaiah's exclusivist binarism.

Lest we are lured into thinking Luke's vision represents a decisive critique against ethnocentrism, his rejection of Third Isaiah is, in fact, not a step toward egalitarianism but a clever setup for a subtle reinstatement of the very position he rejects. He portrays the synagogue crowd as being unable to grasp the connection between Jesus' proclamation of the Jubilee and his omission of vengeance. His Jesus cites the stories of Elijah and Elisha to make this point explicit: "In truth I say to you," Luke goes on using a prophetic formula, "there were many widows at the time of Elijah in Israel [during a severe drought], but Elijah was sent to none of them except to a widow at Zarephath in Sidon" (4:25–26).[22] In a similar fashion, Elisha is said to have cleansed none of the lepers in Israel except Naaman the Syrian (4:27). The contrast Luke highlights for his audience is the favor granted to the ethnic other and the withholding of the same to the chosen people. The point of the Nazareth Manifesto is commendable by itself: the Jubilee Year is here and is being fulfilled now, and its beneficiaries must include the previously excluded ethnic other.

At this point in his narrative Luke takes a fateful step: It is *the Jews* who reject this universalist vision of the Jubilee. In rejecting this vision, *the Jews* declare Luke's Jesus a pretender and conspire to execute him as a blasphemer (4:28–29). If this opening episode recalls how Luke portrays the Jewish plot against Jesus in the Passion Narrative, it is not coincidental. According to Luke's narrative, Jesus is a lone prophet in a sea of ethnic chauvinism who risks his life to call his people back to a form of covenantal universalism, but his people reject his message and ultimately him, to the point of condemning him to death. Writing in the late first century, Luke's story amounts to making Jews responsible for the emerging antagonism between Jews and Luke's followers of Jesus, who are by now becoming predominantly Gentile.[23]

The Nazareth Manifesto represents only the beginning of protracted strife between Jews and Christians. One of the stated purposes of Luke-Acts is revealed in the final confrontation between Luke's Paul and Jewish leaders, in Rome of all places, the seat of the Empire (Acts 28:23–28). The Lukan Paul castigates Jewish leaders for rejecting Jesus as Messiah: "The Holy Spirit was right in saying to *your ancestors* through the prophet Isaiah, 'Go to this people and say, You will indeed listen, but never understand, and you will indeed look, but never perceive'" (emphasis added). The placement of *"your* ancestors" in the mouth of Paul who proclaims himself ready to be damned for the sake of his kinsfolk (Rom. 9:1–5) and who never ceases to take pride in his Jewish credentials (2 Cor. 11:22; Gal. 1:14; Phil. 3:4–6) is jarring enough.[24] Luke's Paul makes one final, decisive pronouncement: "Let it be known to you then that this salvation of God has been sent to the Gentiles; they will listen" (Acts 28:28). Thus the parting of the ways between Jews and Christians is complete, and Jews are made responsible for it.[25]

Seen against this anticlimactic scene in Acts, the fleeting glimpse of the inclusive, universalist vision that begins the ministry of the Lukan Jesus takes on new color. Luke's poison pen uses this vision to hold Jewish intransigence and ethnocentrism responsible for the separation between Jews and Christians, a separation that would lead in time to acrimony, bitterness, violence, and unspeakable atrocities in the history of the Christian West. In Luke, Jesus becomes a divisive figure who ends up legitimating Christian chauvinism.

DOES GOD REALLY LOVE DIVERSITY? CONCLUDING COMMENTS

To peoples excluded as strangers and to nations branded as enemies of "Christian nations" or "the chosen people," this question must be answered resoundingly in the negative. After all, as the Jewish and Christian scriptures have amply documented, writers of these sacred texts are not immune to ethnocentrism. Not only are they prone to triumphalism, occasionally even descending into tribalism, but they are especially adept at turning intimations of universalism and tolerance into self-serving encomia of patriotic fervor, narrow xenophobia, and outright chauvinism. One might claim, perhaps with some justification, that these texts were written at times of want and deprivation, when the threat of annihilation insinuated itself into a message of survival. But history is replete with examples of self-styled victims turning the table on erstwhile victimizers, the oppressed becoming the oppressor, the revolutionary becoming the tyrant. If postcolonial studies have taught us anything, it is that the relationship between the colonizer and the colonized, between the victimizer and the victimized, is not a simple matter of good *versus* evil. Colonization is a cauldron of conquest, violence, and rapacity that traps everyone caught up in it and creates victimizers out of victims.[26] That is the real tragedy of colonization, and the use of the biblical text in Western "Christian" conquests for the last three centuries should give anyone pause who wishes to plead victimhood as a defense for these texts.[27]

But perhaps a glimmer of hope can be found in the subtle, often buried intimations of acceptance and inclusion, intimations that emerge in spite of their ideological captivity. The Servant Songs speak of a universal

God who bestows blessings upon all peoples irrespective of ethnicity and borders, and the New Testament writers extol a self-giving God who would rather empty oneself than claim divine prerogatives. Even Luke's cynicism, which must be held responsible for centuries of separation and exclusion, could not hush up the murmuring hope of Jubilee without vengeance, egalitarianism without discrimination, justice without distinction. If a scripture is sacred not just by dint of a "communal authority" imputed to it, as Wilfred Cantwell Smith has rightly suggested,[28] but also because of its "surplus of meaning" that cannot be exhausted by a single generation of interpreters or, as a reading of these texts from below has shown, even by the scriptural writers themselves[29]—if all that is indeed the case, then it behooves a new generation of readers and interpreters, scholars and ministers and rabbis, theoreticians and practitioners alike to uncover what the biblical texts are all about. Does God really love diversity? It is up to all of us who take the biblical texts seriously to answer the question.

NOTES

1. http://www.youtube.com/watch?v=FNuyDZevKrU [accessed December 6, 2012].

2. Alternatively called Second Isaiah. I use the two interchangeably.

3. The metaphor is, of course, borrowed from music theory; see Said's use of counterpuntal reading in his *Orientalism* (New York: Vintage Books, 1978), and his *Culture and Imperialism* (New York: Vintage Books, 1993).

4. The creation theme is found throughout the Servant Songs: 40:12–31; 43:1–7, 14–15, 16–21; 44:1–5, 21–22; 45:18–19; 48:12–16; 54:4–6.

5. The Servant Songs are unique in this regard among prophetic writings. For creation terminology, see Richard J. Clifford, "Isaiah, Book of (Second Isaiah)," *Anchor Bible Dictionary*, vol. 3 (New York: Doubleday, 1992), 500–501.

6. To formulate creation in this manner—as subordinate to the restoration of Israel—is to follow Gerhard von Rad's assessment of the relationship between the two: Gerhard von Rad, "The Theological Problem of the Old Testament Doctrine of Creation," in *The Problem of the Hexateuch and Other Essays* (New York: McGraw-Hill, 1966), 131–43, and the translation of his 1936 German article "Das theologische Problem des alttestamentlichen Schöpfungsglaubens," collected in *Gesammelte Studien* I (Munich: Kaiser, 1965), 136–47. In response, Claus Wassermann suggests that the polarity between the two is used to show that God's saving of his people was "an island within the mighty universe of God's work as creator"; Claus Westermann, *Isaiah 40–66: A Commentary* (Old Testament Library; Philadelphia: Westminster, 1969), 25. For a summary of the debate between von Rad and Westermann, see Clifford, "Second Isaiah," 500. For a general theme of creation in Second Isaiah, see Klaus Baltzer, *Deutero-Isaiah: A Commentary on Isaiah 40–55* (Hermeneia; Minneapolis: Fortress, 2001), 38–42.

7. All translations are from the New Revised Standard Version (NRSV) unless otherwise noted. Where the NRSV has "The Lord" for the Hebrew Tetragrammaton I have emended it as YHWH, but I have kept "lord" for the Greek *kyrios*.

8. Similar language is used in Isa. 44:21 ("I formed you, you are my servant") and Isa. 44:28 ("Thus says YHWH, your redeemer, who formed you in the womb").

9. In theological terms, "the unity of the world in space and time is a recognition conferred by faith. Its foundation lies in the activity of the one God: 'I am Yahweh who

makes all things' (Isa. 44:24; cf. 45:8)"; see Baltzer, *Deutero-Isaiah*, 42. It should be noted that this statement is itself a universalization of a particular people's faith.

10. Baltzer, *Deutero-Isaiah*, 42.

11. Duane Christensen, "Nations," *Anchor Bible Dictionary*, vol. 4, ed., D. N. Freedman et al. (New York: Doubleday, 1992), 1037–49.

12. For dating, see Westermann, *Isaiah 40–66*, 295–96. It is widely accepted that Third Isaiah presupposes a return to Judah and Jerusalem, though not before the completion of the second temple; see Westermann, *Isaiah 40–66*, 297.

13. While the nations aid in the national salvation of Israel, they serve a more negative role in Third Isaiah; see Westermann, *Isaiah 40–66*, 297. Westermann acknowledges that Third Isaiah "does considerably damp down [Second Isaiah's] universalism."

14. For a view of the returning exiles, under the royal patronage of the Persians, from a postcolonial perspective, see Gale Yee, "Postcolonial Biblical Criticism," in *Methods for Exodus*, ed. Thomas B. Dozeman (Cambridge/New York: Cambridge University Press, 2010), 193–233.

15. This invective against foreigners takes an apocalyptic turn in 63:1–6, in which images of juices from trampled grapes in a wine press form a gruesome metaphor for vengeance against foreigners: "I trampled down peoples in my anger, I crushed them in my wrath, and I poured out their lifeblood on the earth" (63:6). See the discussion in Westermann, *Isaiah 40–66*, 304–5.

16. The citation follows the LXX almost verbatim, except it omits the line, "to heal those who are downcast in their heart," and adds "to let the oppressed go free" from 58:6.

17. My translation. These words could, of course, be read as hostile. For both possibilities, see C. F. Evans, *Saint Luke* (TPI New Testament Commentaries; London: SCM Press; Philadelphia: Trinity Press International, 1990), 273.

18. See, among others, I. Howard Marshall, *The Gospel of Luke: A Commentary on the Greek Text* (The New International Greek Testament Commentary; Grand Rapids: Eerdmans, 1978), 184; Evans, *Saint Luke*, 271; F. Bovon, *Luke 1: A Commentary on the Gospel of Luke 1:1–9:50* (Hermeneia; Minneapolis: Fortress, 2002), 154.

19. The word *dĕrôr* ("liberty") used in Isa. 61:1 is "the explicitly jubilary word for release"; see Christopher J. H. Wright, "Jubilee, Year of," *Anchor Bible Dictionary*, vol. 3, 1028.

20. *Emartyroun autō.*

21. François Bovon suggests that the "completeness of the composition" of this scene implies that Jesus is presented as selecting his own text; see Bovon, *Luke 1*, 153. Inexplicably, however, Bovon immediately hedges his own point without argument.

22. My translation of the original Greek.

23. Bovon thinks this antipathy toward Jesus points to "the fellowship between Jews and Gentiles"; see Bovon, *Luke 1*, 156. But surely the depiction of the lynch mob indicates antagonism, not fellowship. My reading of this episode is closer to that of Jack T. Sanders, "The Jewish People in Luke-Acts," in *Luke-Acts and the Jewish People: Eight Perspectives*, ed. Joseph B. Tyson (Minneapolis: Augsburg, 1988), 51–75, especially 62–63.

24. For Paul's own robust consciousness of his own Jewish identity, see the famous article by Krister Stendahl, "The Apostle Paul and the Introspective Conscience of the West," *Harvard Theological Review* 56 (1963): 199–215. See, more recently, Pamela Eisenbaum, *Paul Was Not a Christian: The Original Message of a Misunderstood Apostle* (New York: HarperCollins, 2009).

25. Whether this climactic scene merits the "anti-Jewish" label is the subject of great debate. For proponents of that label, see, among others, Jack T. Sanders, *The Jews in Luke-Acts* (Philadelphia: Fortress, 1987), 80–83; and Joseph B. Tyson, "The Problem of Jewish Rejection in Act," in *Luke-Acts and the Jewish People: Eight Perspectives*, ed. Joseph B. Tyson (Minneapolis: Augsburg, 1988), 124–37. Those who resist the label include James D. G. Dunn, *The Partings of the Ways between Christianity and Judaism and their*

Significance for the Character of Christianity (London: SCM Press; Philadelphia: Trinity Press International, 1991), 150–51; and Richard Pervo, *Acts: A Commentary* (Hermeneia; Minneapolis: Fortress, 2009), 685.

26. The relation between the colonizers and subjects is neither purely oppressive nor purely resistant but both. Inasmuch as the colonial subjects resist colonization, through which oppression and exploitation are exercised, they also find it nurturing, for it brings order and perhaps even a measure of civilization to precolonial chaos. But when the colonial subjects try to imitate their masters, the result is imperfect and their mimicry turns into mockery, because the clash and mutual interpenetration between the worlds of the subjects and of the colonizers is by nature adaptive, creative, and finally transgressive. The ambivalent colonial subjects are therefore colored by hybridity. See Homi Bhabha's two essays, "Of Mimicry and Man: The Ambivalence of Colonial Discourse" (originally published in 1984); and "Signs Taken for Wonders: Questions of Ambivalence and Authority Under a Tree Outside Delhi, May 1817" (originally published in 1985), collected in *The Location of Culture* (London: Routledge, 1994). Hybridity also characterizes the colonizers since they come into close contact with their subjects and are equally affected. See the discussion in Sze-kar Wan, "Does Diaspora Identity Imply Some Sort of Universality? An Asian-American Reading of Galatians," in *Interpreting Beyond the Border*, ed. F. Segovia (The Bible and Postcolonialism, 2; Sheffield: Sheffield Academic Press, 2000), 107–31; especially 108–11. Robert Young, interpreting Bhabha, suggests that this ambivalence represents a disturbance to the seemingly stable colonial discourse and sows the seed for its eventual demise; see his *Colonial Desire: Hybridity in Theory, Culture and Race* (London/New York: Routledge, 1995).

27. For a continuation of the colonial division between Christian and non-Christian "civilizations," one need look no further than Samuel Huntington, *Clash of Civilizations and the Remaking of World Order* (New York: Simon & Schuster, 1996), whose ideas became hugely influential after 9/11 in the West's attitude and policies towards Islam. It should not surprise us that Huntington's construction of "ideological blocs" has been compared to the Nazi sympathizer Carl Schmitt's *Großräume*; see Carl Schmitt, *Roman Catholicism and Political Form*, translated and introduced by G. Ulmen (Westport, CT/London: Greenwood, 1996; the German original was published in 1923); and Michael Kirwan, *Political Theology: An Introduction* (Minneapolis: Fortress, 2009), 202n12.

28. See Wilfred Cantwell Smith, *What Is Scripture? A Comparative Approach* (Minneapolis: Fortress, 1993).

29. See David Tracey, *The Analogical Imagination: Christian Theology and the Culture of Pluralism* (New York: Crossroad, 1981).

Part IV

About Justice

EIGHT

Diversity, Justice, and the Bible for Grown-Ups

A Jewish Russian-Israeli-American Hebrew Bible Scholar Speaks

Serge Frolov

"God loves diversity? And justice? Says who?"

That, in layperson's terms, would be a traditional Jewish reaction to the titular proposition of the present volume. The intellectual convention that lies at the core of Judaism since its biblical beginnings, and especially since the times of Mishnah and Talmud, is that no claim, even if at first blush it appears incongruous or outrageous, is to be rejected out of hand. At the same time, whoever makes a theological statement, especially one as sweeping and consequential as this one, should be prepared to substantiate it by citing appropriately interpreted prooftext(s), to grapple with alternative construals of the same texts, and to tackle, by exegetical means, any counter-citations an opponent might come up with. That is, if you believe you have something to say about God, you'd better know your way around your scriptures (as well as other authoritative writings of your tradition) and be handy with them.[1] Although I am not the only Jew among this volume's participants, as someone with two decades of intense experience in biblical exegesis I accept the task of discussing (and, if possible, defending) the volume's main thesis within this referential framework.[2]

JUSTICE FOR TREES BUT NOT FOR HUMANS?

In the foundational text of Judaism, known to Jews as the Tanak, to Christians as the Old Testament, and to all and sundry as the Hebrew Bible, the root *tsedeq*, conveying the notion of justice, is very common: it occurs more than six hundred times, mostly in the roughly synonymous nouns *tsedeq* and *tsedaqah*, "justice," and the adjective *tsaddiq*, "just, righteous." Although the root's distribution is somewhat uneven (apart from proper names, it seems to occur mainly in Deuteronomy, Isaiah, Jeremiah, Ezekiel, Psalms, Proverbs, and Job), this produces a strong impression that the Hebrew Bible is heavily preoccupied with justice, if not obsessed with it. It is ascribed to the deity, as seen especially in the theophoric name Zedekiah, "Yhwh's justice," and presented as something that the deity requires of worshippers, as suggested most forcefully by the terse prescription of Deut. 16:20: "Justice, justice should you pursue." Seemingly, the inevitable conclusion is that God does not simply love justice but is virtually mad about it. Yet, as usual, the devil is in the details, or rather in the total lack thereof. The biblical corpus never explicitly divulges what exactly qualifies as justice or provides appropriate examples, thereby implicitly inviting the audience to identify the norms that are promulgated by the deity (*mitzvot*—"commandments" in Judaism; *nomos*—"law" in Christianity) as such.

And that is precisely where the problems begin because not all of these norms would necessarily strike the listener or reader as just—unless, of course, they are assumed to be so simply by virtue of their (alleged) numinous origin. Many would probably qualify as "just" in most, if not all, ethical systems, sometimes even to the point of impracticality. The injunction against charging interest on loans (Exod. 22:24) and the requirement to remit all debts every seventh year (Deut. 15:1–11) are two examples that readily come to mind. Others, however, would not, at least not readily. A well-known and salient case in point is the following passage, found in Deuteronomy 20, just four short chapters away from the "Justice, justice should you pursue" maxim:

> 10 When you approach a city to make war against it, offer it peace. 11 If it responds peacefully and opens up to you, all the people present there will be yours for corvée[3] and to serve you. 12 If it does not make peace with you and makes war against you, besiege it, 13 and if Yhwh your God gives it into your hand, smite all its males with the edge of the sword. 14 Only women, and children, and domestic animals, and all that will be in the city, all its plunder take as spoils for yourself, and you will consume the plunder of your enemies that Yhwh your God gave you. 15 Thus you should act with regard to all the cities that are very far from you, those that are not among the cities of these peoples, the aborigines. 16 But from the cities of these peoples, which Yhwh your God gives you as a hereditary estate, do not let a single soul live.

17 It is, rather, your emphatic obligation to exterminate them—the Hittites and the Amorites, the Canaanites and the Perizzites, the Hivvites and the Jebusites, as Yhwh your God has commanded you, 18 lest they teach you to imitate all the abominable things they were doing for their gods and you transgress against Yhwh your God.[4]

This is hardly the kind of justice modern Westerners usually have in mind when they use the term. In the first part of the passage (vv. 10–15), the text's addressees are not only permitted, but actually required to kill all adult male inhabitants of a captured city, enslave the women and children, and steal everything of value. Even if the city chooses to surrender (an option that is described, in an almost Orwellian fashion, as *shalom*, or "peace"), the only major difference is that men are permitted to live; the residents are still essentially enslaved and robbed. In the second part (vv. 16–18), even this nightmarish scenario turns out to be too rosy when it comes to six indigenous populations of the land of Canaan, allegedly earmarked by the deity for the commandment's audience. These are to be exterminated, without exception, no matter what; for them, even unconditional capitulation presumably would not make a difference. And, in a touch of morbid irony (or, perhaps, absurdity?), the chilling instruction is followed by an ecologically commendable injunction against the destruction of fruit trees around the besieged city, quaintly justified by their inability to move (v. 19):

When you besiege a city for many days, fighting against it to seize it, do not slaughter its trees, wielding an ax against them; just eat from them, but do not cut them down, for is a tree of the field a person to come because of you inside the city walls?

There is justice (or at least compassion) for the trees, it seems, but not for the city's human inhabitants if they are Canaanites, Hivvites, or Jebusites.

Things are even worse when it comes to diversity. There is no biblical term for the concept (for the obvious reason of its relatively recent origin), and as a result we do not even have generalized statements about the deity's commitment to diversity to balance against the deity's actual directives, which indicate lack of such commitment. To be sure, the Hebrew Bible acknowledges the diversity not only of the natural world, which is outlined in considerable detail in Genesis 1, but also of humanity, which is described in the famous "table of nations" of Genesis 10 as split into numerous "countries, languages, families, and peoples" (v. 5). Yet this does not seem to be what the deity had in mind when creating the world. Apart from the sexual dimorphism, which is brought into the picture for the sake of procreation in Gen. 1:26–28 and for that of complementary companionship in Gen. 2:18–24, in the Hebrew Bible human diversity appears as an unfortunate result of human disobedience and hubris. The deity imposes it to prevent humanity from building "a tower with its top in heaven" (Gen. 11:1–9). More remotely, it is also a ramification of Adam and Eve's expulsion from the Garden of Eden (Genesis 3).[5] And, of course, the second part of the Deuteronomic passage quoted above (Deut. 20:16–18) would appear to militate strongly against the idea that God loves diversity: the indigenous populations are targeted for extermination precisely because they are different, because their beliefs and practices—the latter indiscriminately labeled "abominations" (v. 18)—differ from those promoted by the Hebrew Bible. At least as far as the "promised land" is concerned, there does not seem to be any space allowed for religious diversity. Indeed, given that the populations in question are not afforded so much as an option of renouncing their gods and their manner of worship, it is possible to argue that in this land even an unwitting deviation from the biblical norms is punishable by death.

So does God in fact *hate* diversity and justice, at least as they are tacitly defined for the purposes of the present volume? Yes and no. Yes, because the preceding discussion demonstrates that Deut. 20:10–18 can be construed in such a way. No, because this construal hinges upon the unspoken assumption that the purpose of the fragment in question is strictly utilitarian: to instruct the audience concerning the treatment of the conquered population with a special attention to six aboriginal groups residing in the Promised Land. There is, however, at least one indication that the text's rhetorical objective—and, accordingly, its meaning—may be different.

THE CANAANITES THAT NEVER WERE

One big difference between the two main parts of Deut. 20:10–18 is that while the first sets a general rule, referencing any "city" that happens to be at war with the fragment's addressees, the second registers an exception to this rule, applying to specific groups of people. What these groups have in common in the Hebrew Bible is their status as indigenous inhabitants of the land of Canaan. They also have in common the fact that, outside of the biblical corpus, they are not connected to this land. In fact, no extra-biblical sources ever mention the Perizzites, the Hivvites, the Jebusites, and even the Canaanites. The term "Canaan" does occur in Egyptian documents, vaguely and probably inconsistently applied to parts of the Levant, but the inhabitants of these areas are never named after the toponym.[6] The case is different with the Hittites and the Amorites, two well-known populations of the ancient Near East; yet even so, there is no archeological or epigraphic evidence of them in Canaan. The Hittite homeland was in Asia Minor, and their direct control did not extend beyond northern parts of today's Syria,[7] while the Amorites lived in and around Mesopotamia.[8] Chances are, therefore, that the Israelite listeners or readers of Deuteronomy 20 never encountered not only Perizzites or Hivvites but also Hittites and Amorites (except perhaps a few individuals) and therefore never had an opportunity to carry out the commandment to exterminate them.

Two trends traceable in the Hebrew Bible confirm as much. Except for the Jebusites in 2 Samuel 5 (1 Chronicles 11) and 2 Samuel 24 (1 Chronicles 21), there are scant references to the populations listed in Deut. 20:17 in the biblical accounts of the monarchic or post-exilic period—that is, of the times when the latter text was possibly written.[9] The non-Israelite and non-Yhwhistic groups that according to the Hebrew Bible remained in Canaan were different, the Philistines being most prominent among them, and they are not even referred to collectively as Canaanites. Further, the biblical taxonomy of the "nations of Canaan" is not only inconsistent[10] but also self-contradictory, with the Canaanites appearing not as an overarching designation, but rather as one group out of many. In both cases, the implication is that the Hittites (and others) were not part of the world as the author of Deut. 20:10–18 knew it. Accordingly, he or she must have been aware that the fragment's instructions could not be put into practice. The purpose of this author was not to incite genocide of actually existing populations. His or her goal lay elsewhere—but where exactly?

One plausible, and meaningful, answer to this question is offered by Judg. 3:5, which is the only list of the "nations of Canaan" in the entire Hebrew Bible to include exactly the same populations as Deut. 20:17, albeit in a somewhat different order.[11] The former piece summarizes the revelation of Judges 1 that despite the best efforts of Joshua and the tribe of Judah, which the deity chooses to assume leadership after Joshua's death (Judg. 1:2), the Israelites failed to fully exterminate the "nations" in question and settled for coexistence with them. As a result, Judg. 3:6 reports that "[the sons of Israel] took their daughters as wives for themselves and gave their daughters to their sons, and served their gods." The statement forges yet another conceptual link to Deut. 20:10–18, according to which the listed populations should be exterminated lest "they teach [the Israelites] to imitate all the abominable things they were doing for their gods and [the Israelites] transgress against Yhwh." Put differently, Judg. 3:5–6 claims, in agreement with the balance of Judges and in fulfillment of the Deuteronomic warning, that as a result of living among the native inhabitants of Canaan, the Israelites became one with them, one extended family and one extended religious community. And since it was the latter that adopted the religion of the former, not the other way around, in effect the Israelites morphed into Canaanites.[12]

This, in turn, causes a sharply adverse reaction on Yhwh's part: the deity withdraws its support from the newly Canaanized Israelites and throws them behind their enemies seeking plunder or political domination, so that the people find themselves "in exceedingly dire straits" (Judg. 2:15). Justified as it is, this punishment might appear excessively harsh, were it not for Deut. 20:10–18. According to the latter, "the Hittites and the Amorites, the Canaanites and the Perizzites, the Hivvites and the Jebusites" (v. 17) are liable to be exterminated without even being granted a chance to repent, and the book of Joshua demonstrates in horrifyingly convincing detail that this is not an empty threat. Yet, when the people of Israel, for all intents and purposes, become Canaanites (as it follows from Judg. 2:5), their penalty is limited to foreign domination and oppression—a tough plight, to be sure, but also a far cry from the wholesale massacres of Joshua. Moreover, as soon as the people repent and "cry to Yhwh"—that is, cease being Canaanites—the deity appoints a deliverer and helps him or her overthrow the oppressor. Even repeated relapses of Canaanization after the deliverers' deaths and later in their lifetimes do not prevent Yhwh from coming to Israel's help the next time around.[13] This pattern, recurring as many as six times in Judges and beyond, speaks volumes about the deity's special relationship with Israel and commitment to it.[14] Moreover, even with foreign worship showing no sign of abating under most Israelite kings, from Solomon (1 Kgs. 11:1–8) to Manasseh (2 Kgs. 21:1–9), the people's ultimate punishment is exile rather than extermination. Severe as this punishment might be, especially within the framework of the Enneateuch that consistently presents the Promised Land as the nodal point of Israel's relationship with its deity, it still leaves ample space for hope.

In essence, Deut. 20:10–18 plays a pivotal role in revealing a substantial measure of divine grace even in divine judgment—something that must have been of special importance for the people of Israel in exile and after it, desperately trying to come to grips with the loss of their homes, their statehood, and their main, if not only, temple. Seen from this perspective, Deut. 20:10–18 is not about Yhwh's willingness to eradicate religious diversity in Canaan by exterminating non-Israelite populations and thus committing a grave injustice,[15] but rather about theodicy—one of the most fundamental and intractable problems inherent in any monotheistic theology. If the Hebrew Bible is concerned about anybody's faith, it is that of the Israelites, not Canaanite natives.[16] Deut. 20:10–18 is designed to safeguard this faith by helping the Enneateuch highlight the dire consequences of abandoning it while emphatically denying that these consequences expose the biblical deity as harsh, fickle, or impotent.

Of course, even when viewed in the above perspective, the Hebrew Bible still considers death a commensurate punishment for religious apostasy—as confirmed by its explicit instructions to put individuals engaging in foreign worship to death by stoning (Deut. 13:7–12; 17:2–7) and to exterminate the inhabitants of the city doing the same *en masse* (Deut. 13:13–19).[17] What makes a world of difference, however, is the fact that in this case intolerance is directed inward rather than outward—at fellow Israelites rather than at the Canaanites. Its purpose is to preserve a community rather than to eliminate one, and as a result, it contributes to religious diversity rather than detracts from it. Admittedly, capital punishment for renunciation of faith might appear anything but just. Yet even today many would argue that for the sake of diversity it is acceptable to commit injustice, for example, to pass over an otherwise worthy candidate for college admission, hiring, or promotion, which for the person affected may be almost as painful as stoning. In fact, it may be an objective—if not *the* objective—of Deuteronomy, including 20:10–18, to put a spotlight on the inherent tension between diversity and justice.[18] Further, in the Hebrew Bible the Israelites voluntarily take upon themselves the covenantal conditions laid out by the deity, including the obligation to worship Yhwh alone and the penalties for violating that obligation.[19] It would be grossly unjust to punish the Canaanites for not worshipping Yhwh because they never agreed to do so, much less to suffer the consequences of acting otherwise, but it is an entirely different matter with the Israelites.

Finally, what about "the cities that are very far" (Deut. 20:15)? How can the deity be said to love justice if it seems to command its followers to plunder cities and to enslave or kill their inhabitants? In answering these questions, it is important to keep in mind that the Hebrew Bible never mandates Israel's expansion beyond the boundaries of Canaan. That, in essence, leaves it up to Yhwh to decide, on a case-by-case basis, whether a given war is sufficiently justified to grant Israel a victory in it. Significantly, the reference to the deity doing that in Deut. 20:13a is translatable as a conditional clause ("and *if* Yhwh your God gives it [sc. the besieged city] into your hand"; contrast the absolute "which Yhwh your God *gives* you as a hereditary estate" regarding the cities of Canaan in Deut. 20:16).[20] And the phrase "your enemies" in Deut. 20:14 leaves little doubt as to which war outside Canaan would qualify as justified: the one where the opponent is an aggressor trying to do all that, if not more, to the Israelites. Indeed, it is possible that the primary rhetorical purpose of the fragment under discussion is to give Israel's defenders a graphic idea of what will happen to them and their families (as it actually did on multiple occasions) if they surrender to the invaders or fail to repel them. At an even deeper level, the piece may be designed to cause the audience to ponder the possible consequences of Yhwh giving Israel's enemies a free hand against it in response to violations of the covenant, as it happens time and again in Judges and Kings.

Thus, no part of Deut. 20:10–18 has to be read as urging or endorsing unprovoked wars, religious intolerance, and genocide, and as a proof that the monotheistic deity hates diversity and encourages injustice. That, however, does not change the simple fact that this fragment *can* be construed in precisely that way; moreover, that such a construal requires much less effort, background knowledge, and exegetical sophistication than the one offered here. Does its complexity render the latter interpretational avenue deficient by default and therefore largely futile? In the third, concluding part of this chapter I will argue that in fact, the opposite may be the case.

READING LIKE A GROWN-UP

In an article published more than twenty-five years ago, Marianne Saw-icki identified what she called four kinds of religious understanding:

> LITERAL UNDERSTANDING is that which is available to one whose thought is concrete-operational, whose theological outlook is naïve realism, and whose relation to his or her own religious tradition and its symbols is primitively naïve;
> CONVENTIONAL UNDERSTANDING is that which is available to one whose thought is formal-operational and whose theological outlook is dogmatic realism;
> CRITICAL UNDERSTANDING is that which is available to one whose thought is trans-operational, critical, and transcendental, and whose theological outlook is critical realism;
> CONJUNCTIVE UNDERSTANDING is that which is available to one whose thought is post-operational and receptive to symbol, and whose relation to his or her religious tradition is in a state of second naïveté.[21]

Since the interpretation of religious texts is a type of religious understanding, there is no reason why these categories could not be applied to different construals of Deut. 20:10–18. Such application can be instrumental not only in bringing some order to what may sound like a cacophony of competing, often mutually incompatible readings, but also in evaluating them.

The designation of Sawicki's first category leaves little doubt that it would include interpretations that view Deut. 20:10–18 as a faithful transcription of what the people of Israel heard from Moses on the left bank of the Jordan—and what they more or less successfully tried to accomplish under Joshua's leadership.[22] In a naïvely realistic manner, such interpretations seek to understand "what actually happened" without trying to make sense of the reported events or derive lessons from them. The readings that treat the fragment in question as an indication that the deity wants its worshippers to wipe out those whose beliefs and practices differ from those prescribed by the Bible would belong to the "conventional" class.[23] Unlike the literal understanding, this construal is built upon a syllogism—the Canaanites did not worship Yhwh but the Israelites did: Yhwh, through Moses, commanded the Israelites to exterminate the Canaanites. Consequently, those who believe in Yhwh are supposed to exterminate those who do not. This argument involves what Piaget termed formal-operational cognition. At the same time, it not only affirms the formative dogma of monotheism—namely, the postulate that there is only one true deity and that those who worship other gods behave in a manner offensive to this deity—but also seeks to put it into practice.

The "critical" set includes a wide range of interpretations that view Deut. 20:10–18 as inconsequential to modern audiences because it is out of date. Some of these interpretations claim that the fragment merely reflects and improves upon the intolerant and violent *Zeitgeist* prevalent when it was written.[24] Others, aimed at practicing Christians, stress that the advent of Jesus nullified the normative parts of the Old Testament or at least changed their meaning.[25] Likewise falling within the "critical" category, although at its diametrically opposite end, are the writings of militant atheists, which cite Deut. 20:10–18 and similar texts as the ultimate proof that the Bible and religion in general cannot serve as a source of morality.[26]

Finally, the reading outlined above can be classified, in Sawicki's terms, as conjunctive. It uses critical means, both historical (by citing biblical and extra-biblical data about the six groups listed in Deut. 20:17) and literary (by reading the fragment under discussion contextually, against the background of the Enneateuch as a whole), to make it possible for my contemporaries and me to reconnect to a seemingly problematic biblical passage. In so doing, it would appear to attain Ricoeur's plane of "second naïveté" by building upon critical cognition in order to leave it behind. To use Ricoeur's own words, it "seek[s] to go beyond criticism by means of criticism, by a criticism that is no longer reductive but restorative."[27]

The importance of this classification of interpretations lies in its close association with the stages of human cognitive development. Sawicki's literal understanding corresponds to Piaget's concrete-operational stage, reached by children at the age of six or seven; Piaget's counterpart of Sawicki's conventional understanding is the formal-operational stage attained between the ages of twelve and fourteen.[28] Piaget did not discuss the possibility of further changes, but Sawicki, building mainly upon Fowler, tentatively places the beginning of the critical stage at the end of adolescence, and that of the conjunctive stage around the age of thirty.[29] This correlation has major pedagogical corollaries, wherein Sawicki's main interest lies.[30] But it also has consequences for the understanding of religious texts, and specifically of Deut. 20:10–18. The readings that paint Yhwh as inimical to religious diversity and as trying to eradicate it by means that are hardly just are associated with early adolescence, or with the adults who never moved beyond it. Conversely, a substantial measure of cognitive maturity is required to understand that the piece in question aims to uphold that diversity by making it easier for a small and embattled community to maintain its distinctive beliefs and practices.[31]

Put differently, it takes an adult to realize that Deut. 20:10–18 may be a rare, if not unique, indication that the deity of the Hebrew Bible is, in fact, so committed to diversity that it is prepared to commit a measure of injustice for that sake (and only for it). In my view, it is a sign of the interpretation's superiority. Of course, this may just be my (euphemistically termed) middle age speaking. It may also have to do with my Jewish heritage and identity: my community's dogged survival, in many periods and places as the only tiny speck of religious and cultural diversity, is for me an inexhaustible source of wonderment and pride. But even if one or both of these factors are at play, the fact remains that I do not feel intellectually dishonest when I maintain that God loves diversity and justice, even if they stand in some tension with each other, and that the common scriptures of Jews and Christians do say so. Ultimately, this is all that matters.

NOTES

1. This is a great way of preventing "*God* loves diversity and justice" from becoming "*I* love diversity and justice." In order for a theological point to be accepted by the community, the former needs to be grounded in something that the latter considers authoritative, and, of course, in the scripture-based Judeo-Christian tradition biblical interpretation is one of the primary loci of authority.
2. A full disclosure is probably in order here. I cannot be rightfully called a "progressive" because I do not share some major aspects of the agenda associated with this political designation. Among other things, as someone who was born in the Soviet Union and lived there until the age of thirty, I am likely forever destined to take a dim view of any expansion of government's powers, be that in the field of national security or health care. On the latter note, the visual and especially olfactory impressions of the state hospital where my grandmother died more than a quarter century ago haunt me to this day. I do, however, believe that justice is imperative—provided, of course, that pursuit thereof does not devolve into a zero-sum game—and that diversity is beneficial for society, even though it may be difficult to reconcile it with justice. Above all, despite not being a part of political progressivism, I am progressive by the nature of my interests and my occupation (which, fortunately, largely overlap). How can it be anything but, given that scholarship is by definition a quest for the new?
3. *Corvée* is state-imposed forced labor, "payment" from peasants too poor to pay other forms of taxes.
4. All biblical translations are the author's.
5. Significantly, in Gen. 11:6 the deity is quoted as saying that with humans "all being one people and having one language"—in other words, with no diversity among them—"nothing that they propose to do will be thwarted."
6. The "Amarna letters," a collection of texts covering several decades in the mid-fourteenth century BCE, know only political divisions in Canaan. The sole groups mentioned outside the framework of local city-states are 'Apiru/Hapiru and Sutû; see *The Amarna Letters*, edited and translated by William L. Moran (Baltimore: Johns Hopkins University Press, 1992), 392–93 and references there. Of course, this may be because the letters pertaining to Canaan are exchanges between local petty potentates and the Pharaoh as represented by court officials, but it is at least equally possible that neither side ever heard of the Perizzites, and so forth. The case of the Jebusites is especially significant because the Hebrew Bible consistently links them to Jerusalem (e.g., Josh. 15:63, Judg. 1:21; 19:10–12; 2 Sam. 5:6–8; 24:18–24), but there are no traces of them in the missives of 'Abdi-Heba, the fourteenth-century ruler of the city.
7. Amélie Kuhrt, *The Ancient Near East, c. 3000–330 BC*, Routledge History of the Ancient World (London: Routledge, 1997), 1.253. The Neo-Hittite, Late Hittite, or Syro-Hittite states that emerged after the collapse of the Hittite empire proper around

1200 BCE were likewise situated in "north Syria, Cilicia and south-central Anatolia"; see Kuhrt, *The Ancient Near East*, 2.410.

8. For instance, the famous King Hammurabi of Babylon was from an Amorite dynasty; see Kuhrt, *The Ancient Near East*, 1.108. It is also possible that the biblical term *'emori*, usually translated as "Amorites," refers instead to the inhabitants of Amurru, a region in what today is northwest Syria.

9. There is, of course, Uriah the Hittite in 2 Samuel 11, but this appellation is likely a sobriquet rather than a genuine ethnic designation (until recently, a black-haired, darker-skinned European could be nicknamed "Gypsy," "Jew," or "Moor" without actually being one; Karl Marx is one example). With a Yhwhistic theophoric name ("Yhwh is my light"), a reverent attitude towards the Ark of the Covenant (2 Sam. 11:11), and a high rank in the Israelite military (2 Sam. 23:39), Uriah could be referred to as Hittite only in jest.

10. One idiosyncratic feature of Deut. 20:17 is the absence of the Girgashites, listed in Gen. 15:21; Deut. 7:1; Josh. 3:10 and elsewhere.

11. The fact that both lists deviate from the traditional count of "seven nations" by excluding the Girgashites (see above) further strengthens the intertextual connection between them.

12. Marvin A. Sweeney insightfully speaks about Israel's increasing "Canaanization" in Judges; see his "Davidic Polemics in the Book of Judges," *VT* 47 (2004): 527; *King Josiah of Judah: The Lost Messiah of Israel* (Oxford: Oxford University Press, 2001), 116.

13. As the narrative of Judges progresses, Canaanization seems to affect even the divinely appointed deliverers. Gideon manufactures a cultic object that the narrator describes as sending Israel "a-whoring" and becoming a "snare" for Gideon and his family (Judg. 8:27)—the language closely associated elsewhere with foreign worship (e.g., Deut. 7:16; Judg. 2:3, 17; 8:33). Jephtah, by sacrificing his daughter (Judg. 11:30–40), commits an act that the Hebrew Bible identifies as a Canaanite practice (e.g., Deut. 12:31), and Samson (Judg. 13–16) becomes the only living example of intermarriage in the entire book. For a more detailed discussion, see Serge Frolov, *Judges* (FOTL 6b; Grand Rapids: Eerdmans, 2013).

14. Granted, toward the conclusion of Judges the deity's patience begins to wear thin, especially when the Israelites apparently beg Yhwh for help while still worshiping other gods. In chapter 6, Yhwh does not begin to deliver Israel until Gideon destroys the altar of Ba'al, and in 10:14, the deity meets the people's plea with a sarcastic suggestion "to go and cry to the gods that [they] have chosen." Yet, at the end of the day, deliverance is forthcoming even in these cases. Moreover, in 13:2–7 the deity appoints Samson as the deliverer—or, rather, creates him as such—without even waiting for the people's repentance. The shortcut does not work, however, and eventually it falls to Samuel in 1 Samuel 7 to convince Israel to renounce foreign worship, whereupon Yhwh defeats the Philistine oppressors.

15. Tellingly, when the Israelites prove willing to coexist with the indigenous population of Canaan (Judges 1, especially vv. 27–36), Yhwh plays along (Judg. 2:3).

16. Richard D. Nelson astutely notes that "[the] alien 'nations' of the past stand [in Deut. 20:10–18] for contemporary Israelite apostasy and for those whose present disloyal behavior must be eliminated"; see his *Deuteronomy: A Commentary* (OTL; Louisville: Westminster John Knox, 2002), 251–52.

17. It is worth noting that the treatment prescribed for the apostate city in Deut. 13:16–18 strongly resembles, with regard to both content and diction, that mandated by Deut. 20:17–18 for the cities of the Hittites et al. In both cases, the inhabitants of the place are liable to be completely exterminated, and both pieces use the lexemes *to'evah* ("abomination") and *kharam* ("to consecrate," in the sense of "to annihilate"). In Deut. 20:17–18, there is no stipulation that the city's goods should be destroyed rather than plundered (contrast Deut. 13:17–18), but such texts as Josh. 6:18–21 presuppose it. The upshot of these parallels is that the real concern of the Hebrew Bible is about the religious practices of the Israelites rather than those of Canaan's aborigines. Confirm-

ing as much is the failure of Deuteronomy 20—or, for that matter, of any other biblical text—to mention conversion as an option.

18. The text can also be understood as exploring the disturbingly positive correlation between diversity and violence, empirically observed throughout human history. The peace, and concomitant prosperity, that has prevailed in most parts of Europe since World War II seems to be a direct consequence of several rounds of genocide and/or ethnic cleansing, especially between 1914 and 1945, which resulted in the formation of largely monocultural nation-states. Notably, Yugoslavia, where this process had not been completed, saw another series of deadly conflicts in the 1990s. In contrast, although Israel is sometimes accused of genocide or ethnic cleansing of the Palestinians, it would hardly have found itself in its current precarious situation if this were actually the case.

19. Note especially their unanimous "everything that Yhwh has said we shall do" in Exod. 19:8; 24:7—both before and after hearing the commandments.

20. The construction in Deut. 20:13a can also be understood as temporal, which is why most English translations have "when" rather than "if" here (thus, for example, KJV, RSV, NRSV, JPS, NAB, and CEV). Yet there is nothing to prevent the phrase from being interpreted in a conditional sense.

21. Marianne Sawicki, "Religion, Symbol, and the Twenty-Year-Old Demythologizer," *Horizons* 11 (1984): 330–31. As clearly seen in her terminology, Sawicki's classification heavily draws on James W. Fowler's typology of belief patterns (*Stages of Faith: The Psychology of Human Development and the Quest for Meaning* [San Francisco: Harper & Row, 1981]) and, together with him, upon Jean Piaget's genetic epistemology as expanded by Bernard Lonergan (Sawicki primarily cites Lonergan's *The Way to Nicea: The Dialectical Development of Trinitarian Theology* [Philadelphia: Westminster, 1976]). The notion of "second naïveté" comes from Paul Ricoeur (*The Symbolism of Evil* [Boston: Beacon, 1967], especially 349–51; *Interpretation Theory: Discourse and the Surplus of Meaning* [Fort Worth: Texas Christian University Press, 1976]).

22. Despite the wholesale slaughter of the Canaanite natives reported in Joshua 6–11, other parts of the book (15:63; 16:10; 17:12–18) and especially Judges (1:19, 21, 27–35) leave little doubt that many Canaanites not only survived but also remained in control of substantial portions of the land.

23. Studies and commentaries published in the last hundred years or so, especially after the Holocaust, understandably avoid saying so loud and clear. Yet several of them come very close when they postulate that the Canaanite natives deserved extermination for their "wickedness" or "sinfulness": thus, for example, Roger H. Munchenberg, *Deuteronomy* (Chi Ro Commentary Series; Adelaide, Australia: Lutheran Publishing House, 1986), 147; and Eugene H. Merrill, *Deuteronomy* (The New American Commentary 4; Nashville, TN: Broadman & Holman, 1994), 282–83, 286–87.

24. Jeffrey H. Tigay, *Deuteronomy* (JPS Torah Commentary; Philadelphia: Jewish Publication Society, 1996), 189, 471; Christopher J. H. Wright, *Deuteronomy* (New International Biblical Commentary; Peabody, MA: Hendrickson, 1996), 227–30; and Gary H. Hall, *Deuteronomy* (The College Press NIV Commentary; Joplin, MO: College Press, 2000), 310–11.

25. J. G. McConville, *Deuteronomy* (Apollos Old Testament Commentary 5; Leicester, England: Apollos; Downers Grove, IL: InterVarsity Press, 2002). This line of reasoning was, obviously, closed to traditional Jewish commentators, who in consequence limited themselves mainly to arguing that the instruction to offer peace applies not only outside Canaan but also in it; for a concise summary, see Tigay, *Deuteronomy*, 472.

26. Richard Dawkins, *The God Delusion* (Boston: Houghton Mifflin, 2006), 237–50, especially 245–48; Christopher Hitchens, *God Is Not Great: How Religion Poisons Everything* (New York: Twelve, 2007), 97–107. Sawicki notes that critical understanding of religion commonly results in its abandonment; see her "Religion, Symbol, and the Demythologizer," 335–38, 340.

27. Ricoeur, *Symbolism of Evil*, 350.

28. Sawicki, "Religion, Symbol, and the Demythologizer," 322. This is the reason why a literal reading is not represented among the commentaries and studies on Deuteronomy 20. Their prospective readers are supposed to have long outgrown the corresponding cognitive phase. For an overview of Piaget's concrete-operational and formal-operational stages, see Laura E. Berk, *Development through the Lifespan*, 5th ed. (Boston: Allyn & Bacon, 2010), 299–302, 383–85.

29. Sawicki, "Religion, Symbol, and the Demythologizer," 326, 328–29.

30. Among other things, it suggests that many undergrads should be able to digest the study of religion from historical, anthropological, socioeconomic, and other critical standpoints, but a theologically minded instructor will have a hard time advancing beyond dogmatics even with the bright but young graduate students. For further discussion, see Philip L. Tite, "On the Necessity of Crisis: A Reflection on Pedagogical Conflict and the Academic Study of Religion," *Teaching Theology and Religion* 6 (2003): 76–84.

31. Before Antiochus IV Epiphanes in the 160s BCE, the Israelites/Jews were never coerced by the dominant powers to abandon their religion. On Assyrian policies in this respect, see J. W. McKay, *Religion in Judah under the Assyrians, 732–609 BC* (Studies in Biblical Theology, Second Series 26; London: SCM Press, 1973); Morton Cogan, *Imperialism and Religion: Assyria, Judah and Israel in the Eighth and Seventh Centuries B.C.E.* (SBLMS 19; Missoula, MT: Society of Biblical Literature; Scholars Press, 1974). At the same time, through most, if not all, of their history, they were undoubtedly under enormous social and cultural pressure to assimilate.

NINE

The Exiled Native

The Paradox of the Black Scholar

Maria Dixon

Since 2008, I have had a wonderful relationship with a group of women outside of Jinja, Uganda. Brought together through a nonprofit organization established by one of my former students, these women (who range in age from eighteen to seventy-nine) supplied arts and crafts for the nonprofit organization to sell back in the United States. As typical in most service tourism to rural African villages, all of the visitors these women had encountered were white evangelicals who "wanted to make a difference." So when I stepped off the bus for the first time in the summer of 2009, neither the women nor I knew how to process the overwhelming emotions that flooded our souls. As Mama Alice, the project leader, would explain later, they had never seen a black woman who could command respect and honor from the *mazungus* (Lugandan for whites). In me, she said with pride, "We found one who looked like us that they had to listen to—for you are their teacher."

When I returned to the village in the spring of 2010, our always raucous reunions took an even more joyful tone. Although I had recently been elected as the chair of the board for the nonprofit, which gave "the one who looked like them" considerably more organizational power, the women were more celebratory of my change in marital status. For the first time, I was invited to sit under the tree with Mama Alice and other leaders as we listened to reports, grievances, and news from the village. Interspersed in these organizational reports were humorous bits of advice on marriage and baby making and their overwhelming pride at my

161

marriage. It was one thing to be a professor and teach the *mazungus* but to marry one—I had hit the social trifecta. As evening gave way, they each came, as was traditional, and, depending on their station, greeted me by kneeling for blessing. I reflected on this ritual, recognizing how much it meant to be to be a part of the circle of life—the great grandchild of slaves returning home to be blessed and to be a blessing.

Yet little did I realize that watching me this whole time had been one of the older men of the village. He stopped me and asked me a question in Lugandan. With only rudimentary skills, I asked Mama Alice to serve as translator. Repeating the question, he held my hand and looked at me directly and asked, "Why do you need someone to help you talk to one of your own? My daughter, have you forgotten your language? Have you forgotten your *home*?"

That evening, my joy had turned into self-doubt and pity. My feelings of a bond with Mother Africa were in tatters. Was I indeed a sellout? Had I been robbed of all that was essential to my identity? Unable to sleep, I opened my Bible to Psalm 137:

> If I forget you, Jerusalem, may my right hand forget its skill. May my tongue cling to the roof of my mouth if I do not remember you, if I do not consider Jerusalem my highest joy. (NRSV)

This psalm, I realized, was both my salve and the bane of my existence, for it served to remind me of the conflicted nature of both my ontology and axiology as an African American who is also a critical scholar. Committed to speaking for those who have no voice, bringing light to situations others would prefer remain in the dark, and privileging of the prophetic over the priestly, my life as a communication scholar who is also a theologian was dedicated to the concepts of social justice and diversity at all times. Yet, despite the confidence that propels me into the halls of the academy and onto the stages of intellectual debate, I am often plagued by self-doubt that is rooted not in intellect but in identity. It is this self-doubt that washes over me when I pass the many service workers leaving Southern Methodist University by the bus route designed for them[1] as I pull out of the faculty parking lot. It is the same self-doubt that seems to cross the faces of the other African American professors as we sit at our reserved table in the faculty dining room being served by "Ms. Francine" with white-linen table service. Maybe it is not as much self-doubt as it is a nagging feeling that despite all our laudable proclamations of being scholars for our people, the distance between us and "our people" is significant. These scenarios (Ms. Francine; passing the countless African American workers on my way to campus) serve to remind me that while we share a great deal in common, we actually share very little. Yes, we are each black in America, but our experience of that "blackness" is framed by our different class locations.

Haunting the work of many African American scholars is a dance of authenticity and responsibility that is constructed, complicated, and compromised by competing ontologies and axiologies of race. At stake for most African American scholars is a racially ingrained belief that our scholarship must serve as a voice for their people while wrestling with the very reality that the vast majority of the race is ambivalent and/or hostile to our very existence. I believe that this dance between the poles of responsibility and authenticity serves both to create and to constrain the African American scholar's ability and willingness to address issues of social justice and diversity in ways that are reflective, meaningful, and authentic for the larger African American socio-political constituency.

The aim of my endeavor is not to create a critical manifesto in the tradition of Cornel West, Henry Louis Gates, bell hooks, or Victor Anderson. Instead, I am more intrigued by the delicate interpretive dance between meaning and behavior. How have the *intra-racially* constructed meanings of what it means to be an African American scholar and what it means to be an African American served to discipline, provoke, and silence African American scholars? To address this question, I want to explore how the dialectic tension of being an exiled native, which is best illustrated in Du Bois's concept of the "Talented Tenth," creates distinct ontological commitments for the contemporary African American scholar to serve as racial savior. Then placing the Du Boisian frame in conversation with the intra-racial construction of the African American scholar as racial-other, I want to explore how questions of racial authenticity and class ultimately influence the efficacy and authority of African American scholars to address issues of social justice and diversity.

THE EXILED NATIVE: BEYOND BABYLON

In retrospect, it was not surprising that I would turn to Psalm 137. For African Americans there is a powerful kinship between our own story and that of the "Hebrew Children" of the Old Testament. Grounded largely in the stories of their bondage and oppression, the fact that African Americans see ourselves as a people forever scarred by slavery, yet determined not to be limited by those scars in our search for dignity, humanity, and promise, cannot be all that remarkable.

While a majority of the theological and cultural-critical literature on the African American experience often points to the Egyptian Exodus as a dominant frame for understanding the African experience in America, I remain unconvinced of its relevance. Perhaps part of my problem is the origin of the conditions for the Hebrew exodus out of Egypt. For as significant as the narrative of "let my people go" is to the African American theological quilt, it is somewhat ill fitting when one considers the political circumstances leading to Egyptian slavery. The slaves of the

Egyptian exodus were not stolen from their homes but entered Egypt as welcomed immigrants only to be made into slaves by a new political regime several generations later.

Instead, like scholars such as William McClain, I believe that the Babylonian exile is a better discursive fit for beginning to frame the African experience in America. Forced from their homes, language and culture, the Africans of the Middle Passage did not enter America as welcomed immigrants but as oil for the economic machinery of chattel slavery. Like the Babylonians before them, the slave masters of the United States engaged in a systematic campaign to destabilize and erase any ability of the Africans to re-create systems of resistance and self-governance. Furthermore, the questions and emotions that emerge from being in exile are remarkably different from finding ourselves on the wrong end of a political regime change. The ever present question of "Why are we here?" becomes the ongoing cognitive mantra that shapes not only the conversations of those in exile but also their prayers. Thomas Ogletree surmises that what makes this question of locality so damning is the required dance between theodicy and promise and particularity (Why are *we* here?) and socio-locality (Why are we *here*?).[2]

Yet as rich as the Babylonian exile is for our initial musings on the fate of Africans in America, I believe it, too, is limiting when one seeks to frame the African American experience particularly in the twenty-first century. Questions of location and explanation are questions for those who experienced the *process of exile*, not those who are born *after the exile*. Questions of "why are we here" are offered by those who know that there is a possibility other than *here*. For the children born in exile, another phenomenon emerges. They are *exiled natives*. They are uniquely aware that they are different from the others yet strangely the same, which is the political goal for exile—to disrupt the continuity of political and social sovereignty of a given people. The Babylonians did not view every demographic in Jerusalem as equally desirous for exile. Those who were viewed as too illiterate or socially inept to wage resistance against the dominant power were left behind, whereas the ruling class—the educated, the civil leadership, and anyone who could muster the political and social capital necessary for rebellion—were exiled. While it was necessary to disrupt the current Hebrew leadership, it was even more important to disrupt the future of their second and third generations for the full effects of socio-political destabilization to be complete. Consequently, the goal was to ensure that if any of the exiled children emerged as leaders, they would do so as trained in the image of the dominant culture.

Thus, those children reared in Babylonian courts—reading Babylonian literature and studying Babylonian political science, administration, and philosophy—eventually came to know Babylon as normative, thereby forcing Jerusalem and its culture, language, values, and people to become an increasingly distant memory with each passing generation. As a result, I believe that the children of the exile asked different questions as they sat by the rivers of Babylon. No longer did their questions turn on *why* but *how*. Having never seen Jerusalem's lights or heard its language, yet riddled with memories and narratives of its existence, the exiled native child is not plagued by questions of particularity and sociality but those of actualization and consciousness: "Lord,[3] how do I succeed, *here*?" "Lord, am I *allowed* succeeding *here*? Can I eat their food and still belong to *home*?" Additionally, the theological questions change for the children of Babylon 2.0 or the children of the African exile. For while questions of theodicy still swirl, questions of prosperity and institution become more insistent. The exiled child grows weary of sitting at the waters of Babylon pining for a paradise lost. Instead, they are filled with desire to live and thrive in downtown Nineveh. With each successive year, the exiled native child knows somewhere deep inside that should they ever see Jerusalem's gates, they will be more tourists than citizens, unable to speak to or for the people from whom they have descended.

The life of the African American scholar is fraught with the tensions of the exiled native. Fed at the table of America, enjoying its fruits, yet always aware that we do not fully partake in all that America offers, the black scholar lives a bifurcated and complex existence. Noted scholar Harold Cruse summarized our existence thusly:

> The peculiarities of the American social structure, and the position of the intellectual class within it, make the functional role of the negro intellectual a special one. The negro intellectual must deal intimately with the white power structure and cultural apparatus and the inner realities of the black world at one and the same time.[4]

Situated in two worlds and at home in neither, the exiled native knows that negotiation of racial exception and expectation becomes essential. Yet not all African American scholars deal with this dialectical mandate the same way. For some, like Father Patrick Healey, the first African American professor and President of Georgetown University, this tension was negotiated by erasing his race altogether. However, those who choose to attempt the delicate dance between racial identity, vocation, and authenticity find that it is a backbreaking two-step dance to, and at times against, the tune of W. E. B. Du Bois.

"THE TALENTED TENTH": CONSTRUCTING THE AFRICAN AMERICAN SAVIOR CLASS

The contribution of W. E. B. Du Bois to the emergence of the African American scholar in the twentieth century is virtually without question. For countless African American scholars and intellectuals, Du Bois's essay "The Talented Tenth," on the ethical imperatives of the African

American intellectual, is required reading. Related to the work of Alexander Crummell, who advanced the idea that there could be no distinction between a life of letters and a life of blackness in America, Du Bois argued that indeed there was a moral responsibility for the African American elite toward racial uplift and leadership.[5] Rejecting the position that academic scholarship and vocation are individually driven pursuits, he posited that rights and duties of the African American scholar were not to the self but to the larger collective of the race:

> [T]he function of the college-bred Negro . . . is as he ought to be, the group leader, the man who sets the ideals of the community where he lives, directs its thoughts and heads its social movements. . . . *The Talented Tenth* of the Negro race must be made leaders of thought and missionaries of culture among their people. . . . [T]he Negro race, like all other races, is going to be saved by its exceptional men.[6]

For Du Bois, education was not for economic success but for building a proud race in America.

Since its initial printing, Du Bois's concept of the "talented tenth" has been praised, dissected, deconstructed, and dismissed, but it has never been ignored. Despite critiques that his idea was idealistic, utopian, uninformed, or inherently misinformed, the essay has been seminal reading for countless generations of prospective and emerging African American scholars. Whether read as a required reading in a black studies course, presented as a tome of enlightenment by one of the brothers and sisters on campus, or considered as the nexus of race and the life of the mind, Du Bois has become our guide. Henry Louis Gates describes the anticipatory socializing influence of the essay thusly: "[His] essay was read and critiqued, almost defensively, for its vanguardism; but [also for] its vision of the educated bourgeoisie as the truly revolutionary class. . . . [It] exerted an unmistakable sway on us."[7] Consequently, Gates suggests that African American scholars are formed by two powerful forces: their academic disciplines and the philosophy of W. E. B. Du Bois. In summarizing Du Bois's power over the identity of the African American scholar, Gates concludes that the totality of the African American scholarly identity—socially, politically, and ethically—emerges from Du Bois.

"The Talented Tenth" outlines an ethical imperative that has served as the agenda for scholarship and advocacy of African American scholars since its first publication in 1903. Hence, regardless of their location, the work of all African American scholars remains the same: they are to create scholarship that explicates, advocates, and uplifts their race. Du Bois frames this task as the duty and honor of representing the black race in the hallowed halls of the academy. Consequently, African American scholars are to undertake this task with great humility, recognizing their endeavors as both self-sacrificial and noble. Admitting that his concept of the "talented tenth" creates a class differential within the race, Du Bois argues that such differentials are not out of petty economic ambition but out of the need to cultivate a race within a race to save the race.

Accordingly, the effect of Du Bois's imperative as each scholar develops her or his self-perception and meaning of her or his work cannot be underestimated. I do not suggest that the African American scholar is without agency in this framing. However, I do posit that the Du Boisian frame plays a significant role in setting our scholarly agenda and commitments. It shapes our individual and collective expectations of how we are to negotiate our lives in the Ivory Tower. While we are free to pursue any academic discipline we choose, the pull of Du Bois, however nuanced, always asks the question of the African American scholar: "How is your work making a difference in the life of your people?" Although we spend hours ranting and raving about how we should not be the "representative" of our race on panels, search committees, or course discussions, inevitably there is an almost insidious nag in our collective spirits that demands that we accept this role even when we are not asked to provide that voice. In the end, we believe, whether or not we ever articulate it, that our role as scholars must include speaking on behalf of our people.

INAUTHENTIC SAVIORS: CONSTRUCTION OF AFRICAN AMERICAN SCHOLARS AS OTHER

Perhaps the most scathing rejection of the African American scholar as "savior" or voice of the people curiously emerges from the "people." Voices critical of Du Bois's casting of the African American scholar as savior seek to remove the mantle from their shoulders not by questioning their credentials but by engaging in the most powerful psychological assault: they question the racial authenticity of the savior. Questions of racial authenticity are not simply schoolyard insults for members of collective cultures.[8] They are debilitating charges that over time wear on the psyche and efficacy of their targets. For within every taunt and every insult is the reminder from those whom we call family that we do not belong.

Out of the White: Constructing Blackness in American Discourse

Commonly, discourses about authenticity emerge when a group encounters and interacts with difference. Such debates of authenticity, particularly in cases of ethnicity and race, work to destabilize definitions of identity that are rooted only in physicality. Here the group, usually in response to a dominant framework that seeks to categorize their identity as physical, provides a counter-narrative that asserts their uniqueness as more than physical, as cultural, spiritual, or ontological. Particularly for collectives shaped by colonial domination or ethnoviolence, by which phenotypical characteristics are shaped and reshaped by interracial sexual interactions with the "Other," appeals to skin color, hair texture, and even blood content prove inconclusive to determine who is truly, authentically "one of us." Forged in opposition, the concept of racial authenticity presupposes that there is an ontological standard that is mandated for racial survival and by which members must adhere to remain "in good standing." J. Martin Favor argues that the discourse of racial authenticity articulates a fundamental belief that there is a "definition of blackness that is constantly being invented, policed, transgressed and contested."[9]

Defining what and who is black is complex and simplistic. It is complex in the sense that when one looks at the genealogical development of the symbolic meaning of blackness in America, it is clear that it emerges from an elegant dance of the economic, political, and socio-religious development of America. It is also simplistic in that it is a definition that finds its genesis in what Kenneth Burke terms "the human creation of the negative." Burke argues that for every term or concept in the realm of humanity, we discursively create a symbol of negation.[10] Consequently, I posit that the meaning of blackness is constructed in light of whiteness.

Though a full genealogical treatment of the construction of whiteness is beyond the scope of my current endeavor, when defined as the summation of all that is "normal" and laudable,[11] whiteness becomes a state of being that the nonwhite person strives to obtain in order to achieve a state of normality. Yet whiteness and its plethora of implications for class, gender, and societal expectations also become a point of resistance for the nonwhite—a means by which we can define our otherness as unique, important, and authentic. This creates "a damned if you do, damned if you don't" dialectic for exiled native African Americans because, in order to be successful in America, they have to demonstrate that they can compete and excel at the standards for white/American success, be accepted and affirmed by the standards of white/American normality, and live and thrive in the white/American community while simultaneously working to destabilize the white/American system and institutions.

Victor Anderson does a masterful job of exploring this dialectic of being black in the light of the demands of American whiteness. Anderson explains that in response to categorical racism—which dismisses the humanity and genius of the African materially, aesthetically, and cognitively—black leaders engage in a discursive act of racial apologetics.[12] The goals of this apologia are, first, to establish that the qualities of white/American genius are not unique to the white race but are universal, and second, to show that it is neither heroic nor imitative but merely the natural state for blacks to engage in the activities and demonstrate the abilities of white/American genius. What emerges, according to Anderson, is a discourse that argues that the African American heroic genius existed before and thrives in light of categorical racism. He states, "The aim of racial apologetics is to overturn the negative prejudices under which white racial ideology defined black identity and to advance positive black cultural qualities in defense of African Americans' cultural assimilation."[13] Anderson argues that from this apologia emerges the dialectic of *negro/freedom* that culminates in Du Bois's depiction of the two souls of the African American, constantly at war with each other.

The result of Du Bois's two-soul framing is the emergence of what Anderson calls an ontological blackness that becomes as instructive as it is exclusive. Inherent in its apologia is a blackness that is defined and created by the very racism it seeks to destabilize. By mirroring categorical racism, in which the white heroic genius establishes a definition of normative whiteness entangled in a framework of class, ontological blackness frames authentic blackness as a heroic middle-class ideal. Anderson summarizes thusly, "It represents categorical ways of transferring negative qualities associated with the group onto others within the group. It creates essential criteria for defining insiders and outsiders within the group."[14] Therefore, the genius celebrated and extolled by Du Bois as an authentic blackness is a blackness that mirrors the achievements and genius of the white middle class.

The Last Shall Be First: The Racial Authenticity of the "Folks"

However, the criteria of racial authenticity, exemplified in "The Talented Tenth," comes under swift rebuke by scholars such as Houston Baker and E. Franklin Frazier, who are unwilling to ignore the inherent strand of class underlying its construction.[15] Both Baker and Frazier believe that the "true experience" of being black in America would never be experienced by the black middle class or its scholars. Instead, they argue that those on the margins of "respectability," inhabiting the lower classes, are the authentic representatives of all things black. Although some regionalize this "authenticity" by classifying the poor, rural, Southern black as the racial standard bearer, others argue that authenticity could only be located in the black lower middle class.

Signified in the personage of the *folk*, the lower-class African American is constructed as a foil against a definition of blackness that is all too close to nothing more than whiteness in blackface. Favor explains that for Houston Baker and later Alain Locke, the *folks* become a preoccupation and symbol of blackness that extends beyond color to cultural expressions in the arts, dress, and politics. Consequently, a competing definition of what it means to be black in America becomes personified in "the rural folk," who are in the process of becoming the urban proletariat, forming "the basis of the African American experience."[16]

If the black lower classes were to become the repository of authentic blackness, then discursively it requires a decentering and dismantling of the significance of Du Bois's "The Talented Tenth." Frazier eagerly embraced this challenge. In both his *Black Bourgeoisie* and "The Failure of the

Negro Intellectual,"[17] he engaged in a scathing critique of African American middle-class intellectuals. Railing at once against their culture of consumption and what he viewed as a desire to racially assimilate to the point of invisibility, Frazier portrayed African American intellectuals as out of touch, materialistic, and racially unhinged.[18]

Framing the argument as one of assimilation versus integration, Frazier also pointed out that middle-class African American intellectuals have lost the ability to distinguish between the two. Integration, Frazier asserted, is necessary for the advancement of African Americans into the political and economic strata of American society, whereas "assimilation leads to complete identification with the people and culture of the community in which the social heritages of different people become merged or fused."[19] Frazier explained that in their drive toward assimilation African American intellectuals become consumed not only with attaining the symbols of American (white) success but also with erasing any vestiges of their cultural identity and solidarity with the lower classes: "The desire to achieve acceptance in American life by conformity to the ideals, values, and patterns of behavior of white Americans. This is no speculation on my part. Every study that has been made reveals that they think very much the same as white Americans, even concerning Negroes."[20] Consequently, Frazier argued that the close socio-political similarity between African American intellectuals and their white counterparts creates an inability for the scholar of color to grasp the true state and fate of authentic African Americans.

Forged in an educational system bought and paid for by white philanthropy, Frazier suggested that the African American scholar is conditioned and rewarded for addressing topics that are considered viable and appropriate by the larger mainstream audience. Therefore, no matter how "revolutionary" a scholar purports to be, their revolution is still funded and approved by a system that requires submission to particular ideals and values. Frazier wrote, "There is no basis of economic support for them in the Negro community. And where there is support, it demands conformity to conservative and conventional ideals."[21] Thus, African American scholars, according to Frazier, are not intellectuals but opportunistic and repetitive, producing research that is full of platitudes "concerning brotherly love and human dignity" and void of substance and attachment to the lived experiences of the authentic African American. Frazier's damning critique of the intellectual and moral enterprise of African American scholars is not isolated to a small segment of the African American race. The perception of inauthenticity, driven in large part by class, has served to create a general mistrust of the "folks" toward the scholar.

In one of his earliest works, Cornel West addressed the tenuous predicament of the black intellectual. Taking on the issue of intra-racial mistrust and suspicion of the African American scholar, West argues that its origins do not emerge from what he terms a general haughtiness of African American scholars toward their own people, but from "the widespread refusal of black intellectuals to remain, in some visible way, organically linked to the Afro-American cultural life."[22] Despite our public assertions of "being down with the people," West argues that our actions speak to the contrary. According to West, our relatively high rates of interracial marriages, departure from cultural institutions such as the black church, and a seeming preoccupation with obtaining all of the trappings of white middle-class life contribute to a perception that black intellectuals are running away from our racial roots and are severing intimate ties to the black community.

This inherent distance also emerges from a more practical phenomenon: the construction of the "folks" as data and text. The African American scholar for better or worse is framed with the expectation of being a data source for academic fields to better understand the African American population. Whether psychology, religion, communication, or public affairs, the African American scholar is expected to bring the "black voice" into the halls of the academy. Mark Sawyer referred to this dynamic when he stated, "We carry the additional burden of trying to provide a deeper understanding of the issues that confront the black community in the United States and beyond."[23] However, in seeking to elevate that voice, the people are rendered no longer as people but data points. Their words, their writings, their rituals and institutions are sources for analysis. Regardless of our own immersion in any and all aspects of the construction of these discursive products, in the end, as we turn to our scholarly work, we become observers and critics on behalf of the dominant culture rather than brothers and sisters in the struggle.

THE EXILED NATIVE DILEMMA: IF WE SPEAK, WILL ANYONE LISTEN, AND THE TROUBLE WITH THE MOVIE *THE HELP*

With the competing frames and demands of being simultaneously seen as savior and sellout, the African American scholar is forced to negotiate a psychic minefield that could drive anyone crazy. On the one hand, African American scholars, by virtue of their access to places for interracial dialogue on policy and politics, are under a moral imperative to carry those voices that do not have such access into the corridors of power. On the other hand, their class and cultural distance from the "folks" creates a credibility and experiential gap when they speak on behalf of other African Americans or marginalized voices.

Nowhere is this gap more evident than in the inter-racial/intra-racial dialogue surrounding the Academy Award–nominated motion picture *The Help*. Based on the bestselling book written by Kathryn Stockett, *The Help* depicts the intertwined and invisible lives of African American maids in Jackson, Mississippi, in 1960. As with every film on African American life, the film provides ample material for deconstruction. A book and film written by a white woman depicting the lives and feelings of African American maids is an excellent context for concerned scholars to speak out on behalf of the "real" experiences of black women who served white families as domestic help. A number of scholarly blogs, articles, and conference panels were dedicated to the book and the movie. For instance, the Association of Black Women Historians took the exceptional action of issuing a press release condemning the movie.[24]

Perhaps no other African American scholar had a more visible bully pulpit than Melissa Harris-Perry. Professor of political science and noted columnist, Harris-Perry pulled no punches in her assessment of *The Help*. Calling it an "ahistorical," "photoshopping" portrayal of the "real" lives of domestics in the Jim Crow South, Harris-Perry tweeted her impressions live while viewing the movie, which were carried on MSNBC and recounted on a number of national blogs.[25] Her tweeted review included assertions that *The Help* "reduces violent racism, sexism and labor exploitation to a catfight that can be won with cunning spunk."[26] On the day before the Academy Awards, Harris-Perry was even more incensed at the popular embrace of a movie she found so disturbing. Accusing the film of whitewashing the dangers of the Jim Crow South, she argued that the reality of Jim Crow–era domestics was "much closer to a horror film than a lighthearted drama. Just ask those who found themselves at the mercy of Jim Crow justice, at the end of the lynch mob's rope or a burning torch . . . for black maids, the threat of rape was always a clear and present danger."[27]

Harris-Perry's position is not unique and unexpected. Frankly, it is quite tame when one considers the tenor and content of critique lauded in the popular press and at academic conference panels. In a typical, if not pedestrian, Marxist fashion, she critiqued a film because, in her view, it failed to depict the true horrors of the period. As tempting as it is to discuss the state of critical scholarship, I am more intrigued by the irony that all of Harris-Perry's academic and political analysis was crafted for the consumption of white audiences. Her review was not posted in venues with diverse readers and viewers; Harris-Perry's critique was found on MSNBC, *The Nation*, and in several black scholarly blogs such as *Black Snob*.[28] Consequently, even a generous assessment of the number of African Americans consuming Harris-Perry's critique could not be totaled as more than eighty thousand people.[29]

Her review appears even more disconnected from the lived experiences and opinions of the "folks" when contrasted with the response of the vanguard of African American media outlets such as Black Entertainment Television, *Ebony*, and *Jet*. With a majority readership/viewership consisting of working-class African Americans that is ten times that of Professor Harris-Perry's more limited audience, these outlets offered vocal support of the movie. Almost serving as an unofficial public relations team, these magazines and their online outlets heralded each box office record and award nomination of *The Help*. Many comments offered by readers on websites and letters to editors clearly supported the actresses and the film, although many were saddened that once again African American actresses were applauded for work in films in which they were featured as domestics. Simply put, the film found great support from African American filmgoers, book purchasers, and civic organizations, such as the NAACP, although it was savaged by a majority of the African American intelligentsia.

Perhaps most damning was the disconnection between black intellectuals and those they purported to defend—domestics. Apparently overlooked by each critic was the fact that domestics of all ages and races celebrated the film and its actresses. When asked, many of domestics articulated their belief that the movie celebrated their humanity and made them visible to a world that ignores them every day. Most notably, the National Domestic Alliance (NDA), which organized viewings of *The Help* and Oscar parties all over the country, stated that the movie served as an accurate depiction of their members' plight. The organization observed that "Barbara Young, who has worked for 17 years as a domestic worker . . . cried when Davis' character was separated from a white child—[because] she had endured several such partings in real life." The NDA pointed out that the movie also served as a clarion call to mobilize their members to change laws and working conditions for all domestics. The NDA is now actively engaging the political process to pass a domestic workers bill of rights that is influenced not by intellectuals such as Melissa Harris-Perry but by Oscar winner Octavia Spencer.

In reality, then, Viola Davis, the actress and daughter and granddaughter of South Carolina domestics, and her co-star, Octavia Spencer, a native of Montgomery, Alabama, not Seattle-born Melissa Harris-Perry, brought the voices and plight of actual domestics to light. Davis explained in interview after interview that her mother's and grandmother's experiences as Jim Crow–era maids were anything but rosy but that they informed her performance. She also mentioned that her mother has been supportive of her depiction of Abilene.[30] Both Davis and Spencer vigorously engaged in debate and conversation about the plight of domestics and defended the racial authenticity of the movie. When noted columnist and author Tavis Smiley expressed his dismay that Davis and Spencer were being nominated for portrayals as domestics, Davis and Spencer responded. Here is an excerpt of their conversation:

> "I want you to win," Mr. Smiley said, "but I'm ambivalent about what you're winning for." Ms. Davis was direct. "That very mind-set that you have and that a lot of African-Americans have is absolutely destroying the black artist," she said. "The black artist cannot live in a

revisionist place," she added. "The black artist can only tell the truth
about humanity, and humanity is messy. People are messy. Caucasian
actors know that." Ms. Spencer pointed out Anthony Hopkins won for
playing a cannibal and Charlize Theron for portraying a serial killer—
that white actors were never taken to task for their choices in playing
troubling roles. "I don't have a problem with nominating these two
earnest, hard-working women. . . . We've never seen this story told
from their perspective."[31]

In their response, Davis and Spencer revealed the "real" problem that
some African American intellectuals have with Abilene and Minnie. They
are maids. The reality that within the so-called post–civil rights era of the
twenty-first century, African America media images still includes maids
flies in the face of the Du Boisian utopia that African American scholars
are socialized to believe should exist: a world in which success is ultimately defined as the goal of every African American to achieve middle-
class whiteness.

My intention is not to question the political or racial commitments of
Harris-Perry or other African American scholars critical of *The Help*. Instead, my goal is to provide an exemplar of the gap that can and does
exist between African American scholars and the individuals for whom
they seek to be a voice. The mandate of Du Bois is lived out in a material
reality in which we are inevitably disconnected from those we seek to
serve. This disconnect renders our voice on their behalf often as uninformed and inauthentic. Scholar Mark Sawyer summarizes this plight
bluntly by pointing out, "[W]e are ciphers. . . . [B]lack intellectuals are not
the leaders in the way in which we once might have claimed."[32]

HOMELESS: THE NATIVE EXILE SCHOLAR

Clearly, I have written myself into something of a dealer's dilemma with
two competing trajectories: neither of which is particularly palatable.
Each track unsatisfying, each one as untenable and distasteful as the
other: yet both so easy to write. On the one hand, it would be quite easy
to argue that African American scholars can still speak out on behalf of
the voiceless and for causes of diversity and social justice. Despite a clear
disconnect from the political, social, and even racial views of our brothers
and sisters in the economic lower classes, I could argue that we have a
duty to speak out on their behalf anyway. To advocate for them even
when "they don't know better" or "can't do better," until they can. I
could then turn to the moral imperative for those who sit in the courts of
Babylon to make known the plight of those who remain exiled, and speak
of the debt that we owe those who have gone before. However, such
musings would leave me in a position of moral authority, spouting easy
and virtuous platitudes that are likely to please progressives with a con-

science. Such a position would also only reify the paternalistic (but well meaning) approach taken by white progressives over the last seventy-five years when advocating for communities of color.

On the other hand, I could accept the absolute implausibility of my ability to speak authentically on behalf of the young sister with the baby on her hip who actually thinks that orange extensions are fashionable. The reality, if I would dare to admit it, is that she and I have no more in common than she and one of my European-American colleagues from an equally privileged background. While she might feign respect for my white colleague, she might label me an oreo, wanna-be, or outsider—frankly, anything but respectable. I would be a foreigner to her and equally as suspect. I could also admit that my attempts to come to her defense whether in the courtroom or in my academic writings are constructed not from walking her walk, but from observing her, hearing of her lot secondhand, or knowing her as some distant cousin far removed from my daily interaction and reality. I could share the reality of the survivor's guilt that hits me every time I pass the bus stop or the school children, knowing that each day I participate in the very system that is crushing them, held there not by fear but by desire and pleasure. I could explain how by speaking out for the rights of gays and lesbians, for immigration reform, or for the rights of all to practice their religions (even if it is not Christian), I am more likely to be exiled further (as if that is possible) from my racial home.[33] Yet the articulation of such complaints leaves me open to being labeled a self-indulgent scholar with racial identity issues, or worse yet, one who has dared to speak of the insecurities plaguing the thoughts of many of the Talented Tenth's third generation.

In the end, it might be best if I simply admit that black scholars are not leaders nor are we revolutionaries. Revolutions are not led by the middle class: they are only co-opted and financed by them. In the battle for social justice and diversity, our best path is to interrogate our own complicity and create work that is accessible not only to those in Nineveh but also to those sitting in the "hood." Perhaps by admitting that we have lost the nuances of our *authentic* discourse (rather than only always demanding alternative meanings of authenticity) and seeking in some tangible way to relearn our mother tongue, we can become less commentators on the evolution of revolution and better collaborators within it.

NOTES

1. Curiously, the public transportation to and from Highland Park, Texas, begins as early as 6 am and ends roughly at 7 pm, whereas it continues late into the evening in other parts of the Dallas Metroplex.

2. Cheryl Sanders, *The Holiness-Pentecostal Experience in African American Religion and Culture* (New York: Oxford University Press, 1996), viii–ix.

3. Within the African American tradition, the designation "Lord" for God is appropriate and historically accurate. However, I acknowledge the androcentric and hierarchical nature of this term.

4. Harold Cruse, *The Crisis of the Negro Intellectual: A Historical Analysis of the Failure of Black Leadership* (New York: Morrow, 1967), 451.

5. Henry Louis Gates and Cornel West, *The Future of the Race* (New York: Alfred Knopf, 1996), 122; W. E. B. Du Bois, "The Talented Tenth," in *The Negro Problem: A Series of Articles by Representative Negros of To-day,* ed. Booker T. Washington (New York: James Pott, 1903), 37.

6. Du Bois, "The Talented Tenth," 37.

7. Gates and West, *Future of the Race,* 5.

8. J. M. Favor, *Authentic Blackness* (Durham, NC: Duke University, 1999), 2.

9. Ibid.

10. Kenneth Burke, "Definition of Men," *The Hudson Review* 16, no. 4 (Winter 1963): 491–514.

11. Critical studies of whiteness include Thandeka, *Learning to Be White* (New York: Continuum, 2000), as well as the works of Hume, Locke, and Thomas Jefferson, who cast whiteness as the normative ideal structuring American understandings of race.

12. Victor Anderson, *Beyond Ontological Blackness: An Essay on African American Religious and Cultural Criticism* (New York: Continuum, 1995), 79.

13. Ibid., 78.

14. Ibid., 79.

15. See also E. Franklin Frazier, "Failure of Negro Intellectual," *The Negro Digest* (February 1963) or Houston Baker, *How Black Intellectuals Have Abandoned the Ideals of the Civil Rights Era* (New York: Columbia University Press, 2008), 7.

16. Favor, *Authentic Blackness,* 12.

17. E. Franklin Frazier, *Black Bourgeoisie* (Glencoe, IL: Free Press, 1957); Frazier, "Failure of the Negro Intellectual," 35.

18. Ibid., 35–37.

19. Frazier, "Failure of the Negro Intellectual," 29.

20. Ibid.

21. Ibid., 31.

22. Cornel West, "The Dilemma of the Black Intellectual," *Cultural Critique* (University of Minnesota, 1985): 113.

23. Mark Sawyer, "The Crisis of the African American Intellectual: What's To Be Learned from Cornel West v. Melissa Perry Debate," *Huffington Post* (February 21, 2012), www.huffingtonpost.com/mark-sawyer/cornel-west-melissa-harris-perry_b_1285666.html [accessed December 6, 2012].

24. Black Entertainment Television, "*The Help* Hurts Black Women's Image, Say Black Female Historians" (March 12, 2011), www.bet.com/news/national/2011/08/12/-the-help-hurts-black-women-s-image-say-black-female-historians.html [accessed December 6, 2012].

25. @MHarrisPerry.

26. Harris-Perry, Melissa. @MHarrisPerry-Live Tweet from *The Help*.

27. Melissa Harris-Perry, *The Last Word with Lawrence O'Donnell* on MSNBC.

28. Danielle Belton, "Melissa Harris-Perry Hates Her Some Help," *Black Snob* (August 8, 2011), http://blacksnob.com/snob_blog/2011/8/11/melissa-harris-perry-hates-her-some-help.html [accessed December 6, 2012].

29. Quantcast MSNBC Viewer Demographics (November 11, 2012), http://www.quantcast.com/msnbc.com [accessed December 6, 2012].

30. Although supportive of her daughter's portrayal, Davis's mother did not watch the movie because of the memories it evoked; see *CBS Morning Show*, "Interview with Viola Davis" (February, 15, 2012).

31. Melena Zik, "Viola Davis on a Mind-Set That She Says Harms Black Actors," *The Carpetbagger* (the awards season blog of the *New York Times*), February 12, 2012, http://

carpetbagger.blogs.nytimes.com/2012/02/14/viola-davis-on-a-mind-set-that-harms-black-actors/ [accessed December 6, 2012].

32. Sawyer, "The Crisis of the African American Intellectual."

33. Pew Research Center. "Gay Marriage Gains More Acceptance," *Pew Research Center Publications* (October 6, 2010), available at http://pewresearch.org/pubs/1755/poll-gay-marriage-gains-acceptance-gays-in-the-military [accessed December 6, 2012].

TEN

Justice Is at the Core

Law, Justice, and Gender Equality in Islamic Feminism

Qudsia Mirza

Justice lies at the core of the Islamic belief system. Its importance is so fundamental that believers are exhorted to "stand firm in justice, witnesses for Allah,"[1] even if it results in self-incrimination. Because of Allah's commitment to justice, the Muslim duty to do justice surpasses the duty even to oneself. The Qur'an is replete with references to justice: divine, distributive, adjudicative, and retributive, and it gives constant reminders to the believer of the overriding necessity to attain justice in all aspects of life. The Qur'an categorically links faith with justice and the faithful are commanded to be just, to uphold justice, and are reminded that justice is next to godliness ("be always just, that is closest to righteousness").[2] There is justice to kith and kin, to the orphan, to the destitute, to the slave, to the wayfarer, and to the needy[3]; the Qur'an directs that "when you judge between the people, you do it with justice,"[4] and "that when you speak, hold the scales even."[5] In short, Islam considers Allah's commitment to justice unsurpassed, it is perfect and absolute, and therefore Muslims have the obligation to bring about justice in the world.

The importance of justice is emphasized in all areas of human interaction—to strangers, between family members, within the community, in the interaction between communities and nations and in the interface between human beings and nature.[6] Muslims have an obligation to establish a just society on earth and the command to do justice is a "structural public obligation that flows from private religious confession."[7] Conse-

quently, justice permeates the entirety of Muslim individual and communal endeavor.[8] However, in both classical and contemporary times, in
both Muslim majority societies and diasporic communities, the ideal of
justice has been aspirational rather than real as it fails to contain a substantive notion of equality.

The call to Muslims to practice justice in the world has not been without its problems. This is particularly so in the public and private relations
between men and women and also in the realm of the family. The classical Islamic tradition is replete with the rulings of jurists in family law—
replicated in modern legal codes—which cannot be justified within the
context of modernity and, most importantly, are incompatible with the
ethical thrust of Islam. The entrenchment of laws that advance a notion of
justice that omits the idea of equality between the sexes is unsustainable
in the light of Islamic principles and ideals; it is contrary to the very
essence of Islam. Thus, equality is central to the Islamic conception of
justice.

This chapter analyzes the concept of justice in Islamic law and within
the wider tradition, and outlines how the notion of gender equality has
largely been omitted from such conceptions of justice. I argue that such
omissions are particularly apparent in the area of family law, which has
considerable implications for the wider status and role of women in Muslim societies. The chapter continues with an outline of what constitutes
"Islamic law," clarifying the important distinction between *Shari'a* and
fiqh. A feminist reading of the sources of Islamic law reveals that this
confusion between the two has been detrimental to the development of
gender justice and equality in Muslim legal cultures. Focusing particularly on interpretive methodologies for reading the Qur'an (the primary
source of *Shari'a*), I demonstrate how feminist scholars are challenging
deeply entrenched notions of the relationship between the sexes by fashioning a "hermeneutics of liberation." They are utilizing the central belief
of Allah's unity (*tawhid*) with the ideal of the welfare of the public (*maslaha*) and offering new readings of gender equality and justice in the
Qur'an. These new interpretations are then put forward as the theological
foundation for the reconfiguration of legal rights for Muslim women.

JUSTICE IN THE ISLAMIC TRADITION

Given the centrality of justice and the fact that the Qur'an urges us constantly to strive for justice, it is surprising that there are so few organized
studies on the nature, character and scope of justice in the classical Islamic tradition.[9] Although the terms used to describe justice pervade the
Qur'anic text with great regularity, neither in the Qur'an nor in the Sunna
are there detailed explanations of what the constitutive elements of justice are or, indeed, how they can be materialized. Muslim theologians,

jurists, and philosophers have not systematically reflected on the concept of justice. This is not to say that justice has remained unexamined or static. On the contrary, Muslim understandings of justice have differed greatly in different times and contexts with societies and communities holding a variety of opinions and establishing differing societal norms over the meaning of justice and how it should be implemented. Qur'anic references are largely to just and virtuous behavior rather than justice in the abstract, and the relevant verses have then been used to "construct" more systematic conceptions of Islamic justice. As Gudrun Kramer outlines, the meaning of justice in the classical Islamic tradition has been understood to refer to "a wide range of ideas and ideals, from straightness and evenness to fairness, equity, and impartiality, from the reciprocity of rights and duties to balance and harmony, the golden mean, and, quite simply, abiding by the law."[10]

A plethora of terms is used to describe justice including *taqwa* (piety), *istiqama* (uprightness), *ihsan* (goodness), and *salah* (righteousness).[11] The word most frequently used to describe justice is *'adl*, which means "to be upright," "to set straight," or "to be balanced," all of which denote following the righteous path and urging the believer to be fair, impartial and unbiased. In the legal context, *'adl* in *fiqh* and in the *Hadith* collection signifies moral integrity and probity, an upstanding individual who has conducted herself with conscientious honor. Doctrinally, both the Mu'tazili[12] and the Shi'a have bequeathed important interpretive legacies in their understanding of *'adl* in the Islamic tradition. In Mu'tazili thought, justice is one of the fundamental attributes of God. Here, as Majid Khadduri outlines in his discussion of Islamic texts, "the value of justice exists independent of religious texts; our sense and definition of justice are shaped by sources outside religion, are innate and have a rational basis."[13] In contrast, the Ashari school of thought avers that justice is derived from religious texts — that is, the text defines what constitutes justice, and this cannot be challenged. In both Mu'tazili and Shi'a thought, God's justice is all-encompassing in that all His acts are deemed to be irrevocably beneficial for humanity and the rest of creation. God is thus constrained by His own attribute of justice.[14]

Whilst *'adl* has an expansive meaning, two other words are used to describe justice in a more specific way: *qist*, which denotes equity and fairness, the opposite of *zulm*, which itself is etymologically related to the ideas of darkness and opaqueness; and *ihsan*, mentioned above, of comporting oneself in a way that is fair to others. *Qist* relates theologically to God's purposes in creation and, more extensively than *'adl*, is concerned with social relations among human beings. Thus, *qist* denotes a sweeping sense of communal justice that encompasses a Muslim's relationship with God, as well as her relationship with the wider society in which she finds herself.[15] Modern notions of justice emphasize this aspect in a communal sense and that one's place in the *umma* or community of Muslims is paramount for the well-being of the individual and her status within society.

Despite the fact that the notion of justice occupies a central position in the Islamic tradition, contemporary reformist Islamic scholars and activists decry the marginal importance that is accorded to notions of justice in many parts of the Muslim world. This is most notable in the area of gender equality and women's rights and in particular, the family laws and jurisprudence of majority Muslim nations. Although justice itself has been integral to Islam since its inception, the notion of gender equality has been rendered marginal or nominal at best in the practice of Islamic justice. This is despite the fact that the Qur'an, which is the primary source of Islamic law (*Shari'a*), clearly enunciates the principles of justice, human dignity (*karamah*), equality (*musawah*), equity ('*insaf*'), love, and compassion (*mawaddah wa rahmah*)[16] as essential in Islam. Thus, contemporary reformers criticize the stark disconnect between these elements and the laws and directives passed in the name of Islam and assert that it is necessary to take a holistic view of justice and equality in order to reestablish the true ideals of Islam. The question that needs to be addressed urgently is this: To what extent does the notion of gender that is encapsulated in orthodox interpretations of scripture truly reflect the principle of justice intrinsic to *Shari'a*?

SHARI'A AND *FIQH*: THE CONCEPT OF LAW

Before we can examine this question and also address the broader issue of law and justice, a distinction needs to be made between the two most commonly used terms to describe Islamic law, *Shari'a* and *fiqh*. The relationship between the two is complex. The former literally means "the way" and is "revealed or canonical law," with the Qur'an as the preeminent source of *Shari'a*. The other primary source is the Sunna, which are the sayings and deeds of the Holy Prophet Muhammad collected in the vast *Hadith* writings. As such, *Shari'a* is much more than a codified collection of laws as it encompasses the principles that direct the believer toward justice and ethical conduct in life. The secondary sources include the principles of consensus (*ijma*) by which the *ulama* (religious scholars) reach a workable decision and *qiyas*, whereby the notion of analogy is utilized in order to set a precedent. In addition, we can add nontextual sources of law such as *istislah* (public interest), *istidlal* (inference), and principles commonly referred to as aims of the law (*maqasid al sharia*) that, inter alia, include the protection of life, religion, property, and others.[17] At this point, it is important to note that the Qur'an is of divine origin, the word of Allah, and has universal and normative effect both in temporal and spatial terms.

Fiqh, however, is the human attempt to understand the *Shari'a,* and this takes the form of positive laws, legal rulings and jurisprudence—the law of jurists—which is fallible and changeable.[18] The science of interpretation by jurists is known as *usul-al-fiqh,* the "roots of jurisprudence," and jurists use the hermeneutic tool of *ijtihad.* This term, meaning "endeavor, self-exertion," is etymologically linked to the concept of *jihad,* meaning "struggle," and is the jurist's method by which rulings are made on new issues in the light of revelation. The distinction between *Shari'a* and *fiqh* has become obfuscated with the result that the terms are often used interchangeably and thus, incorrectly. Some contend that the two are inseparable and that *Shari'a* can only be known by way of *fiqh.* Others argue that there is a fundamental difference between *fiqh,* which is always spatially and temporally specific, and *Shar'ia,* which, as "revealed law," is all-prevailing. This is particularly problematic for modern reformist scholars, as they are "finding contradictions between inherited legal norms (derived from *fiqh*) and Islamic ethical values (derived from the Qur'an)."[19] This "entanglement" between *Shari'a* and *fiqh* manifests itself most strikingly in terms of gender and the establishment of social and legal rights for women in the Islamic tradition. In formulating new Qur'an-based legal initiatives, such scholars are said to be developing a "modern *fiqh*" utilizing a "feminist *ijithad.*" A clear distinction is made between this *fiqh* and *Shari'a.* Modern *fiqh* can also be distinguished from classical *fiqh* in terms of both subject matter and method.[20]

The notion of a bounded and homogenous "Islamic law" or the application of an "Islamic legal code" is also problematic as neither *Shari'a* nor *fiqh* correspond easily to a "Western" conception of legality. Islamic law covers a broader range of issues than those under the rubric of "Western" law, as it encompasses matters such as devotion and worship, personal moral frameworks, family relationships, and social and public welfare. There is also, of course, the fundamental doctrinal split between Sunni and Shi'a Islam with each side comprising a number of different schools of jurisprudence or legal thought (*madhab*).[21] Every *madhab* has developed within differing historical and interpretive contexts. As a result, the rulings between each *madhab* on a particular legal question can be so at variance with each other that it is difficult to provide a singular and definitive answer under the rubric of "Islamic law." Historically, the first three or four centuries of Islamic thought were periods of great intellectual innovation and dynamism. By the end of the fifth century AH,[22] the four main *madhab* were instituted, the contours of Islamic thought were established, and these *madhab* were effectively entrenched in all the major parts of the Muslim territories.

There are also distinctions in the nature of legal rulings themselves. There are two types of such rulings: those that are concerned with devotional and spiritual issues or matters of ritual (*'ibadat*) and those that are social, transactional, or contractual (*mu'amalat*). The distinction between the two is significant as this determines whether legal precepts can be challenged, and the extent to which they are open to change and modification. Rulings in the *'ibadat* category regulate the relationship between Allah and the believing Muslim. As such, the possibility of altering or amending these rulings is very limited. In contrast, rulings in the latter, *mu'amalat* category regulate interhuman relationships and offer much more capacity for change. Implicit in this mutability of *mu'amalat* rulings is the recognition that humanity is in a constant state of flux and striving to advance and progress. Consequently, the interpretations of religious texts need to be revised constantly in order to keep pace with societal changes that occur because of the passage of time and because of the differences in social contexts. Rulings on the family and gender relations are in the domain of *mu'amalat,* which means that jurists in the classical tradition have viewed them as social and contractual matters and therefore open to rational consideration and change. The paradox, however, is the need to retain the transcendental nature of scripture while formulating interpretations that reflect social change. The dilemma can be articulated thus: If the *Qur'an* is considered to be atemporal and ahistorical, eternally relevant at all times and in all contexts, how can this be reconciled with the idea of historical change and social and cultural specificity?

Allied to this is the pressing question of who has the authority to create and interpret the Islamic tradition, a question that contemporary feminists are formulating as a crisis in the notion of authority.[23] From the very time of Islam's inception, women were at the forefront in both the production and the interpretation of religious knowledge. However, the further we travel from that time, and certainly by the time that the four main schools of jurisprudence had crystallized, the marginalization of women as the producers of religious and legal knowledge was firmly entrenched. From this point on, women were secondary in the law-making process and unable to participate in the legal domain as jurists or in any official interpretive capacity. Their role was relegated to being transmitters of religious knowledge in a private or unofficial capacity at home and in the mosque.[24]

The lack of women in key interpretive positions has had a significant effect on the development of Islamic law. We see a fixity or stagnation in many legal precepts associated with the status and rights of women. Legal rulings have become fossilized as rigid interpretations of medieval *fiqh,* which have little or no bearing on the lives of many Muslim women in modern times. Islamic religious and legal literature has been produced largely by men who have inscribed an androcentric and patriarchal ethos into it, thereby obliterating the egalitarian impulse that lies at the heart of Islam.[25] As Leila Ahmed contends, interpretations within the Islamic tradition have resulted in the negating of the "ethical voice of Islam," a voice that unambiguously points to egalitarianism, as this has been subsumed over the centuries under an overarching patriarchal bias.[26] There is thus an incompatibility between this ethos and the reformist calls for a return to "authentic" Islam in which the ideals of gender justice and equality are present. The feminist project is to reinterpret biased scriptural interpretations and institute authentic and ethically correct interpretations upon which progressive laws can be founded. Furthermore, feminists are highlighting the fact that the classical tradition has obscured the interpretation of the Qur'an, as the focus has been on understanding the exegetical literature itself rather than the text of the Qur'an.

One of the key arguments that feminists are making is that the Qur'an has historically been interpreted in a decontextualized and literalist manner. This methodological approach to the Qur'an has given rise to interpretations that are prejudicial to women and have become entrenched in Islamic legal and theological literature. Contemporary reformists are developing an Islamic feminist hermeneutics with interpretations of the Qur'an[27] that reveal the patriarchal underpinnings embedded in the classical Islamic tradition. These interpretations are focused both on this area of Qur'anic exegesis and on the area of Islamic jurisprudence in order to "develop alternative women liberatory interpretations."[28] These then produce more nuanced notions of gender equality that conform to the lived realities of women today.

A related problem is that both classical and contemporary Islamic literature contains depictions of women in which they are constructed solely as sexed and erotic female bodies and the quintessence of seduction. They are viewed as the source of moral and social chaos — of *fitna*.[29] This distorted and artificial construction of female sexuality is well entrenched and is the result of, *inter alia*, male interpretive communities promoting a particular version of female (and male) sexuality throughout the centuries of the Islamic tradition. The resulting sexual ethics promotes detrimental understandings of the status and role of women in all areas of life: sexual chastity, virginity, rights and obligations in marriage and divorce, the segregation of the sexes, veiling and bodily modesty, and the gendering of both public and private spaces. The feminist mission is to redress such discriminatory and injurious renderings and to highlight the fact that many detrimental laws relating to the rights of women have been implemented on the basis of distorted "constructions" of women.

The feminist endeavor is framed within the contours of an explicitly Islamic paradigm that incorporates the idea that gender justice can be achieved through the formulation of equality laws that reinstitute the ethical voice of "authentic" Islam. Feminists are fashioning a hermeneutics and interpretive framework from which legal rights that guarantee equality for women may be configured. To this end, the reform of Islamic law is imperative and seen as one of the principal means by which the inequality and injustice that women have endured through erroneous readings of the Qur'an and Sunna can be addressed. Thus, the medium of

law plays a pivotal role in the realization and implementation of the
contemporary feminist project.

GENDER AND THE NOTION OF EQUALITY

One of the most revolutionary aspects of the coming of Islam was the
way in which the new religion addressed the relation between the sexes
by instituting basic human rights for women as well as introducing the
notion of gender equality as an integral part of a just society.[30] References
to equality abound in the Qur'an.[31] The text contains verses that refer to
the equality between women and men and the fact that women and men
are created equal; that both were created from a single soul (*nafs wahi-
dah*);[32] and that such equality is applicable to both women and men in
terms of their life on earth and in the hereafter. The language employed
by the Qur'an in these verses is enormously important. In each verse of
this kind, the word "women" is used as well as the word "men." Therefore, these Qur'anic verses aver clearly to an explicit sense of equality
between the sexes. In terms of temporality, one sex was not created before the other, there is no hierarchy of the sexes with one sex superior to
the other, and one sex was not created from the other. There are multiple
verses in the Qur'an that demonstrate clearly that women and men have
been created for the mutual benefit of each other. The Qur'an teaches
"love and tenderness" (*Ar-Rum* 30:22) between women and men; that
men and women are like each other's garments (*Al-Baqarah* 2:188); that
"You are spiritually akin one to another" (*Al-'Imran* 3:195); and that "the
believers, men and women, are friends one of another" (*Al-Tawbah*
9:71).[33]

There are, undoubtedly, problematic verses in the Qur'an that, in a
literal interpretation, treat the sexes unequally and give priority to men
over women (*Al-Baqarah* 2:223, 229 and *An-Nisa* 4:4–5, 35). There is in the
classical tradition an interpretational orientation that marginalizes the
importance of context in the reading of the Qur'an. The emphasis has
been upon disregarding the coherence and unity of the Qur'anic text and,
instead, adopting "the practice of textual segmentalism . . . a verse-by-
verse, sura by sura, linear, segmental analysis."[34] This interpretive methodology has allowed jurists to disregard or relegate the contextual whole
of the Qur'an and the gender equality therein, in favor of this fragmented
approach. Furthermore, classical jurists' opinions on the interpretation of
such verses have been incorrectly conflated with the divine will, com-
pounding the problem by embedding an uncritical acceptance of this
juristic vision of gender roles. Contemporary theorists are highlighting
the vast majority of Qur'anic imperatives that contain a categoric assertion of equality and asserting that a holistic approach to the reading of

the Qur'an should be adopted rather than interpreting specific (and minority) verses in this atomistic manner.

The notion of equality is particularly pertinent in the area of family law because of the central role that the family plays in Muslim life; some of the greatest inequities against women exist in this area of law. The centrality of family law is also important as many of its rules and imperatives are linked with the status of women and their role in wider society. Women's dignity in public and private life is affected by inequality within the family; women's rights to movement in the public domain, their rights to property, to citizenship and nationality, their employment rights, their treatment under criminal laws, and their ability to participate fully in political life are all impinged upon and shaped by existing family laws.[35] As Islam clearly mandates justice, equality, human dignity, love, and compassion in all social interaction—including in the very basis of society in Islam, the family unit—the continued presence of such laws is antithetical to the very essence of Islam.

Many contemporary Muslim majority societies have implemented family laws that contain standards and principles developed by classical jurists (*fuqaha*) in social environments and in historical times that are very different from the societies of today. The *fuqaha* of the classical tradition incorporated the social, political, and cultural norms of their age and "a set of assumptions about law, society and gender that reflected the state of knowledge, normative values and patriarchal institutions of their time."[36] As such, the concept of gender equality in the form we understand it today simply did not exist and therefore was not incorporated by the *fuqaha* in the notions of justice that became established in the classical tradition. This fixity took place relatively early on as many of these ideas had become set as *Shari'a* precepts by medieval times. Thus, juristic thinking from these times disconnected the idea of justice from gender equality and became entrenched in the classical Islamic tradition.

Conceptions of justice began to change by the start of the twentieth century, and the idea that equality should be an integral component of justice began to circulate.[37] However, it was difficult for these innovative notions to establish themselves, given the power and longevity of the older constructions of justice and equality that were so strongly anchored in Islamic jurisprudence and the classical tradition. At this juncture, it is important to note a perspective that has critically affected the development of Islamic law in many Muslim majority societies. Colonialism has had a profound effect on the development of Muslim nations, and the area of law is one obvious dimension of colonial rule that has had the most lasting and damaging effect. This is because the colonial project was based firmly on depicting Muslims in an Orientalist fashion, and this took the form of representing Islam and its laws as fixed, unchanging, and also implacably opposed to women's rights. The depiction of women and their "construction" as passive victims of an overbearing masculinist

Islam was central to the success of the colonial project. The nationalist movements that arose to challenge colonial hegemony also used women as central figures in their call for the "restitution of Shari'a." In many cases, the anti-colonial movements perpetuated existing negative representations of women as well as perpetrating further misrepresentations and, in their calls for a return to *Shari'a*, denied women equal rights under the law.

The problem was particularly acute in family laws under colonial control. The older constructions of justice/equality were amended so that the classical juristic concepts, already limited in affording women substantive equality, were made even more harmful by being combined with regressive parts of colonial laws and the negative elements of local customs and practices.[38] These were then codified, and the legacy of their classical and colonial background is strong: such laws still exist in many postcolonial Muslim countries and are managed by executive and legislative bodies that often have a specific political or ideological bent. This adjustment in personnel has also engendered profound change: the development of laws and their control has transferred from classical jurists and religious scholars to government bodies that have maintained premodern interpretations of the *Shari'a*.[39] This situation poses particular problems for feminist groups proposing new interpretations of scripture upon which more progressive laws can be established in societies where governments themselves have sanctioned such laws.

CAMPAIGNING FOR GENDER EQUALITY: THE CONTRIBUTIONS OF ISLAMIC FEMINISM

The rapid "democratization" of religious knowledge and the fragmentation of religious authority we are witnessing in contemporary times has created a flourishing environment in which rising numbers of Muslims are participating in debates on "normative" Islam. Allied to this is an invigorating reappraisal of many of the foundational precepts of Islam and such notions as orthodoxy, authenticity, tradition, and progress.[40] Foremost among these is the urgent call to reevaluate the notion of gender justice and what the meaning of equality between the sexes is in modern times. The reform of laws that determine the nature and scope of rights for women in Muslim societies is one of the most direct means by which justice for women can be achieved. Musawah is an international group of scholars and activists theorizing and campaigning around the issue of gender equality in Islam.[41] They state that creating equality within the context of the family is possible through a holistic approach that brings together Islamic principles derived from the Qur'an and the Sunna, universal human rights norms, fundamental rights, and constitutional guarantees, and combines these with the contemporary experience and realities of women and men today.[42]

Islamic feminists are placing religion—and the norms, values and laws derived from religious precepts—at the very heart of their calls for the reconfiguration of women's rights in Islam.[43] They are concerned with the reform of the "internal" dynamics of Islamic law and its interpretation—that is, reform from within the Islamic epistemic and methodological framework. The development of Islamic feminism, defined by Margot Badran as "a feminist discourse and practice articulated within an Islamic paradigm,"[44] has gathered such momentum that it can be identified clearly as an international coalition of scholars and activists advancing new interpretations of scripture and tradition, and arguing for the adaptation and modification of Islamic precepts in line with the needs of women in contemporary societies. As mentioned above, such interpretations are based upon an understanding of Islam and *Shari'a* as shifting and contested rather than as fixed and static—the latter an all-too-common representation of both Islam and *Shari'a* throughout history. By perpetuating the notion that Islamic norms are fixed in patriarchal tradition, *Shari'a* standards have been characterized as immutable and dangerous for Muslim women.[45]

Islamic feminism offers a counterpoint to prevailing orthodoxies and an emancipatory agenda that incorporates revitalized interpretations of the sources of Islamic tradition in order to effect equal rights for women. This is the overriding objective of Islamic feminists. However, this body of thought is characterized by great diversity of opinion, and it is therefore more appropriate to talk about the multiplicity of Islamic *feminisms*—different schools of thought that can be distinguished along cultural, geographical, and (often significant) doctrinal lines. This diversity of feminist *ijtihad* ranges from the creation of new interpretive methodologies in scriptural exegesis to analyses that are more critical of the relationship between Islam and feminism. Nevertheless, many are challenging the hegemony of the orthodox interpretive processes of classical Islam and are offering a clearly defined agenda for reform that includes the significant reconfiguration of laws regulating gender relations.

The institution of new legal rights for women is viewed as one of the principal means by which gender discrimination in Islam can be addressed and remedied. Feminists are actively using the heterogeneity of Islamic law, and its potential to carry a variety of interpretations, to champion reconstituted legal rights for women. This project entails advancing new interpretations of the sources of Islamic law and theorizing a "feminist theology" with a "Qur'anic hermeneutics of liberation" at the vanguard of this endeavor. There is a rich body of work on such hermeneutical efforts. Writers such as Amina Wadud, Asma Barlas, and Fatima Mernissi have developed interpretations of the Qur'an and the Sunna that bring to light the gender egalitarian impulse they see as implicit in these religious sources. Their project entails challenging both accepted ideas of interpretive authority and traditional interpretations of scripture within the classical tradition.

Islamic feminism is located within the broader reformist and progressive movement. Indeed, Omid Safi contends that "there can be no progressive interpretation of Islam without gender justice" and that the success of the larger progressive movement depends fundamentally on the degree of change that can be achieved in the area of gender justice.[46] Women's rights are an important dimension of progressive thought because they are seen as a gauge for determining the broader issue of justice and pluralism in Muslim majority societies.[47]

The progressive movement stresses the importance of epistemological and methodological pluralism in interpretation, of critical thinking and the need to maintain the division between religion (which may be divinely ordained—that is, the Qur'an as a source of *Shari'a*) and religious knowledge (such as *fiqh* literature, which is humanly constructed). As Duderija asserts, "Knowledge of the tradition is not to be confused with the tradition itself."[48] The accent on the "constructedness" of much of the Islamic tradition also highlights the centrality of human agency in reading and interpreting such texts. Implicit in this is the recognition that interpretation is a dynamic process that results in a diversity of opinions. This multiplicity of opinion, *ikhtilaf*, humanly created, is well rooted in the legal tradition. Indeed, its importance in the legal corpus can be seen in the very existence of the multiple schools of jurisprudence—each school can hold very different opinions from the others on any given subject. *Ikhtilaf* has been immensely useful, as it has allowed for the reform of legal rules and directives for the benefit of society throughout the history of the Islamic tradition.

Methodologically, progressive scholars claim that *ikhtilaf* can be used to produce a range of views on an issue and, utilizing the concept of the welfare of the public or public interest (*maslaha*), a variety of determinations can be made for the benefit of society. The welfare of the public should be paramount as a guiding principle as well as a hermeneutic tool in formulating law. *Maslaha* should be combined with the notion of *maqasid* or the purposefulness of law. Once this is taken into account, the purpose or aim of any reading of scripture should be to facilitate and implement the principle of the general welfare of society. In his analysis of *maslaha*, Khaled Abou El Fadl considers whether an ethical norm could serve as the basis of a binding obligation in the Islamic legal order. He focuses on the constituent moral elements of *maslaha* and argues that these unequivocally include the imperatives of justice and righteousness.[49] Farid Esack supplements this argument by adding that the objective of Islamic law is to realize and implement dignity and justice in Muslim life. If there are laws instituted that do not fulfill this obligation, they are open to amendment or repeal.[50]

In this way, *maslaha* is acknowledged as the leading hermeneutical rule and all manifestations of law should be scrutinized so that they are in compliance with the obligation of justice. Contemporary progressive scholars criticize the classical tradition for underutilizing *maslaha*. They also claim that, historically, the tradition has not adequately integrated *maqasid*, the purposefulness of Islamic law, and the objectives of justice and equality. The application of this hermeneutic can be seen in the reading of Qur'anic verses 4.35 and 2.229, which have been interpreted in the classical tradition in a way that has instituted a gender hierarchy with men as "superior" to women and possessing the right of "protectorship" over women.

As the above discussion indicates, much contemporary feminist work is being conducted in the field of Qur'anic exegesis.[51] In his analysis of contemporary readings of the Qur'an, Chandra Muzzafar points out that our understanding of this text is limited as the *ulama* have utilized a selective rather than a holistic interpretive approach, which has "resulted in an obsession with superficialities . . . an injustice to God's revelation."[52] He proposes that readings of the Qur'an should focus on justice and compassion as the guiding principles of the text and directs our attention to the concept of *tawhid*, the Oneness and unity of Allah. This principle is the most fundamental tenet in Islam and the primary article of faith and, as both belief and concept, is closely linked with the pursuit of justice in the life of the believer. The unity of Allah is also linked to the unity of humankind and the recognition that this unity is only achievable when there is communal justice. As Muzaffar declares, "It is only by striving for justice that *Tawhid*, a spiritual idea, can be transformed into *Tawhid*, a living social reality."[53]

In campaigning for gender equality, Musawah also emphasizes the unity of humankind as the key Islamic principle that affirms that all humans are born equal in worth and dignity. Regardless of gender, they are all entitled to exercise "equal rights to political participation and leadership, equal access to economic resources, equality before the law, and equal autonomy in the economic, social, cultural and political spheres."[54] All humans, as agents of Allah, are entrusted with the task of carrying out Divine will, and this set of duties and responsibilities is not defined in gendered terms. It is incumbent upon all Muslims to contribute to the formulation of laws, policies, and practices in order to realize justice and equality within their families, communities, and societies.[55]

Progressive scholars such as the late Abu Zayd also assert that, viewing the Qur'an in a holistic sense, it is clear that it holds justice as an overriding principle. This imperative of justice should be used as the most hermeneutically privileged tool,[56] and any verses in the Qur'an that appear to be discriminatory against women should be read in the light of this guiding principle. If this approach is adopted, then discriminatory verses are said to have limited application to times in Islamic history when societal norms dictated that women were dependent upon men. Furthermore, feminists challenge the notion that is embedded in the classical tradition that the "superiority" of men and their duty of "protectorship" are innate, normative, and universal. Feminists such as Asma Barlas[57] suggest that these views, which are socially contingent, have been perpetuated throughout history and have had the effect of entrenching essentialized views of men and women. These views have been enormously detrimental to women. Like other feminist scholars, Barlas also underlines the concept of *tawhid* in her Qur'anic exegesis and stresses the internal coherence and textual unity of the Qur'an.[58] There are certain ethical guiding principles contained in the Qur'an such as justice, the dignity and equality of all humans, and mercy and compassion, which operate as primary and essential rules of interpretation. These principles are closely linked, and all emanate from the notion of the unity of God, which is all-pervasive and infuses the entire outlook of the Qur'an.

There is a dialectical relationship between the past and the present in feminist and progressive work and an emphasis upon the "historicity" of the Qur'an. This is an obviously contextual approach that highlights the socio-historical nature of the text. Barlas posits that we must read the Qur'an in the light of the historical context in which it was revealed and, in a movement of recontextualization, interpret the text in the light of the present and the changed social circumstances of this time.[59] Such an approach takes into account and accommodates changing norms on gender and sexuality. It also challenges the understanding of the tradition as fixed and unchanging and demonstrates the multiplicity of interpretations that can exist. It allows the interpreter to distinguish between those verses that should have universal and timeless application and those that should be restricted to their socio-historical context.

CONCLUSION

The concept of justice in the Islamic tradition has been limited by its omission of a substantive notion of gender equality. In the words of Azizah Al-Hibri, the central belief for feminist Muslims is that "there is no metaphysical, ontological, religious, or ethical primacy for the male over the female."[60] The feminist endeavor offers "a hermeneutics of liberation," a framework for advancing notions of gender justice and equality that challenge both classical and contemporary depictions of women and regressive notions of gender relations. In their evaluation of the sources of Islamic law, feminists conclude that the corpus of legal rulings on the relations between the sexes and gendered rights in the tradition is humanly constructed and, as such, the result of many past communities of interpretation. The legal tradition, therefore, is the repository of a great diversity of opinion and is dynamic, vibrant, and ever-changing. In advancing the notion of the utilitarian notion of the welfare of the public and the recognition of the diversity of opinion that subsists in the tradition, feminists are advancing a hermeneutics located firmly within an Islamic epistemological framework.

The new interpretations of scripture offer great scope for the reform of discriminatory laws in the Muslim world, and there is a pressing need for legislators and those wielding political power to take these interpretations into serious consideration when formulating laws. It is a great misfortune that such proposals are often dismissed by those in political leadership. Such reform will help realize the full potential of women in these societies as autonomous human beings, of equal dignity and worth with men, who are able to enjoy the rights and entitlements due to them within ethically correct interpretations of the Islamic tradition. Thus, it is incumbent upon every Muslim—male and female—to engage in *ijtihad* and to challenge incorrect readings of scripture, to strive for justice, fairness, and equality, and to ensure that the true ideals of Islam are realized.

NOTES

1. The version of the Qur'an used in this essay is Muhammad Zafrulla Khan's *The Qur'an* (London: Curzon Press, 1981). The verse quoted here is from *Qur'an*, 4:136.
2. Qur'an 5:9.
3. Chandra Muzzafar, *Rights, Religion and Reform* (London: Routledge, 2002), 173.
4. *Qur'an*, 4:59.
5. *Qur'an*, 6:153.
6. Muzaffar, *Rights, Religion and Reform*, 173.
7. Shabbir Akhtar, *Islam as Political Religion* (New York: Routledge, 2011), 126.
8. Human beings are viewed as vice-regents of God on earth and the upholding of justice is one of the preeminent duties of the believer; see Muzaffar, *Rights, Religion and Reform*, 175.
9. For analyses of justice in Islam, see Majid Khadduri, *The Islamic Conception of Justice* (Baltimore: John Hopkins University Press, 1984); Lawrence Rosen, *The Justice of Islam: Comparative Perspectives on Islamic Law and Society* (New York: Oxford University Press, 1999); Lawrence Rosen, *The Anthropology of Justice: Law as Culture in Islamic Society* (Cambridge: Cambridge University Press, 1989); R. S. Khare (ed.), *Perspectives on Islamic Law, Justice and Society* (Lanham, MD: Rowman and Littlefield, 1999); Gudrun Kramer, "Justice in Modern Islamic Thought," in *Shari'a Islamic Law in the Contemporary Context*, ed. Abaas Amanat and Frank Griffel (Stanford, CA: Stanford University Press, 2007); Nimet Barazangi et al., *Islamic Identity and the Struggle for Justice* (Gainesville: University of Florida Press, 1996); Nasim Hasan Shah, *Law, Justice and Islam* (Lahore: Wajidalis, 1989); and A. Smirnov, "Understanding Justice in an Islamic Context: Some Points of Contrast with Western Theories Philosophy," *East and West* 46, no. 3 (July 1996): 337–50.
10. Kramer, "Justice in Modern Islamic Thought," 24.
11. Mahmoud Ayoub, "The Islamic Concept of Justice," in *Islamic Identity and the Struggle for Justice*, ed. Nimet Barazangi et al. (Gainesville: University of Florida Press, 1996), 23.
12. The Mu'tazili is a school of Islamic philosophical thought that was formulated primarily in the cities of Basra and Baghdad (of what is now modern Iraq) between the eighth and tenth centuries CE. Mu'tazili thought attempts to synthesize reason and revelation in the belief that it is human intellect that directs a person to know God, His

attributes, and the boundaries of moral behavior. Thus, the commands of God are accessible to rational thought and inquiry as knowledge is drawn from reason. It is reason that allows us to determine what is just.

13. Khadduri, *The Islamic Conception of Justice,* 9

14. Ayoub, "The Islamic Concept of Justice," 20.

15. Ibid., 22.

16. Musawah, *Framework for Action* (Selangor: Sisters in Islam, 2007), 5. For the organization "Musawah: Equality in the Muslim Family," visit http://www.musawah.org/about-musawah/framework-action.

17. See, generally, Wael Hallaq, *A History of Islamic Legal Theories* (Cambridge: Cambridge University Press, 1999) for the historical development of constituent elements of *Shari'a.*

18. For completeness, we should also mention *qanun*, or state law.

19. Yvonne Yazbeck Haddad (ed.), "Introduction," in *Islamic Law and the Challenges of Modernity*, ed. Yvonne Yazbeck Haddad and Barbara Freyer Stowasser (Walnut Creek, CA: AltaMira Press, 2004), 4.

20. Ibid., 4.

21. My focus is on Sunni Islam, which is divided into four *madhab*: Hanafites (after Abu Hanifa), Malikites (after Malik *b.* Anas), Shafi'ites (after al-Shafi'tes), and Hanbalites (after Ibn Hanbal).

22. The abbreviation "AH" stands for "After Hijra," which refers to the migration of the Prophet Muhammad to Medina in the twelfth century CE.

23. See, for instance, Margot Badran, *Feminism and Conversion: Comparing British, Dutch and South African Life Stories* in Karin van Nieuwerk (ed.), *Women and Islam* (Austin: University of Texas Press, 2006), 205; Ziba Mir-Hosseini, "Gender Equality and Islamic Law," in *New Directions in Islamic Thought*, ed. Kari Vogt, Lean Larsen and Christian Moe (London: I. B. Taurus, 2009).

24. Omaima Abou Bakr, "Teaching the Words of the Prophet: Women Instructors of the Hadith (Fourteenth and Fifteenth Centuries)," *Hawwa* 1, no. 3 (2003): 306–28.

25. Leila Ahmed, *Women and Gender in Islam* (New Haven, CT: Yale University Press, 1992), 88.

26. Ibid., 63–67.

27. See also new interpretations of the Sunna.

28. Adis Duderija, *Constructing a Religiously Ideal "Believer" and "Woman" in Islam* (New York: Palgrave Macmillan, 2011), 5.

29. For an account of how women are constructed in this way, see Khalid Abou El Fadl, *Speaking in God's Name* (Oxford: Oneworld, 2001), 245.

30. See Mir-Hosseini, "Gender Equality and Islamic Law," 108. For an analysis of gender equality in Islam, see Ahmed Souaiaia, *Contesting Justice: Women, Islam, Law and Society* (Albany: State University of New York Press, 2008); Mohammad Hashim Kamali, *Freedom, Equality and Justice in Islam* (Cambridge: Islamic Texts Society, 2002); and Zainah Anwar (ed.), *Wanted: Equality and Justice in the Muslim Family* (Selangor: Musawah, 2009).

31. See, for instance, 2:229; 3:195; 4:12–13; 4:33; 4:35; 4:58; 16:98; 33:59; 49:14.

32. *Sura an-Nisa* 4:2.

33. For a summary of key Qur'anic verses, see Musawah, *Framework for Action,* 9.

34. Adis Duderija, "The Interpretational Implications of Progressive Muslims Qur'an and Sunna Manhaj in Relation to Their Formulation of a Normative Muslima Construct," *Islam and Christian-Muslim Relations* 19, no. 4 (2008): 415.

35. Musawah, *Framework for Action,* 4.

36. Ibid., 3.

37. For an overview of the relationship between justice and equality, see Mohammad Hashim Kamali, *Freedom, Equality and Justice in Islam* (Cambridge: The Islamic Texts Society, 2002).

38. However, in some cases, such as India, the indigenous personal laws (which included family law) were not substantively altered by colonial administrators in any significant form.

39. Musawah, *Framework for Action*, 4.

40. Duderija, *Constructing a Religiously Ideal "Believer"*, xi.

41. Musawah's *Framework for Action* provides a conceptual framework for equality and justice in the Muslim family. Musawah declares that equality in the family is necessary because many aspects of our current Muslim family laws and practices are unjust and do not respond to the lives and experiences of Muslim families and individuals. The framework has been developed by a group of Muslim activists and scholars who have come together to initiate Musawah. The core group, coordinated by Sisters in Islam (Malaysia), comprises a twelve-member planning committee of Muslim activists and academics from eleven countries. The framework was conceptualized and written through a series of meetings and discussions with Islamic scholars, academics, activists, and legal practitioners from approximately thirty countries.

42. Musawah, *Framework for Action*, 2.

43. There is a growing body of feminist literature exploring women's rights in Islam, and the manner in which this work is challenging restrictive, traditional notions of gendered rights. For an overview, see Qudsia Mirza, "Islamic Feminism: Possibilities and Limitations," in *Law After Ground Zero*, ed. John Strawson (London: Cavendish, 2002).

44. Margot Badran, "Islamic Feminism: What's In a Name?" *Al-Ahram Weekly Online* 569 (January 17–23, 2002), http://weekly.ahram.org.eg/.

45. Natasha Bakht, "Were Muslim Barbarians Really Knocking on the Gates of Ontario? The Religious Arbitration Controversy—Another Perspective," *Ottawa Law Review* (Summer 2005): 67–82. The article is available online at http://papers.ssrn.com/sol3/papers.cfm?abstract_id=1121790.

46. Omid Safi, "What Is Progressive Islam?" *ISIM Newsletter* 13 (December 2003): 48.

47. Duderija, *Constructing a Religiously Ideal "Believer"*, 120.

48. Ibid., 131.

49. Khaled Abou El Fadl, "The Place of Ethical Obligations in Islamic Law," *Journal of Islamic and Near Eastern Law* 1 (2005): 31–32.

50. Farid Esack, "Islam and Gender Justice," in *What Men Owe to Women: Men's Voices from World Religions*, ed. John C. Raines and Daniel C. Maguire (Albany: State University of New York Press, 2001), 187. For a good summary of the arguments put forward by El Fadl and Esack, see Duderija, *Constructing a Religiously Ideal "Believer"*, 51–152.

51. See, for instance, Amina Wadud, *Qur'an and Woman* (New York: Oxford University Press, 1999), Asma Barlas, *"Believing Women" in Islam* (Austin: University of Texas Press, 2002); and Amina Wadud, *Inside the Gender Jihad* (Oxford: Oneworld, 2006).

52. Muzzafar, *Rights, Religion, and Reform*, 177.

53. Ibid., 180.

54. Musawah, *Framework for Action*, 10.

55. Ibid.

56. Nasr Hamid Abu Zayd, "The Nexus of Theory and Practice," in *The New Voices of Islam: Rethinking Politics and Modernity, A Reader*, ed. M. Kamvara (Berkeley: University of California Press, 2006), 153–76.

57. See also Asma Barlas, "Muslim Women and Sexual Oppression: Reading Liberation from the Quran," *Macalester International* 10 (2001): 117–46; Asma Barlas, "The Qur'an and Hermeneutics: Reading the Qur'an's Opposition to Patriarchy," *Journal of Qur'anic Studies* 3, no. 2 (2000): 15–38; and Asma Barlas, "Texts, Sex, and States: A Critique of North African Discourse on Islam," in *The Arab-African and Islamic Worlds: Interdisciplinary Studies*, ed. Kevin Lacey and Ralph Coury (London: Peter Lang, 2000).

58. Barlas, *"Believing Women" in Islam*, 13.

59. Ibid., 22–23.

60. Azizah Al-Hibri, "Islamic Jurisprudence and Critical Race Feminism," in *Global Critical Race Feminism*, ed. Adrien Wing (New York: New York University Press, 2000), 53.

ELEVEN

Transgender Spirituality

Finding Justice through Activism and Love

Gordene MacKenzie and Nancy Nangeroni

> The Transgender Spirit transcends the simplistic cultural dictum that anatomical sex is synonymous with gender expression. . . . It is a rainbow that is far too splendorous in its diversity. The expression of one's whole gender must be intuitive, fluid, and in a perpetual state of becoming. There can be no rules to govern how Spirit must manifest. [1]

Gender is at the root of what makes lesbian, gay, bisexual, transgender, and queer (LGBTQ) people "different," whether by their own gender identity or expression or by the gender of those they love. It is also at the root of our historic and present-day persecution by religions that have excluded, denigrated, and in extreme cases advocated violence against our spirit and our flesh. In the face of such persecution LGBTQ persons have shepherded a spirituality that transcends conventional "norms" for gender roles while holding sacred the love of justice, community, and family.

It is beyond the scope of this chapter to address lesbian and gay spirituality. We instead focus on a re-envisioning of diverse gender expression and identity as both activism and a spiritually holistic practice. We believe that divinity exists within each and every one of us, so that acceptance and promotion of diversity and justice are necessary elements of any holistic spiritual practice. We will attempt to make connections between the liberation of gender and the recognition of the sacred nature of all life. We also explore the complex and changing relationship between some mainstream U.S. Christian religions, as well as modern paganism, and transgender persons.

Stories, which for LGBTQ persons frequently include coming-out stories and documentation of discrimination, have the power to heal and help create change. In the spirit of the "personal is political,"[2] we share some of our own stories to establish a context for these writings, as well as stories and thoughts of others, to give shape to the transgender portion of the gender movement that we have been privileged to witness during our lifetimes.

In a binary gender system, where only one of two options (male or female, masculine or feminine) are sanctioned by the wider culture, the expression of complex truths of gender identity and sexual orientation has been and continues to be a cause for persecution. We see the consequences of the historical harm when, in much of the world, people of diverse gender have been prevented from expressing their true gender by threats and violence of the most brutal nature. Reports issued by the ACLU, Human Rights Watch, and those gathering statistics for the annual international Transgender Day of Remembrance confirm that discrimination and gender violence is epidemic and in some areas may even be on the rise.[3]

The struggle for gender liberation and justice, born out of this continuing persecution, has a long history. For example, transgender activist Leslie Feinberg documents that during the Catholic Inquisition, Joan of Arc, the leader of the successful French peasants' rebellion against England, was tried for witchcraft, blasphemy against the Church, and paganism. In 1431, the Inquisition dropped the charge of witchcraft and "denounced Joan for asserting that her cross-dressing was a religious duty compelled by voices she heard in visions and for maintaining that these voices were a higher authority than the Church."[4] Joan of Arc's peasant followers considered both her and her cross-dressed clothing sacred.[5] She was told that if she adopted female clothing in prison, her life would be spared. After a failed attempt at wearing women's clothing and unable to submit to the Church's authority, the nineteen-year-old Joan stated, "For nothing in the world . . . will I swear not to arm myself and put on a man's dress."[6] Joan of Arc was burned at the stake in 1431. When she was presumed dead, the flames were extinguished and the hot ashes were scraped away by the witch hunters, who publicly exposed her naked, cremated body in order to prove that she was a "woman."

In the "new world," colonizing missionaries, seeking to conquer and convert First Nation people to Christianity, unleashed dogs to tear to pieces two-spirit persons, whom they referred to as "sinful sodomites." In some (though not all) of the First Nations in North America, two-spirit persons[7] occupied varying institutionalized spiritual roles, such as naming children and acting as a mediators to the divine and between the sexes and genders.[8]

In the United States during the 1990s, the struggle for social justice and human rights for transgender persons began to publicly challenge the mistreatment of and violence against transpeople who were stigmatized because their gender was different. During this decade public struggles in the realm of spirituality also emerged as transgender activists began the fight for inclusion in mainstream churches. They began re-creating and reclaiming a transgender spirituality.

The witch hunting of transgender bodies continues today as major social institutions, including mainstream U.S. religions, law, and mass media, publicly rebuke, misname, or deny transpersons civil and human rights. Thankfully, change is also happening as transgender activists and advocates work for equality and justice.

We have been and are privileged to participate in the transgender liberation movement that is built on the women's liberation movement, the gay and lesbian liberation movement, and the civil rights movement. Nancy published the first nationally distributed transgender activist newsletter,[9] and Gordene founded and facilitated the first transgender and transsexual support group and hotline in Albuquerque, New Mexico, in the mid-1980s through the early 1990s, and also authored *Transgender Nation* in 1994.[10] Together, we produced and hosted GenderTalk radio from 1999 to 2006 and GenderVision,[11] a cable TV program designed to educate people on transgender issues, from 2007 to 2008. At the time of this writing, Nancy serves as the chair of the Massachusetts Transgender Political Coalition (MTPC), and Gordene is an educator who teaches about and advocates for transgender rights. Our activism has taken us to the statehouse, the streets, into the transgender spiritual movement and into mainstream churches fighting for equality and justice. Our work is a fulfillment of our spiritual commitment to creating change.

OUR PERSONAL STORIES: GORDENE

My spirituality cannot be separated from my activism. Participating in social and global human rights work for transgender persons connects me with the spirit of justice and love. This activist work renews my spirit.

Losing My Religion

Like so many others of my era, I was terrorized by a rigid patriarchal and hierarchical religion. As a second grader in a small parochial school in Albuquerque, New Mexico, I was told by my teacher that if you were not a baptized Catholic, you would burn in hell forever. This statement sent shock waves throughout my body. I worried that my father, a follower of Ernest Holme's *Science of the Mind*, would burn in hell for eternity. My days and nights were haunted by images of my father on fire, unable to escape the bounds of hell. Worried I could not save him and fearful of ending up in hell myself, I obsessively thought about souls. Every day I saw yellow and magenta souls teetering between limbo and hell, burning, screaming, and suffering.

In fourth grade I lost my faith in the cruel, hierarchical Catholicism to which I had been exposed to in the late 1950s and early 1960s. Back then, one had to fast to receive communion. One fall day the whole school attended a funeral mass for a classmate's younger sister. The mass started at 1:00 pm; I had not eaten all day. During communion I hungrily took the host in my mouth, wanting to bite it but worried that if I did, I would be cast into hell. Returning from communion, I felt dizzy, as if I was going to pass out. My knees shook while bright lights and stars danced before my eyes. When I raised my head I saw Jesus Christ walking off the cross on the altar. He carried his bleeding sacred heart. Shoving it toward me, he screamed, "Eat the sacred heart." The nuns lifted me up by my elbows. The entire church had cleared but I had not noticed it. They mistakenly thought I had had a holy vision. My "reward" was to spend the rest of the day in the library reading about the lives of Christian martyrs and saints. Terrified by the violent vision, I refused to enter the church. When my parents dropped me off at church on Sunday, I did not go in but instead sat on the wall outside of the church, watching nature and listening to the birds until mass was over.

Finding My Spirituality in Gender Liberation

To me, the complexity of gender has always been a path to the divine. At age five, I chopped off my braids, handing them to my horrified mother. My freed atoms danced ecstatic. I peeled off the cultural skin of girl, trading it for boyhood as I pulled on a pair of gray corduroy jeans and a plaid shirt. Momentarily liberated, I luxuriated in the warm southwest sun free of the shackles of what "girl" meant in the late 1950s and 1960s in middle-class white America. I chanted over and over at the top of my lungs, "I'm a boy, I'm a boy," as I made the swing go higher and higher. I was kissing the clouds. In high school I frequently went by the name of Joshua Van Gogh, the name I chose to represent the femme male spirit animating me. As Joshua, I felt at one with the divine, which for me was the natural world, particularly mountains, gold sandstone bluffs, magical cottonwood trees down by the river, and every kind of creature. Joshua gave me courage and voice.

Over the years I have explored many alternative spiritual beliefs and practices. In the late 1970s, which was a time of spiritual awakening and searching in the United States, I co-founded Tekhma'at, a federally recognized earth-based religion that denounced hierarchies, embraced diversity, and emphasized the development of our natural abilities for healing ourselves and the natural environment. In graduate school, still feeling the stirrings of a complex gender, my attention focused on its cultural meanings. I challenged the medical definitions, the dominant discourse on transsexuals at the time. Privately I wondered if I was transsexual, as I often felt more male than female. I asked friends, most of them male, if they thought I looked more male than female. Knowing nothing of my internal struggle, they told me how feminine I appeared. This did little to quiet my inner spiritual struggle. I wondered if I should have surgery. I researched transgender issues and activism for my doctorate.[12] When I conducted my first research interview with a feminist transwoman, she told me I had a very "male soul." As mentioned earlier, I co-founded and co-facilitated the first cross-dresser and transsexual support group and operated the first transgender hotline in the mid-1980s in Albuquerque, New Mexico.

My gender journey is still complex. When I discovered the transgender community, it felt like coming home. At transgender conferences in the early 1990s, I became aware of a profound spiritual energy that is released when gender is liberated. This sense was confirmed for me at a conference in the southwest when I met Yvonne Cooke-Riley, a transgender activist and spiritual leader. Yvonne managed the International Foundation for Gender Education's book display. As I passed by, I heard her speak without sounding the words: "Let me know if you can hear me?" I responded psychically that I did. She heard me.

OUR PERSONAL STORIES: NANCY

To me, spirituality is a search not for meaning or some higher force in which to believe, but rather a search for a better understanding of the nature of reality, drawing upon science as well as the teachings of wise women and men, both contemporary and historical.

Catholicism, the religion I was steeped in, taught that a male deity wields absolute power over everything, with priests the exclusive interpreters of God's wishes. But what was to stop a priest from lying about God's wishes for his own gain? Organized religion presented too much opportunity for exploitation, even if it also provided avenues for good works.

I tried praying. I asked God to make me a girl. Later I asked God to rid me of the desire to be one. But my prayers went unanswered, and I saw no religious benefit in the life of my family. As I transitioned from the ignorance of childhood into a disillusioned adolescence, I lost all fear of eternal damnation. I refused to take the "leap of faith" required to believe in Catholicism. I entered adulthood a skeptic.

Then a series of setbacks left me reeling. I failed at every serious relationship attempt. My career choice proved a lot less fulfilling than I had hoped, and I could not make sense of my transgender compulsion. I enjoyed my indulgences in femininity, but they left me feeling ashamed and grew into self-hatred. I hungered for relief, even if that relief were to come from a tragic ending. Doubting any afterlife, I figured that death more likely led to dissipation of life force, molecules joining with the universe in chaos devoid of self-awareness, perhaps reconstituting into a force again, but a different force, a different consciousness. Death meant a quiet ending. So I lost my fear of death, and even invited death to take its best shot at me, as I rode recklessly on my motorcycle.

Inevitably, I crashed. Yet, instead of dying, I was rescued from the roadside and nursed back to life. The loving care, unasked-for help, and generous indulgence of strangers made a profound impression on me. My desperate, lonely life was displaced by gratitude for the kindness I was receiving. I began to develop faith in the basic goodness of people. This faith, energizing my recovery from my injuries, became the foundation of my transgender activism. While recovering, I gradually realized that I could no longer afford to avoid or deny my transgender nature. To do so would be to risk another disaster. So I finally rejected for all time the words of my mother, who confronted me at about age fifteen, telling me, "You know what transvestites are, right? They're perverts." These words were just more of the spiritual poison that had been holding me crippled for too many years.

I decided to choose as friends only those with whom I could be forthcoming about my gender dilemma and who would accept me as I am. Still, it took me years to come out as transgender and join the "gender" community. When I finally did, I found within that community a fountain of acceptance and helpful wisdom. With such help, I began to see my gender expression and identity less as a matter of social norms than as a matter of personal integrity. This changed perspective made it more important to be true to myself than to avoid harassment or, worse, to pretend to be "normal." Fearless I was not, but denial and hiding had nearly killed me. I envisioned creating a space in our culture for mobility across the gender divide, to enable those who cross over to carry with them the seeds for more equitable social systems.

As I learned more about other people like me, I learned that authorities had long tacitly approved violence against transgender persons, whether as a means for thinning the herd of so-called deviants and perverts, or simply as an unfortunate circumstance that affected only those about whom few really cared. Investigations of violence and murder against transgender persons were skipped or at best cursory, and perpetrators remained unchecked. The prevailing attitude towards trans victims was often "they got what they deserved."

In 1994, I began connecting with other trans-identified folks who felt the need to do more, including other transsexuals who, like me, had been forced out of the closet by our gender transitions. Together, we turned our limited resources against the forces of violent gender oppression. In 1995, I publicly committed myself to contesting injustice against transgender people on a national basis. I helped lead demonstrations, including one in Falls City, Nebraska, at the trial of one of the murderers of a young transman, Brandon Teena, as well as in places like Colorado Springs, Chicago, Washington, DC, and elsewhere. I began doing a weekly radio program out of MIT, "GenderTalk," promoting a progressive view of gender. In my hometown of Cambridge, Massachusetts, I led the fight against the racist and transphobic defense in court and in the newspapers of the murderer of transwoman Chanelle Pickett.

In late 1998, I led a candlelight vigil in Allston, Massachusetts, for murdered transwoman Rita Hester, and then fought against transphobic media coverage of her death. The story caught brief national attention, inspiring what has become the annual International Transgender Day of Remembrance. Intended as a reminder of the violence and discrimination routinely perpetrated against transgender people, this day also serves as an expression of community. Participants include both those who identify as transgender or queer and those who identify as allies, recognizing our common humanity and interest in ending gender-related violence.

SPREADING GOSPELS OF HATE AND FEAR

Sadly, there are people who actively spread a gospel of hate and teach people to fear diversity and difference. Right-wing Christian groups in the United States commonly use biology to condemn transgender people as "unnatural." They create hate for gender difference. From the pulpit to the courtroom and beyond, the word "natural" is deployed to denigrate gender-diverse people, branding them as malignant, a "problematic assumption . . . used to oppress groups of marginalized people."[13] When we observe nature without prejudice, it is not as simple as previously thought. Progressive researchers in the sciences, such as biologist Bruce Bagemihl, counter false claims of what is "natural" in the animal world by providing numerous examples of sex and gender diversity throughout nature.[14] Bagemihl notes that because of homophobia, the majority of scientists, who often identified with the species they studied, omitted mention of the sex and gender diversity that they observed in animals.

Bagemihl estimates 40 percent of animal species exhibit some amount of same-sex courtship behavior and/or pair bonding and/or gender diversity. For example, shrimp, oysters, and at least fifty different types of coral reef fish either completely reverse their sex and mating or are gender fluid, going back and forth between sexes and genders. He observes, "When animals do something we like, we call it natural. When they do something we don't like, we call it animalistic."[15]

The Christian Right's disdain for gender diversity is captured in Focus on the Family's assertion that "transgenderism violates God's intentional design for sex and sexuality, we believe that this is a cultural and theological battle that we must engage and win."[16] The extreme Christian and political right takes this battle seriously. They believe they are on a divine mission to initiate discriminatory legislation and to prevent progressive civil rights legislation for transgender people. Tennessee legislator Richard Floyd, who has repeatedly introduced legislation to deny transgender persons gender-based access to bathrooms, when asked by a reporter what would happen if he came across a transwoman preparing to go into a women's dressing room, responded that he would "stomp a mudhole in him and stomp him dry. Don't ask me to adjust to their perverted way . . . and put my family at risk."[17] When Mitt Romney was governor of Massachusetts he nearly disbanded the governor's commission on Gay and Lesbian Youth because a press release that included his name was "on the same page as the word 'transgender.' He was not happy. He was going to shut down the Commission."[18] Biomedical ethicist Alice Dreger sees evidence of this cultural war in dangerous fetal engineering experiments whose goal is to eradicate diversity in the womb.[19]

An effort to pass legislation intended to end the rampant discrimination and hate crimes against transpersons in Massachusetts was staunchly opposed by two organizations, MassResistance and the Massachusetts Family Institute, the latter funded by the Christian Coalition. These organizations adopted tactics used in other states, labeling the bill as the "Bathroom Bill," a moniker so effective it was widely repeated by local news outlets. In November 2011, the Transgender Equal Rights bill was passed in Massachusetts, but an important provision—nondiscrimination in public accommodations (which includes everything from outdoor space, public restrooms, and locker rooms to service in a restaurant)—was omitted over Christian Right–fed fear of gender insecurity in bathrooms and locker rooms. Christian Right opponents claimed, without evidence, that protecting the right of male-to-female transgender individuals, including those who do not enjoy "passing privilege" (i.e., whose male origin is incompletely erased), to use women's bathrooms and locker rooms would "put vulnerable women and children at risk."[20] Despite supportive testimony by leading women's advocacy organizations, including the National Organization of Women (NOW) and Jane Doe, this argument prevailed.

Kent Monkman, a Cree artist and activist, uses art to challenge Christian Eurocentric attacks on gender diversity through his art. His monumental installation "Theatre de Cristal," a fourteen-foot crystal-beaded tipi with a cross-shaped floor screen, projects a video of his two-spirit persona, Miss Chief Eagle Testicle, who appears in much of his art. Theatre de Cristal references the mirrored palace in which a Native Iowa dance troupe performed in 1845 for King Phillipe of France. The troupe was brought there by George Caitlin, an American painter who romanticized and painted Native Americans but "thought that two-spirits[21] were a 'disgraceful degradation.'"[22] On another level the crystal tipi (intentionally or not) references and critiques the homophobic Crystal Cathedral mega-church. In 2011, the pastor of the Crystal Cathedral declared that people wanting to remain in the choir had to sign a covenant stating that God intends sex to take place only in marriage between a woman and a man.[23] The Catholic Church, which bought the bankrupt Crystal Cathedral, projects that it will become the most significant Catholic Center after the Vatican![24]

CHRISTIAN TRANSGENDER SPIRITUALITY

There have always been people whose gender differs from a limited western hierarchical gender and sex binary. Many struggle to find spiritual accommodation for their place in the world. Contemporary transgender activists must challenge deeply entrenched prejudices to find a place of respect within mainstream Christianity in the United States. However, a small minority of transgender persons is welcomed as legitimate members of their churches. For example, transgender author and activist Joanne Herman acknowledges that "many LGBT people have been hurt by religion used in hate."[25] She recalls, "I have always felt welcomed at Old South Church in Boston (United Church of Christ) as a transgender person, and I feel proud to be part of a congregation that does Christianity right."[26] Based on a proposal submitted by Joanne, the board of deacons at the Old South Church voted in 2008 to include "gender identity and gender expression" in their document titled "The Inclusive Dimension of God's Grace."[27]

Yet not all feel welcomed by their congregation. Marcia and Ken Garber, parents of a beloved transgender son, CJ, who died of an overdose, were treated unkindly when members of their Catholic parish learned that their son was transgender. They are now tireless activists who have been instrumental in helping pass transgender equal rights legislation in Massachusetts. After CJ's tragic death the Garbers left their transphobic parish and found a parish more accepting of diversity. They also work with Dignity, a Catholic LGBT advocacy group.

Some transgender activists like Virginia Ramey Mollenkott feel a spiritual commitment to do transgender justice work within the institutional Christian church. For her, this work means getting Christian churches "used to dealing with us."[28] Mollenkott grew up in a right-wing fundamentalist Protestant church that made her think that God was disgusted by her. She laments that religious fundamentalism often tends to "shrink God into a more 'manageable,' anthropomorphized, and always male-oriented perspective."[29] She believes that so-called literal Bible interpretations are used to promulgate an oppressive theology that excludes gender-variant persons from participating fully in the faith community. Mollenkott warns that violence, oppression, and hate do not come from God. As a Christian spiritual leader, she uses religious doctrine to support a non-binary view of gender that she calls "omnigender." It includes gender-different people, regardless of their sexual preference.[30] Mollenkott believes a Christian journey means being totally honest with one's self, others, and God. This means that transgender people must come out and tell their stories in their faith. Research shows that this can be life-saving work, as the risk of suicide and internalized self-hatred is even higher for transgender youth than LGB youth, whose risk far exceeds that of heterosexuals of the same age.

Mollenkott is hopeful that if transgender persons remember that God loves them unconditionally, they can find the courage to speak the horrors of their oppression, which will end their own internalized shame. It will also, she argues, educate and help move the church toward greater compassion, depth, and acceptance of transgender people, hopefully inspiring them to assist in doing the necessary justice work for social transformation.

TRANSGENDER MINISTERS AND TWO SPIRITS

Some transgender people are called into the ministry. This path can be exceedingly challenging, even in faiths that welcome diversity. Rev. Laurie Auffant, who identifies as transgender, found herself without a congregation after members of her Unitarian Universalist church objected to her ministering because of her gender presentation. She now ministers to the community, though she does not serve a congregation.

Other ministers thrive with the support of their church, like Malcolm Himschoot, the subject of the 2005 documentary *Call Me Malcolm*. Rev. Himschoot, like so many others, struggled with being transgender and at times felt as if God and his church hated him. He lost his family, friends, church, and himself. The film shows that the support he gained from his new Christian community at Iliff Theological Seminary empowered him to begin his gender transition. The film documents his final year of seminary as he embarks on a road trip to visit with transgender activists and advocates across the country. Perhaps the film's most powerful moment is when Malcolm visits with Pauline Martinez, the Dine' (Navajo) mother of F.C., a Na'dleehi (two-spirit) who was murdered for being gender-different. Malcolm learns that for traditional Dine' gender is not limited to a simple binary system, but is far more complex. In some traditional Native American cultures, two-spirit people are considered a blessing and a gift, which is how Martinez viewed F.C. At the end of his journey,

the film shows that Malcolm has learned multiple perspectives of identity, faith, and love and is filled with possibilities.[31]

Lydia Nibley's 2011 documentary *Two Spirits* documents two-spirit
teenager F.C. Martinez, who felt half man and half woman and "self-
identified as a gay male."[32] We learn that F.C. believed that being a
Na'dleehi (two-spirit Dine'/Navajo tradition) was "cool." F.C. proudly
wore pink nail polish, eyeliner, and headbands to school. F.C. was brutally murdered by a local teenager who, after he bludgeoned F.C. to death,
bragged that he had "bug smashed a fag."[33]

TRANSCENDENCE TRANSGENDER GOSPEL CHOIR

Transcendence, the award-winning all-transgender gospel choir and subject of an award-winning documentary titled *The Believers,*[34] was founded
by transgender musician Ashley Moore in 2001. Moore's mother told
Ashley that her father had been transsexual, which, according to her
mother's faith, meant that he was an "abomination." Shocked by her
mother's transphobic attitude, Ashley set out to correct the misinforma-
tion and hate toward transgender persons in churches. For Moore, the
founding of the transgender gospel choir began a mission to change
Christian attitudes toward transgender people and to renew her faith.
None of the choir members had ever sung before, and finding their voice
was a challenge. Moore followed the advice of a musician friend who
told her not to worry about feminizing her voice but "just sing from your
heart," which is what the whole choir does as they spread a musical
gospel of acceptance and diversity, underscored by their diversity in race
and gender. A line from one of their award-winning songs, "I am so glad
you are in my life. I am so glad you came to save us," affirms that
transgender persons are divinely loved. Ashley observes that when the
choir first walks out on stage, "people think what the hell is this," but
when they sing people are swept up in the music and it changes them.[35]

BEYOND THE CHURCH WALLS: EARTH-BASED AND MODERN PAGAN TRANSGENDER SPIRITUALITY

Some transgender persons find their spirituality in earth-based practices,
including modern paganism. Yet some of them have begun to speak and
write about the discrimination and prejudice they have experienced in
various branches of modern paganism. Much of this discrimination is
rooted in fixed ideas about sex and gender, the link of gender to biological sex, and the communication that males and females are inherently
different. While ideas about sex and gender vary within Christian and
neo-pagan groups, the impact on gender-different people is often the
same.[36] Many neo-pagan transgender persons, like their Christian

counterparts, actively challenge their exclusion from some circles, rituals, and religions. Their success is as mixed as the success of their Christian counterparts. A growing body of literature recognizes that gender-variant persons have been spiritual leaders in paganism and earth-based religions throughout the ages.[37] There are also well-known transgender spiritual leaders who are recognized as world authorities on the modern interpretation of the tarot and other esoteric practices.[38]

A recent anthology, *Gender and Transgender in Modern Paganism*, challenges harmful ideas about gender that are deeply embedded in some branches of the modern pagan community. Several events occurred during the world's largest pagan convention in 2009, which inspired the creation of the anthology. Gina Pond, a co-founder of the open source Circle of Cerridwen who self-describes as a "fairly butch-looking woman," was excluded from a male ritual dedicated to her patron god because of her birth sex. Pond was angered by the exclusion and a comment made by a male ritual participant who told her that she would be better off at the woman's Dianic ritual down the hall. At the same conference Pond's wife, Sara Thompson, experienced bigotry and covert exclusion from some of the Dianic rituals and workshops.[39]

Pond and Thompson challenged the exclusion of gender variant and transgender persons from rituals, particularly in some of the Wiccan-derived paths reliant on binaries. Thompson wrote a letter to the conference organizers, detailing the discrimination experienced at the conference. Both Thompson and Pond also created a direct action ritual at the 2011 Pantheacon, and eventually they edited the anthology to critically interrogate assumptions about gender binaries in the neo-pagan community. For instance, the volume critiques the idea that "women should worship a goddess and men should worship a god," and the notion that women are "expected to participate in women-only rituals." Pond and Thompson thus reject the use of hetero-normative language found in rituals, and advocate for multi-gender deities. In their view, paganism must evolve to stay relevant.

Yet, as fair-minded editors, Pond and Thompson also included opposing views in their anthology. One of the opponents is Ruth Barrett, who rejects transgender inclusion. She participates in a Dianic sect that regards the exclusion of transwomen from the Dianic tradition as an "act of religious freedom." Barrett also believes that the Dianic tradition "is a religion for genetic females," and that "transgender people need to make their own rituals."[40] Still, the Circle of Cerridwen at the 2011 Pantheacon began a conversation on the exclusion of transgender and gender-variant persons and included a ritual of direct action that challenged assumptions about gender. This moment of inclusion, however, was brief. Already during the next year, in 2012, Pantheacon Z. in Budapest invited to a ritual "genetic women only." One critic of this exclusionary ritual stated that as a public religious event for which people had to pay, the Pantheacon should not allow discrimination.[41]

Another contributor to the anthology makes yet another significant point. Neo-pagan transgender and intersex shaman, activist, and author Raven Kaldera contends that transgender people have to come out because it is part of their spirit work. Kaldera also affirms that he invited the gods of gender transgression to teach him their mysteries. The gods and spirits told him that he had to transition and they would guide him through the process. He warned that if you are not "fully living your sacred gender, then everything that the gods and spirits will do to you will be about forcing you to come to terms with this. If you resist, if you keep putting it off, things will just get worse and worse. When you come to terms with your gender and live it, your life will improve."[42] Foxfetch, a neo-pagan transsexual man, agrees with Kaldera on the importance of recognizing and reclaiming diverse gender deities. He urges that "we need third gender, multi-gender, beyond gender deities." Foxfetch asserts, "Our bodies are sacred too. We too are God, are Goddess."[43]

As part of his spirit work, Kaldera reflects on and educates about transgender persons who have died due to gender intolerance. He states:

> The Dead of our tribe are angry. They rage, they weep, they cry out. They rage because we are being killed in the streets, because we are turned away when we seek food and shelter and work and health care, because we are ridiculed and often unloved, because we are exiled from our families and clans, because we are beaten down until we break and take our own lives. Because to live in our country is to live in a war zone. Our Dead are angry, and they demand this of us: that as much as we are able, we will do what has to be done to make sure that there are no more fallen in this war. In order to save each other, we must band together and take care of each other, because alone we go down.[44]

TRANSGENDER DAY OF REMEMBRANCE

In November of 1998, Boston's LGBT community recoiled in horror at the discovery of the latest victim of transphobic violence. Rita Hester, a popular figure in the local rock'n'roll scene, who also happened to be a transsexual, had been brutally stabbed to death in her Brighton apartment. Like so many killings of transgender persons, the victim was subjected to enough brutality to kill her many times over. A local community of queer activists, family, friends, and allies—over 250 people in all—came together and held a speak-out and candlelight vigil in Rita's honor. They formed a human stream of light winding its way through Rita's old Allston stomping grounds. One year later, a memorial vigil was held in San Francisco; the following year Boston and a few other cities joined in, and by now hundreds of observances are held each year in twenty-seven countries. Gathering to mourn its dead, the transgender community makes a clear statement of dignity, humanity, and determination to change the way in which our people are regarded by society at large.

The Transgender Day of Remembrance is the first internationally observed transgender event. It has always served as a vehicle for publicizing the violence and discrimination suffered by members of our community.[45] In 2011, Boston's Transgender Day of Remembrance observance, held at the Cathedral Church of St. Paul in downtown Boston, included welcoming remarks from Episcopalian diocesan bishop, Rev. M. Thomas Shaw, who surprised and deeply moved participants when he said that he wanted to apologize for the way in which Christians hurt transgender people by "misrepresenting God" to them. He went on to speak about how the Church was made more whole by the full participation of transgender persons.[46]

Unitarians have been similarly welcoming of this event. The Arlington Street Church in Boston, a Unitarian Universalist congregation long known for its support of activist causes, hosted many activist gatherings for transgender causes, including the city's first candlelight vigil honoring a transgender murder victim, Chanelle Pickett, in 1995, as well as the organizing meeting for the Rita Hester vigil in 1998. In February 2012, the First Parish Unitarian Universalist of Cambridge awarded Nancy the "Courageous Love Award," stating:

> The award honors Ms. Nangeroni's years of dedicated service to the transgender community, her perseverance in educating the general public about transgender life and issues, and her critical role in passing the Massachusetts Transgender Equal Rights Act. She also started a nationwide campaign to end violence against transgender people.[47]

These murders are jarring reminders of the injustice that disproportionately targets trans women of color. The National Coalition of Anti-Violence Programs[48] has reported that violence against lesbian, gay, bisexual, and transgender people has increased 23 percent from 2009 to 2010, with people of color and transgender women as the most common victims. Of the victims murdered in 2010, 70 percent were persons of color, while 44 percent were transgender women.[49]

KINDRED SPIRITS

> I remember you, they all said. But do we remember who we are? And as their campfire glowed more deeply, they did remember. We are family. We are the clan who has lost our name—even our pronouns. How can we rekindle our visions and share them with the world?[50]

In the early 1990s, a new transgender community began to coalesce around annual conventions held at various times within cities across the United States. In 1991, the first "Southern Comfort" convention, an annual conference for transgender persons, activists, academics, advocates, and members of the medical community, was held in Atlanta, Georgia, quickly becoming the most popular among them. At that first Southern Comfort, transgender spiritualist Holly Boswell, a writer and presenter on alternative spiritual approaches to being transgender, called for the forming of a spiritual circle during the last afternoon of the conference. About twenty-five people, including Nancy, attended the first circle, giving participants an opportunity to envision themselves as connected not only to one another but also to a larger world in which being transgender had a rightful, spiritual place.

According to a fellow transgender spiritualist, Yvonne Cook-Riley, who spoke on GenderTalk radio in 2002, "There were a lot of people involved in Wicca, witchcraft, some of the other alternatives . . . but they didn't relate it to the concept of how a transgender person would recognize their own path, their own spirituality." Yvonne explained that this was the first time transgender and spirituality came together in the community and that it was "the first time that anything was acknowledged other than what I would call debating the religious Bible issue."[51] Yvonne believes that childhood isolation of transgender persons deprived them of their spiritual heritage: "Most crossdressers back when they were children understood the dynamics of shifting from the masculine to the feminine. They had no idea that it was a spiritual journey."[52] She credits Holly Boswell with helping to lead the spiritual awakening of the transgender community: "Holly had the energy and foresight to put it in words, and she began developing the story for the spiritual movement within the transgender movement." Holly told us, "It seems that once you approach gender shifting from a spiritual perspective, this notion of binary gender becomes a little silly."[53]

In 1993, Holly hosted a gathering of thirteen invited transgender leaders, including Nancy, for a weekend in the southern Appalachians north of Asheville, North Carolina, to explore transgender spirituality. The group held discussion circles, experimented with rituals gleaned from earth-based beliefs, and communed with nature in an attempt to gain a better understanding of our own transgender spirits and their relationship to the world. Nancy later described the event as "a pivotal spiritual experience which catapulted me forward with bolstered confidence and insight onto my transgender path." Among the participants, Angela Brightfeather Sheedy wrote of gaining "the ability to see why being transgendered is a gift from the Creator, and to have the ability to make that gift work for me." This dynamic weekend birthed the "Kindred Spirits" (KS) group that began to meet regularly in Asheville. The group is now a global network that is still based in the southern Appalachian Mountains near Asheville. It is communal in nature but inspired by Holly Boswell's vision.

Kindred Spirits is the oldest transgender-founded spiritual tradition in the United States. The organization has and continues to provide a safe space for transgender persons and allies to explore, practice and create spiritual traditions. Boswell believes it is the spirit that makes one transgender. Yvonne Cook-Riley writes, "Kindred Spirits is the forum to learn and teach in the world of the 'two-spirit.' It is a place to explore ancient healing traditions, as well as a celebration of other types of healing and understanding. For me, it provides access to the way of life of the Shaman, and the many techniques that the shamanic circle embraces."[54]

Kindred Spirits has four major concepts. They are expressed in the group's mission statement: "Every 'thing' is a living manifestation of Spirit . . . harmony and balance between all beings must be respected. . . . The diversity of all life forms is to be honored and celebrated. . . . All beings are divine and enjoy direct access with Spirit." Boswell reminds us that not only does the survival of a species depend on diversity, but that Nature loves diversity. Kindred Spirits encourages us to tell our truth. The mission statement affirms this goal: "To transcend gender stereotyping is to dare to be fully oneself, fully human, as Spirit intended." This truth-telling and truthful living includes refashioning old myths and re-inventing the tools. Boswell told GenderTalk Radio listeners, "One of the primary prerequisites to any of our gatherings is that we come in with no expectations. To come in any other way is very self-defeating. It requires a leap of faith, really, you really just have to surrender to spirit and trust that everything that needs to happen will happen."[55]

In 2002, we (Gordene and Nancy) participated in a Kindred Spirits Circle, led by Holly Boswell. We trekked through the Appalachian Mountains, swimming, drumming on top of the mountain, eating blackberries, chanting, and leaping over fire. When I, Gordene, stood on top of the Appalachian mountain in North Carolina, I felt a gentle turquoise wind move through my body. Gender atoms swirled, liberating all of my gender. On top of Max Patch Bald Mountain in the wind and the rain, I felt my male spirit renewed and set free.

Attentive to the natural world, Boswell looks to the widespread diversity found in plants, animals, and humans as "evidence of Spirit expressing its diversity." Kindred Spirits has reclaimed their transgender deities, compiled their history and, under the guidance of visionary fairy Holly Boswell, created a compelling origin myth. Every year transgender persons and a few allies, seeking spiritual connection, gather in the Appalachian Mountains, where, led by Holly and other participants, they perform rituals, create a circle, and engage in sacred fun. A quote included on the Kindred Spirit website describes what many participants experience in the Kindred Spirit circles:

All began in love; all seeks to return to love. Love is the law, the teacher of wisdom, and the great revealer of mysteries. . . . The processes of gender transgression are simply a way for Spirit to transcend the passing whims and dictates of human cultures in order to more freely manifest its glorious diversity in Nature—and in our very flesh. This process forms the root of Transgender Spirituality.[56]

The Kindred Spirit origin story concludes:

Your ancestors welcome you home. Your energy is needed now in the world, to help restore balance and harmony. Your lineage is older than the fall of Adam and Eve, so you can help them. Show the men and the women how they are one, and remind them that they are one with all beings. You have the power. Heal each other, and as you do so, go forth and help heal the world.[57]

TOWARD THE GENDER LIBERATION OF THE SPIRIT: A CONCLUSION

Despite escalating cultural wars waged by the U.S. Christian religious and political right on transbodies and exclusionary practices by some branches of modern paganism, change is happening slowly, whether through inclusion or legislation. Transgender activists committed to challenging exclusionary spiritual practices are making a difference by creating awareness, educating, and inspiring their congregations and circles. More, but not enough, transgender people in the United States are being welcomed into spiritual congregations and open circles as others join them in the struggle for equality and respect. Transgender persons also reclaim and create their own spiritual traditions. Globally, there is currently little information on trans-inclusion in non-Western religions, as transgender persons in some countries are fighting to survive against repressive regimes that criminalize and threaten their very existence with brutal police abuse and worse discriminatory practices.[58]

Some progressive churches are making efforts to be transgender inclusive. In 2012, the Episcopal Church voted overwhelmingly in favor of allowing transgender people to be ordained. At its triennial General Convention in Indianapolis, the Church House of Deputies approved a change to the nondiscrimination canons to include gender identity and expression. The church also voted to make it illegal to discriminate against transgender people in the church.[59] However, U.S. churches are still free to discriminate against diversity. For instance, the Catholic Church follows an unpublished document that forbids the church from accepting the gender of a transgender Catholic.

Some modern pagans are working at building bridges between Dianic and transgender communities. The 2013 Pagan Gathering Festival will offer a mystery ritual and ritual rites of passage for transgender pagans that will be led by transgender activist Melissa Murphy. She has been in conversation with Dianic leaders who have excluded transwomen from their women-only rituals in the past. One Dianic leader, Ruth Barrett, agreed to co-lead the ritual with Murray, provided she attends the conference. In addition, several Dianic leaders have publicly acknowledged that transwomen are women. The festival now includes plans to hold separate Dianic circles for anyone who identifies as a woman, as well as a "genetic women only" circle.

Love of justice is an effective agent of change for transgender activists and allies. But, as we demonstrate, it is not always easy or immediately successful. As more stories of transgender struggles are heard and more people join in the effort to educate, heal the injustices, and stop the violence, change will happen. Whether that change is in Christian churches, earth-based religions, modern pagan circles, transgender spiritual traditions, or atheist communities, all of them will contribute toward justice and gender liberation of the spirit.

NOTES

1. See the website of Holly Boswell's Kindred Spirits, available at http://www.trans-spirits.org.
2. The saying was created and used in the late1960s and early 1970s by feminist Robin Morgan and the Redstockings, an activist group, to call attention to the sexism and violence in women's lives and the effort to bring political awareness of it to create change.
3. See American Civil Liberties Union (ACLU LGBT Rights project) at http://www.aclu.org/lgbt-rights; Human Rights Watch LGBT Rights at http://www.hrw.org/topic/lgbt-rights; International Transgender Day of Remembrance statistics—Ethan St. Pierre at http://www.transgenderdor.org/?page_id=192; and Kimberly McLeod, "Transgender Deaths: Where Is the Outcry?" *The Root* (September 1, 2012): 1–2.
4. Leslie Feinberg, *Transgender Warriors: Making History from Joan of Arc to RuPaul* (Boston: Beacon Press, 1996), 35.
5. Ibid., 32.
6. Ibid., 35.
7. Terry Tafoya is interviewed on GenderTalk Radio (www.gendertalk.com/, #390, December 16, 2002). Tafoya traces the origin of the term *two-spirit* and explains that it means having both male and female energy. See also Sue Ellen Jacobs, Wesley Thomas, and Sabine Lang (eds.), *Two-Spirit People: Native American Gender Identity, Sexuality and Spirituality* (Urbana/Chicago: University of Illinois Press, 1997), 3. The authors discuss how the "word two-spirit emphasizes the spiritual aspect of one's life."
8. For additional information, see Feinberg, *Transgender Warriors*; Walter Williams, *The Spirit and the Flesh: Sexual Diversity in American Indian Cultures* (Boston: Beacon Press, 1986).
9. Nancy Nangeroni, *In Your Face* (Cambridge, MA: Self-published, 1995–1998).
10. Gordene MacKenzie, *Transgender Nation* (Bowling Green, OH: Bowling Green State University Popular Press, 1994).
11. See http://www.GenderVision.org.
12. Gordene MacKenzie, "Transsexual Ideology, Transgenderism, and the Gender Movement in America: A Sociopolitical Analysis of Gender Bipolarism" (PhD thesis, University of New Mexico, 1991). The thesis was published as *Transgender Nation*

(Bowling Green, OH: Bowling Green State University Popular Press, 1994). The book is dedicated "To the Gender Revolution."

13. Noel Sturgeon, *Environmentalism in Popular Culture: Gender, Race, Sexuality and the Politics of the Natural* (Tucson: University of Arizona Press, 2008), 22.

14. See Bruce Bagemihl, *Biological Exuberance: Animal Homosexuality and Natural Diversity* (New York: St. Martin's Press, 1999). Also see Joan Roughgarden, *Evolution's Rainbow: Diversity, Gender and Sexuality in Nature and in People* (New York: Saint Martin's Press, 2004).

15. Bagemihl, *Biological Exuberance*, 77.

16. See www.focusonthefamily.com/socialissues/social-issues/transgenderism/our-position.aspx.

17. See http://www.autostraddle.com/republicans-try-to-stomp-a-mudhole-in-trans-rights-128134/.

18. Scott Kearnan, "Romney a Wimp? Not So Much," *Boston Spirit Magazine* 8, no. 5 (September/October 2012): 20.

19. See Alice Dreger, Ellen K. Feder, and Anne Tamar-Mattis, "Prenatal Dexamethasone for Congenital Adrenal Hyperplasia: An Ethics Canary in the Modern Medical Mine," *Journal of Bioethical Inquiry* (September 9, 2012): 277–94.

20. The quote is from a lobbying invitation distributed at the Massachusetts Family Institute in April 2009.

21. Terry Tafoya observes that two-spirit persons have both male and female energy inside of them; see the interview with Tafoya on GenderTalk Radio (www.gendertalk.com, #390, December 16, 2002).

22. Karen Kramer Russel, *Shapeshifting: Transformations in Native American Art* (Salem, MA: Peabody Essex Museum/New Haven, CT: Yale University Press, 2012), 17.

23. The full covenant states, "I understand that in an era where images of family relationship and personal sexuality are often confused, Crystal Cathedral Ministries believes that it is important to teach and model the biblical view. I understand that Crystal Cathedral Ministries teaches that sexual intimacy is intended by God to only be within the bond of marriage, between one man and one woman." Also see Karen Kramer, "Anti-Gay Covenant Provokes Controversy at Crystal Cathedral," *Christian Beliefs* (March 17, 2011): 17.

24. Sotyan Zaimov, "Former Crystal Cathedral May Become Most Significant Catholic Center after the Vatican," *Christian Post Reporter* (August 9, 2012): 1.

25. Joanne Herman, *Transgender Explained for Those Who Are Not* (Bloomington, IN: AuthorHouse, 2009), 75.

26. Ibid., x.

27. Ibid., 106.

28. Virginia Ramey Mollenkott and Vanessa Sheridan, *Transgender Journeys* (Eugene, OR: Resource Publications, 2010), 32.

29. Virginia Ramey Mollenkott, *Omnigender: A Trans-Religious Approach* (Cleveland, OH: Pilgrim Press, 2001), 25.

30. Ibid. For additional information, see the interview with Mollenkott on GenderTalk Radio (wwwgendertalk.com, #339, December 9, 2001).

31. *Call Me Malcom*, directed by Joseph Paralagreco (FilmWorks & United Church of Christ, 2005). For additional information, see the interview with Rev. Malcom Himschoot and Joseph Paralagreco on GenderTalk Radio (www.gendertalk.com, #538, November 26, 2005).

32. For more information, see http://twospirits.org/people-in-the-film/.

33. For more information, see http://fredmartinezispunk.weebly.com/fredfc-martinez-jr.html.

34. *The Believers*, directed by Todd Holland (Frameline Films, 2006).

35. Ashley Moore is interviewed on GenderTalk Radio (www.gendertalk.com, #371, August 5, 2002).

36. Sarah Thompson, Gina Pond, Phillip Tanner, Calyxa Omphalos, and Jacob Polanshek (eds.), *Gender and Transgender in Modern Paganism* (Cupertino, CA: Circle of Cerridwen Press, 2012).

37. Randy Conner, *Blossom of Bone: Reclaiming the Connections between Homoeroticism and the Sacred* (San Francisco: HarperSanFrancisco, 1993).

38. See, for example, Rachel Pollack, *The Forest of Souls: A Walk through the Tarot* (St. Paul, MN: Llewellyn, 2002); Rachel Pollak, *The Kabbalah Tree* (St. Paul, MN: Llewellyn, 2004).

39. Gina Pond, "Preface," in *Gender and Transgender in Modern Paganism*, 3–8.

40. Ruth Barrett, "A Dianic Perspective," in *Gender and Transgender in Modern Paganism*, 93–98.

41. See http://www.incitingariot.com/2012/02/gender-exclusivity-at-pantheacon-2012.html.

42. Raven Kaldera, "The Third Voice," in *Gender and Transgender in Modern Paganism*, 76.

43. Foxfetch, "Awakening The Transsexual Gods," in *Gender and Transgender in Modern Paganism*, 42.

44. See www.ravenkaldera.org/gender/for-transgendered-spirit-workers.html.

45. Angela Alberti, "Vigil Honors Transgender Murder Victims," *Bay Windows: New England's Largest GLBT Newspaper* (November 22, 2010): 1–2.

46. See http://blog.transepiscopal.com/2010_11_01_archive.html.

47. See http://www.standingonthesideoflove.org/tag/nancy-nangeroni/.

48. See http://www.avp.org/documents/NCAVPHateViolenceReport2011Finaledjl finaledits.pdf.

49. See http://www.theroot.com/views/your-take. Kimberly McLeod, "Transgender Deaths: Where Is the Outcry?" *The Root* (September 1, 2012): 2.

50. This is an origin myth of Kindred Spirits written by Holly Boswell. It is available on the Kindred Spirit website at http://www.trans-spirits.org.

51. See the interview with Yvonne Cook-Riley on GenderTalk Radio (http://www.gendertalk.com, #372, August 12, 2002).

52. See the interview with Yvonne Cook-Riley on GenderTalk Radio (http://www.gendertalk.com, #372, August 12, 2002).

53. See the interview with Yvonne Cook-Riley on GenderTalk Radio (http://www.gendertalk.com, #346, February 11, 2002).

54. See http://www.trans-spirits.org/spirit_of_transgender.html.

55. See the interview with Holly Boswell on GenderTalk Radio (http://www.gendertalk.com, #346, February 11, 2002).

56. http://www.trans-spirits.org/spirit_of_transgender.html.

57. Ibid.

58. See the Human Rights Watch Reports on human rights abuse of transgender persons in Uganda, South Africa, Iraq, Turkey, Kuwait, The Netherlands, and elsewhere at http://www.hrw.org/search/apachesolr_search/transgender.

59. James Kaleem, "Episcopal Church Approves Ordination of Transgender People," *Huffington Post* (July 10, 2012).

Part V

Two Responses

TWELVE

Reflections on "God Loves Diversity and Justice"

A (Modern) Human Rights Perspective

Patricia H. Davis

The Preamble to the Universal Declaration of Human Rights states, "Recognition of the inherent dignity and of the equal and inalienable rights of all members of the human family is the foundation of freedom, justice and peace in the world."[1] From a human rights perspective, the question of God's love of justice and diversity may be a bit beside the point; human rights are founded in an agreement by the human community that dignity should be protected and upheld in all people's lives.[2] Human rights take an agnostic view of God's existence, being, and/or preferences/loves. Religious faith is an aspect of human culture to be protected for individuals, and defeated (not as faith *per se*) when it is a proxy for exploitative political, economic, social, cultural, or civil power.

I am a Christian who has chosen to work toward upholding human dignity and justice within this secular framework rather than a religious one. There are many reasons for this choice, the principal one being the seriousness with which I take Dietrich Bonhoeffer's admonition that in this time we must live in the world as if God were absent: "God as a working hypothesis in morals, politics, or science, has been surmounted and abolished; and the same thing has happened in philosophy and religion."[3]

This is true for two reasons. First, because the theological strategy to insert God where God is not required (e.g., reason, science, ethics, politics, philosophy)—*Deus ex machina*—has been revealed to be unnecessary

219

and dishonest.[4] Second, because "the Bible directs [us] to God's power-lessness and suffering."[5] God doesn't give answers or guidance for justice or diversity—God "wins power and space" in the world by God's weakness.[6]

The modern human rights movement was born—nay, it erupted—in an anguished response to the immense, efficient, cold evil—mass murder, cruelty, and degradation—of the second global war. The movement came into being with the hope that Auschwitz, Belzac, Treblinka, Sobibor, Nanjing, Nagasaki, Dresden, and Stalingrad were not final words about the status of the human spirit. The Universal Declaration of Human Rights was promulgated (and ratified by the UN General Assembly without dissenting vote) in 1948 in recognition that neither diplomacy nor economic or military might, nor religion, nor any other force on earth had been sufficient to hold back the "barbarous acts" that had "outraged the conscience of mankind."[7] The UDHR is a global affirmation that human beings are better than mass rapes, genocides, and ridiculously lethal bombs—and that human dignity is an inherent and irrevocable birthright for every person—from birth until death (and even for bodies in death).

The human rights movement is, thus, a modernist movement with deep historical roots (in the Magna Carta, natural law, the American and French Revolutions, the Enlightenment, and even reactions to the trans-Atlantic slave trade).[8] It stands philosophically uncomfortable in a postmodern and otherwise colonialized (and postcolonial) world—proclaiming its own text and doctrine—defiantly deeming them to be universally "true" and applicable to all humanity.[9] The claim of human rights to universality is defensible. The UDHR was adopted and ratified—as a "deathbed" declaration—by the nations of the world, at a time when the world was in moral *extremis*. Its power inheres in the confidence and positive affirmation of the nations of the world at such a moment, and the continuing utility of human rights claims and policies based on the UDHR and other global human rights agreements. In addition, the words and ideals of the UDHR stand as (or in the place of) "sacred" text—powerful, convicting, and true.

One personal anecdote on the transforming power of human rights covenants and declarations from Kigali, Rwanda (2007): I was one of several (Western) facilitators at a human rights conference for African women leaders—social workers, church workers, educators, lawyers, judges, and legislators—from Congo, Rwanda, Kenya, Burundi, and Sudan. The idea of universal human rights was new to these women, whose countries had experienced and were experiencing genocide, rape as a weapon of war, the kidnapping and conscription of their children as soldiers and sex slaves, and the brutal murder of innocent family members and neighbors in their homes and on their streets.

As part of the conference, these women read the UDHR along with relevant corollary human rights documents: the African Charter on

Human and Peoples' Rights,[10] the UN Convention on the Rights of the Child,[11] and the UN Convention on the Elimination of all Forms of Discrimination Against Women (CEDAW) (also called the "international bill of rights for women").[12] Their first reaction to hearing and reading these was incredulity. They demanded to see the signatories for each document—not believing that the world had agreed on these principles of human dignity, justice, and freedom. They read the documents repeatedly. And they vowed to carry them back to the women they served in their home countries.

The other conference facilitators and I expressed wariness at this prospect. We cautioned them not to act naively or rashly, or as if these rights were guaranteed merely because the documents were signed and ratified.

The women understood the risks and advantages *in situ* better than we did, however. In the ensuing months, we heard repeatedly of empowering encounters with these documents. A representative from Darfur related the following declaration (in translation from Arabic) from a woman in a camp for internationally deplaced persons (IDPs) there: "Now that I know that being raped is against my human rights—and the world says that's true—I am determined to live and fight for my children."

Despite, however, the power of human rights ideals, it is a fundamentally temporal/historical movement, with the problems, blind spots, issues, and inherent faults and frailties of any such movement. Critics can easily find idolatry, fear,[13] divisive politics, imbalances of power, and proneness to cultural misadventure and mistake. And the UDHR's authors seemed cognizant of the potential for even greater problems: hypocrisy and irrelevance. As Pamela Milne correctly notes, "[R]ights are only as strong as the society that supports them" (42).

Nevertheless, I would argue along with Milne that the UDHR is a "better" text for defining and protecting justice than the Bible or any other ancient sacred text, because it is historically more evolved—with a notion of justice "wider and deeper than the biblical notion"—and because it is less ambiguous about what justice demands (42). In addition, Milne's insight relating to one of the strengths of neo-paganism also applies to the human rights movement—it is not "burdened by an ancient canonical text against which [it] struggle[s]"[14] (46).

At least two authors in this volume, Sze-kar Wan and Serge Frolov, expressly struggle with biblical texts—to wrest ideas of justice and diversity from them. Readers must admire the linguistic, intellectual, and creative prowess of each of these contributors. But their impulses to find justice (in the Servant Songs of Isaiah [and Luke] and in Deuteronomy 20, respectively) seem strained and improbable. Texts that need to be read through such excruciatingly twisted "grown-up" lenses to locate justice and appreciation of diversity are not merely neutral puzzles for academic inquiry—they are dangerous incitements to injustice.

Frolov's claim that "whoever makes a theological statement [such as 'God loves diversity and justice'] should be prepared to substantiate it by citing appropriately interpreted prooftext(s), to grapple with alternative construals of the same texts," and so on is undoubtedly true (147). His "grown-up" reading of horrific texts defends Yhwh's cruel and genocidal commands against the Canaanites in Deuteronomy 20 as (at worst) moot. Nevertheless, he admits that those who read with "less effort, background knowledge, and exegetical sophistication" (153) will obviously conclude that Yhwh is "harsh, fickle, or impotent" (152). From a non-biblical scholar perspective, if scholars really desire to reclaim dangerous texts such as this—loaded with ammunition for (more childlike?) potential genocidaires?—in a world that's a hair trigger away from self-annihilation, perhaps they should do so in private and hide the work from the ruthless "children."

Sze-kar Wan comes much closer to admitting the genocidal tone of the Servant Songs and Luke: "[W]hile the restoration of Israel is good news to Israel, it means devastation to the locals. Israel's jubilee implies condemnation to the ethnic Other" (139). Wan asks, "Does God love diversity?" He finds the answer from these texts to be a "resounding" no. But even Wan seeks to find the silver lining in the texts—in "often buried intimations of acceptance and inclusion, intimations that emerge in spite of their ideological captivity" (141).

Why this effort for reclamation? An effort that reveals Milne's point, in fact, that the modern idea of justice has moved far beyond the Bible. Why not let these chauvinistic and dangerous passages rest with other ancient texts in the purview of experts and "adults"? Or perhaps consign them to the shelf of cautionary texts, documents, and films (along with *Mein Kampf*, *Triumph of the Will*, and *Birth of a Nation*) that contaminate our perspectives (cultural, emotional, and intellectual) on such deep levels that we rarely see or admit their power. Keep them where they belong—to be handled with care—and out of the reach of those who would use them blindly. Let these learned interpreters (who obviously know and care about justice) be the analysts (and prophets) who uncover the shadow impulses of the texts, and the ways in which these make unwanted appearances in our midst. But let's not pretend that these texts are benign, or that they in any way point to justice (much less a justice that "God loves").

This volume provides three additional answers to the question of identifying God's love for justice and diversity: in the dynamics of power in relationships (Rieger, Johnson); in the prophetic voice (Ellis); and in the undivided nature of the Divine who IS justice and diversity (Singh).

Rieger makes the important argument that there is no justice without diversity, and that "diversity" without justice is merely oppression—that we are called to "take sides" as God chose the Israelites against Egypt: "[Justice] objects to the distortions of relationships in favor of new relationships based on justice and equality" (124). Rieger rejects the notion that inversion of power (the last becoming first) is a model for justice. Yet his relational model of justice also stumbles on the Bible—and especially the biblical account of the conquest of Canaan. As Rieger correctly notes, "The Bible contains numerous conquest fantasies, according to which the Israelites conquer Canaan, break down the walls of its cities, kill the inhabitants, and take over the land" (124).

How to reconcile this genocidal impulse with transforming justice? [15] Rieger relies on a secondary source to postulate a history in which the Israelites joined forces with liberated peoples in Canaan to "usher[] in liberation from an unjust monopoly of city states." [16] Thus, he brings an interpretation to the narrative which only serves to illustrate the model of "justice" that he proposed at the outset.

Susanne Johnson similarly locates the possibilities of justice in the disruption of exploitive power relationships—especially including class exploitation as a "reality that cuts across gender, race, ethnicity, immigrant status, sexual orientation, age, and religious identity" (90). For Johnson, justice is the goal of a political struggle against Empire, carried out through broad-based organizing that "bring[s] people together across [the same] lines of class, gender, race, ethnicity, nationality, geography, immigrant status, and religion" (107).

Interestingly, religion and faith seem to take a marginal position in this struggle. For Johnson, class struggle against economic oppression is neither defined nor "solved" by faith or faith communities—except for a hope that a "fugitive Christianity," which is vitally interested in the working class, may emerge when the "status quo bureaucracy" of the institutional church (which domesticates rather than transforms) is broken (106). In Johnson, the reader finds an outline of a humanist view of justice—a prize to be won through struggle of the unified oppressed on earth. Although she quotes Bonhoeffer approvingly, her work actually demonstrates Bonhoeffer's insight that in the "world come of age" God has been pushed to the sidelines—we must live before God as if God does not exist. [17]

Mark Ellis announces the end of Jewish history—the end of history for "a people that carries the indigenous prophetic as its baseline and eschatological essence" because of Israel's (and "worldwide Jewry['s]") violation of the Palestinians (58). For Ellis, this history cannot be recovered by "progressives" who expropriate the prophetic "without the prophet" (59). Progressives are so much rooted in empire, and so well established in the elite classes, that despite their intent, they remain "empire enablers" [18] (66).

Comfort, if it is to be found, is in the name Ellis attributes to God: "*I AM, WHO LOVES THE PROPHETS*" (62). The prophets provide the foundation for justice, and the prophetic is the "center of Jewishness" (63). The prophets know, however, that God "demands atheism at the very core of faith . . . the willingness to suffer without the possibility of rescue" (69). Thus, Ellis takes Bonhoeffer a step further—God is no longer present as *Deus ex machina* for modern *questions* (Bonhoeffer); for Ellis, God is similarly not present to *rescue* humanity from hypocrisy, blindness, and its own devices.

Yet, for Ellis, there also seems (surprisingly) to be a note of hope: "*I AM, WHO LOVES THE PROPHETS*, loves you." Wherever the prophetic remains—if it remains—it champions justice: "the dignity of the person, the very reason for a social order, the political as a vocation, religion as a purveyor of a destiny beyond the immediate . . . embrace, reconciliation, forgiveness, and the ultimate meaning of life" (69).

This final note of hope—resonating with other similar final notes in this volume (perhaps necessary theological retreats for "People(s) of the Book"?) is somewhat jarring in this context. The logic of the essay suggests that God is absent, the people (Jews and non-Jews) have killed history, and the authentic prophetic voice has died because of unjust human actions. It is important to note, however, that the prophetic, if it exists for Ellis, is not the transcendent voice—God is not there to speak or rescue—but a human voice proclaiming justice, dignity, and integrity—beyond Constantinian religion.

In Nikky-Guninder Kaur Singh's chapter, perhaps human rights advocates can find the closest affinity. For Singh, the focus is not on something outside of oneself or others but rather on the beauty of the "multiverse," which is diverse and unified in the Divine. Singh, a Sikh feminist, explains that "God" does not exist in the Sikh context. Rather, the Divine is a singular plentitudinous reality—"One Being Is" (13). And, according to Singh's feminist interpretation of Sikhism, "Divine . . . *is* diversity and justice." There is no separation of subject and object/lover and loved, as Singh states: "From the One issue myriads and into the One they are ultimately assimilated"[19] (14).

Importantly, Sikh scripture, as interpreted by Singh, embraces temporality, humanity, and the earth as the location for just action: "Amidst nights, seasons, solar and lunar days/Amidst air, water, fire and the netherworld/The earth is placed, the place for righteous action" (26). Diversity is affirmed in the unity of the Divine. Ethical regard is required toward the entire universe. Singh writes, "The thought of the transcendent Divine permeating our multiverse energizes us to work for equality, health care, education, our ecosystem, and justice for each and all" (29).

Does God love justice and diversity? From a human rights perspective it doesn't matter, except that "God" and sacred scripture are dangerous tools in the hands of those who would obfuscate, co-opt, and oppose either/both. The human rights movement established itself in the ruins of civilizations rife with religion and idolatry. God wasn't there, didn't care, and certainly didn't rescue Africans shipped to North America by the millions, Native Americans driven off their lands and slaughtered, millions of innocents who died at Auschwitz, or Tutsis being slaughtered by Hutus (and then vice versa) in Rwanda. God isn't there, doesn't care, and doesn't rescue when babies' heads are bashed against trees in the Congo and children enslaved by warlords murder their parents and dismember them. God isn't there, doesn't care, and doesn't rescue when little girls are prostituted and little boys are forced into slavery all over the world today.

Perhaps we should let go of hopeful sayings and happy endings concerning God? Maybe it's time to "come of age" with the world, and to listen to the words of Dietrich Bonhoeffer (from Tegel Prison and the last months of his life): "When we speak of God in a 'non-religious' way, we must speak of [God] in such a way that the godlessness of the world is not in some way concealed, but rather revealed. . . . [O]ur coming of age leads us to a true recognition of our situation before God. God would have us know that we must live as [people] who manage our lives without God. . . . Before God and with God we live without God."[20] If God does not care, we must. If God is not there, we must be. And if God does not rescue, we must try.

NOTES

1. United Nations, Preamble to the Universal Declaration of Human Rights (New York: United Nations, 1948), http://www.un.org/en/documents/udhr/index.shtml.

2. Jack Donnelly, *Universal Human Rights in Theory and Practice* (Ithaca, NY: Cornell University Press, 2003).

3. Dietrich Bonhoeffer, *Letters & Papers from Prison* (New York: Touchstone, 1997), 360.

4. Ibid., 359–60.

5. Ibid., 361.

6. Ibid.

7. Ibid., 360.

8. For a recent exposition of the history of human rights law, see Jenny S. Martinez, *The Slave Trade and the Origins of International Human Rights Law* (New York: Oxford University Press, 2012).

9. Most human rights advocates in this time are very aware of the possibilities that the UDHR (and United Nations and International Criminal Court) are also prone to (cultural, economic, and political) hegemonic tendencies. Donnelly, in *Universal Human Rights*, for example, proposes that human rights are universal in that they apply to all people, but they are historically contingent and culturally particular (1–3).

10. Organization of African Unity, *African Charter on Human and Peoples' Rights (Banjul Charter)*, June 27, 1981, CAB/LEG/67/3 rev. 5, 21 I.L.M. 58 (1982), http://www.unhcr.org/refworld/docid/3ae6b3630.html [accessed December 6, 2012].

11. United Nations, *Convention on the Rights of the Child* (New York: United Nations, 1989), http://www2.ohchr.org/english/law/crc.htm [accessed December 6, 2012]. This convention is, incidentally, signed and ratified by every nation in the world except the United States and Somalia.

12. Office of the High Commissioner on Human Rights, *Convention on the Elimination of all Forms of Discrimination against Women* (New York: United Nations, 1979), http://www2.ohchr.org/english/law/cedaw.htm [accessed December 6, 2012].

13. The United Nations has not declared any conflict "genocide"—including Bosnia, Rwanda, or Darfur—since its adoption of the Convention on the Prevention and Punishment of the Crime of Genocide in 1948. This designation would require the response and involvement ("to prevent and punish") of all of the nations, which signed the Convention (New York: United Nations, 1948—http://www.hrweb.org/legal/genocide.html).

14. Except, in the sense that every movement is inevitably burdened (directly or indirectly) by the canonical texts of its culture[s].

15. Ellis asks this question another way: "Is that what advanced seminary training is for, reconciling God and injustice?" (62).

16. Rieger takes this interpretation from Norman Gottwald's *The Hebrew Bible: A Brief Socio-Literary Introduction* (Minneapolis: Fortress Press, 2009). Interestingly, Rieger places this reading in opposition to the genocidal view represented in "the book of Joshua *in its entirety*" (128, note 19; emphasis added).

17. See Bonhoeffer, *Letters & Papers from Prison*, 341, 361 ("God is being increasingly pushed out of a world that has come of age, out of the spheres of our knowledge and life").

18. Ellis writes, "Know that you have become a bystander in the abuse of Holocaust memory and that your progressive understandings will not allow you to break out of your own imprisonment, which you, muttering under your breath, lay at the feet of the Constantinian Jewish establishment. It should be so placed. And also at your own feet. At your own cowardice" (68).

19. Singh, quoting Gurinder Singh Mann, *The Making of Sikh Scripture* (New York: Oxford University Press, 2001), 101.

20. Bonhoeffer, *Letters & Papers*, 362, 360.

THIRTEEN

Should God Remain?

*A Response from the Perspective of Peace
and Conflict Studies*

Victoria Fontan

Recently, I met God in Sweden. We were both keynote speakers at a conference on the future of peace and conflict studies.[1] It was to be the first keynote speech of my career, and I was so proud to have been selected to perform right after him at this high-profile conference. On the way to Sweden, I doubted myself. Did the organizers really know what they were doing when they invited me to deliver a keynote? Maybe it was a mistake. After all, who belongs as a keynote speaker right next to God? A white, potbellied, middle-aged male? Should I perhaps also add, a Christian, white, potbellied, middle-aged male?

So, God spoke on that day, yet not very eloquently. He focused half his speech on the Cold War, and since most of us in the room were not even born then, it was, let us say, rather boring. In retrospect, I wish it had stayed boring, since fossilized reminiscences can be harmless when compared to an anti-Semitic rant. I knew God had anti-Semitic tendencies, so I was careful to listen to his every word, and then it all came flooding—the need for us all to read the Protocols of the Elders of Zion, the "well-known fact" that Jews have money and are responsible for the recent economic crisis, the bonding that Jews inflict economically on the rest of the world, their endless domination, and so forth.[2] Colleagues behind me were quivering with excitement at his every word, reeling in pleasure, in ecstasy before their God. After all, we were in Europe, where anti-Semitism is still prevalent underneath a repentant surface. He took twice his allocated time, since he is God, and then the coffee break arrived. I asked some colleagues what they thought about what had just been said. Some replied that they had not listened and others said that there was no point in denouncing his anti-Semitism, since he had been going at it for years. A handful of us were shocked.

Then it was my time to speak. I chose not to dignify his anti-Semitic rant with any direct response. I told God that his mainstream vision of peace and conflict studies might have been useful at some point. However, now it was time for it to be set aside, so that we could finally decolonize our discipline, bring to it diversity, justice, and, above all, equity in peace. His public response was scathing: "If you publish these ideas, your career will be over." It was unequivocal, brutal, and, dare I say, emblematic of my discipline.

God does not love anyone but Christian, white, potbellied, middle-aged males. The rest of us in his discipline are only given space for cosmetic purposes, as "ethnic" ornaments in a high-power business office, or the token African or Asian scholar at a conference roundtable. God does not love diversity, nor does he stand for justice. To me, a feminist peace and conflict studies scholar, God is in the way of diversity and justice. He needs to be uncovered for his bigotry, and then he must be made to retire.

DRAMA TRIANGLE

From a peace and conflict studies perspective, this book does not ask important questions: Does God exist? Can God continue to exist? Should "he" undisputedly remain God? Shihada, Singh, and Johnson still refer to their religions as a "beacon" of peace, love, justice, and equity, accusing patriarchy, capitalism, or men's bigotry as an obstacle to God's or the Divine's work, will, and legacy to us mere mortals. As Rieger points out, any exceptionalism can be interpreted as supporting the worst human rights abuses. To elevate one's people or religion may very well be utilized by *genocidaires* in various parts of the world. While it does not justify genocide, exceptionalism, named by Ellis as the prophetic, is the other side of the same coin. Persecution, conflict, and war are a reflection of manmade patriarchal value systems. As Milne points out, our societies construct our religious concepts according to their own value systems. What is it in our own society that warrants persecution and victimhood?

The notion of the prophet suffering for its people places this narrative within Karpman's Drama triangle.[3] This Drama triangle is the best-kept secret of today's psychological discourse, and it pervades peace and conflict studies. It is the root of the patriarchal epistemology that has enslaved us humans since Neolithic times.[4] Individuals can stay for years going over the script of their lives on a therapist couch without knowing about it, since it is at the root of our patriarchal culture. Entire societies are made to embody this triangle in their historical accounts, their social narratives, and most importantly, their religious scripts. The Drama triangle analyzes human interactions as being locked in a script of being and interacting with the Rescuer, the Persecutor, and the Victim. Everybody takes turns at playing those roles in this Manichean vision of life. Of importance here is that visions create a reality, which from God's creation of peace and conflict studies in his image can be very problematic. Indeed, many foundation courses in peace and conflict studies still view God as one of the founding fathers of the discipline, even though many others, including women, have been instrumental in developing the field.[5] The fact that God, well into his eighties, is still considered an inescapable keynote speaker at important peace studies conferences speaks for itself. It indicates the pervasiveness of patriarchy in peace and conflict studies as a discipline. It prefers short-term solutions built on hierarchies between victim and rescuer over dialogue, holism, and self-organized community-based initiatives, and it considers only a fraction of female authors as relevant to its normative foundations.

THE NEW MISSIONARIES

God rules this Drama triangle. There are peoples who are closer to God than others, and let's face it, many, though professing diversity, actually believe that their religion is better than others. Milne, again, makes this point explicit in her discussion. This is actually what organized religion expects its followers to believe, whether it is being articulated within the dynamics of a false consciousness or made explicit in the idea of "we give the greatest gift to the world." God thrives on the Drama triangle, since it validates him as the ultimate "peace builder," as if communities across the world did not know how to build peace on their own. From a mainstream peace and conflict studies perspective, our God, who "fathered" the discipline back in the 1960s, believes that peace and conflict are a matter of calculus and the application of the same few solutions all over the world.

Peace in our scriptures is being managed through three distinct blocks.[6] When a conflict is ongoing, peacekeeping is being administered in the same way a fire brigade would run to a fire. The ethics of the peacekeepers are not questioned, since, according to the Drama-triangle-based epistemology of our discipline, they are the benevolent saviors. As a result, they can rape women and children as they please and will be protected by their hierarchy; they are free to become the persecutors to their helpless victims.[7] Then comes the phase of peacemaking, when the different patriarchal actors of the conflict come together to agree to a ceasefire and manage it. This phase usually takes place in a Northern capital, since we in the global North are experts in peace. We do not harbor any social problems and have fully developed democratic systems in which all our citizens are equal and fulfilled. Genocide, riots, or acts of terrorism are anomalies of our systems that we are quick to ascribe to the devil tempting us, impersonated in democratically elected Adolf Hitler, depraved youth gangs, and evil terrorists.[8] After this phase comes the happily-ever-after phase of peace building when we, the well-educated Northerners, come to save the rest of the world as well-meaning peace missionaries. We also give the greatest gift to the world: sustainable peace.

Our Ivy League universities grant us the diploma that will allow us to apply our solutions to the rest of the world, the "savages" that require, for their salvation, to be evangelized into development, good governance, democracy, human rights, and nonviolence. We are able to uproot their indigenous populations for the sake of development and to upturn their elections results when their democratization phases do not go according to our plans. We reserve the right to bomb them with our drones if they persist in not understanding our peaceful messages, and we can detain them indefinitely as enemy combatants if they dare to just look differently threatening and practice another religion. We, the missionaries of peace, have to apply tough love to the rest of the world, because we know best; we are the chosen ones.[9] We affectionately refer to this God's gift as liberal peace.[10] It is this mainstream of peace and conflict studies that our God stands for. Peace building may be imperfect, but it needs to be administered for the sake of a new world order. We in this script take turns to become Rescuers and Persecutors, and when these roles do not go according to plan, we then become Victims. God thrives within a Drama triangle. "He" cannot be part of the after-Drama life.

DECOLONIZING PEACE

Decolonizing peace and conflict studies needs neither a savior nor a decolonizer.[11] It is a process that stems from the realization of peace having become a tool of neocolonialism. My God called me trouble in Sweden, since I am the one who denounced the prophet, and in turn he then denounced me and promised me eternity without a career. Luckily, the decolonization of peace is not ascribed to a single scholar. It is a form of liberation theology for my academic discipline, resting on the same realizations made by Wan in this volume. It questions the birthright that well-intentioned Northerners have to evangelize for peace in the Global South. It challenges a Cartesian epistemology deeply rooted in the patriarchal Drama triangle, and it offers alternative lenses to understand our world, outside this Drama triangle. It uncovers initiatives for peace that do not require international funding, or any peacemaker knight in a shiny SUV. It summons God and "his" army of peacemakers to their well-deserved retirement. It does not challenge them into retirement. This postcolonial peacemaking process exists outside God's world, and it survives and thrives without "his" benevolent help. It renders God redundant, unnecessary, and harmless. Many in "his" ranks are ready to see God step down.

The first time I saw God's necessity strongly doubted by a supposed agent of "his" power was when I visited the Mejicanos neighborhood of San Salvador. There, I met a Catholic priest, Father Antonio Rodriguez Lopez, who has been living in this gang-controlled neighborhood for more than twelve years. He has tried to facilitate the rehabilitation of former gang members, supporting them in their decisions and initiatives to lead peaceful and humble lives, outside any Drama triangle. His efforts have not suited any of the political parties sharing power in El Salvador, whether at the municipal or the national level, since this type of initiative is self-organized and none of them can act as a Savior. A self-organizing community is the nightmare of any "peacemaker" or political boss since no help or salvation is necessary, hence threatening the *raison d'être* of those entities. In his sermon a few days earlier, he had made a very important statement: "If God existed, he would care about your misery." Father Antonio belongs to a long tradition of liberation theologians in Central America and, as Monsignor Romero before him, his life is being threatened for denouncing governmental corruption and economical exclusion in El Salvador.

"Should God remain?" is the question that this book ought to have asked outright. A vision of God has been appropriated by many different religions, as it has by peace and conflict studies, where its self-proclaimed God has been reigning over the discipline for far too many years. God and "his" hierarchy of experts, scholars, and its caste system of Northern and Southern elite-educated professionals have organized peace as a religion that validates exceptionalism as much as it does anti-Semitism. It is no mistake that Johan Galtung has been allowed to spill his hate speech for so many years as part of a discipline that celebrates the expertise of some over others, the missionary work of liberal peace for the greater good, and all the abuses that derive from that.

CAN GOD BE REINVENTED?

God ought to retire, and perhaps, as Monsignor Romero once said about his potential death, be resurrected in the heart of peoples. The decolonization of peace witnesses and documents just that. It expands into a holistic Cosmovision the possibility of self-organized communities to decide about their own future and generate their own opportunities. I came across so many of these initiatives throughout the world. From the gang of Pink Saris in India, enforcing gender and caste equity in rural communities, to the community group of Somalis raising more than two hundred abandoned babies, self-organized peace is thriving, and it decolonizes our own vision of peace on a daily basis, one step at a time. I dream of the day where I will not be called to carry out capacity-building workshops in another part of the world, but where local expertise will finally be revealed to its own community. We can all embody unconditional love, diversity, and justice. We all have the potential to be holistic human beings. We are all God, and the network that we can be across races, nations, and organized religions can reveal unconditional love, diversity, and justice to the world. There can be no people special over others, no people giving the greatest gift to the world. There can only be human beings. God is not transcendent; its expression can be immanent to every one of us.

Where does that leave us, the champions of organized religion, the theologians who have made our whole careers splitting hairs into so many parts to justify our tenured salaries, our "peace missions" per diems and giant SUVs? There is space for all of us within decolonizing peace. As I witnessed in El Salvador, life outside the Drama triangle of politics can lead to great danger. A student of mine from the University of Innsbruck, Michaela, spent months accompanying communities in Guatemala that tried to live outside the State's Drama triangle. She explained to me how her presence as an "international" within the community gave a strong message to the state that if it wanted to pull the community into the triangle, rendering them victims, the rest of the world would know. Michaela spent months eating the same food as her family, drinking the same water, sleeping on the same floor, and suffering from the same squalid living-conditions-related illnesses. She did not "save" the community by returning to her fortified five-star hotel at night. This community does not need any saviors. This type of association between self-organized communities and outsiders may well exist within the remit of decolonizing peace. Theologians should do the same. If they send God to retire, if they tend to their own liberation outside a Drama triangle, in equity, and without any "gifts" to be brought to the world by self-appointed chosen peoples and their prophets, then they might finally find in their lives a god that loves diversity and justice.

NOTES

1. See http://www.esf.org/index.php?id=9306 [accessed December 6, 2012].

2. See http://www.haaretz.com/news/diplomacy-defense/pioneer-of-global-peace-studies-hints-at-link-between-norway-massacre-and-mossad-1.427385. For a response from a Jewish peace and conflict studies scholar, see http://www.haaretz.com/opinion/an-open-letter-to-johan-galtung-peace-making-and-anti-semitism-can-t-go-together-1.428974. For a rebuttal of Galtung's organization on the anti-Semitic charges, burying

him even deeper, see https://www.transcend.org/galtung/statement-may-2012/ [accessed December 6, 2012].

3. Stephen Karpman, "Fairy Tales and Script Drama Analysis," *Transactional Analysis Bulletin* 7, no. 26 (1968): 39–43.

4. Riane Eisler, *The Chalice and the Blade: Our History, Our Future* (New York: Harper and Row, 1987). For an Asian viewpoint on the same issue, see Min Jiayin (ed.), *The Chalice and the Blade in Chinese Culture: Gender Relations and Social Models* (Beijing: China Social Sciences Publishing House, 1995).

5. Elise Boulding, *Cultures of Peace: The Hidden Side of History* (Syracuse, NY: Syracuse University Press, 2000).

6. See, for example, Johan Galtung, "Violence, Peace and Pace Research," *Journal of Peace Research* 6, no. 3 (1969): 167–91.

7. Gerald Caplan, "Peacekeepers Gone Wild: How Much More Abuse Will the UN Ignore in Congo?" *The Globe and Mail* (2012), http://www.theglobeandmail.com/news/politics/second-reading/peacekeepers-gone-wild-how-much-more-abuse-will-the-un-ignore-in-congo/article4462151/.

8. Victoria Fontan, *Decolonizing Peace* (Portland, OR: Dignity Press, 2012).

9. For an edifying illustration of this, see President Obama's Nobel Lecture: http://www.nobelprize.org/nobel_prizes/peace/laureates/2009/obama-lecture.html [accessed December 6, 2012].

10. For a discussion on liberal peace, see Oliver Richmond, *The Transformation of Peace* (London: Palgrave, Macmillan, 2007).

11. Fontan, *Decolonizing Peace*. I thank Bert Jenkins for this valuable remark in relation to the "decolonizer."

Index

About the Contributors

Patricia H. Davis, JD, PhD, is director of research and training for the Frederick Douglass Family Foundation and a consultant for the Department of Justice, nongovernmental organizations, and law enforcement agencies across the country geared to combat human trafficking. Among her publications are "Human Trafficking, Sex Tourism, and Child Exploitation on the Southern U.S. Border" (with Jim Walters—2011) and "The Pickle Case: Labor Trafficking as Civil Rights Violation" (with Bill Bernstein and Robert A. Canino—2013).

Maria Dixon, PhD, is associate professor of organizational communication at Southern Methodist University in Dallas, Texas. Her primary research interests are strategic communication in nonprofit and religious organizations and power and identity in organizational life, as well as religious organizational conflict. A contributing author for Patheos.com, her work is also featured in *Management Communication Quarterly*, the *Journal of Communication and Religion*, and *Business Communication Quarterly*.

Marc H. Ellis, PhD, recently retired as university professor of Jewish studies, professor of history, and director of the Center for Jewish Studies at Baylor University. He is the author of more than twenty books, including *Toward a Jewish Theology of Liberation* and *Encountering the Jewish Future*. He has been a senior fellow and visiting scholar at Harvard's Center for the Study of World Religions and Center for Middle Eastern Studies. Currently, he is senior visiting professor of peace and conflict studies at the University for Peace in Costa Rica.

Victoria Fontan, PhD, is associate professor of peace and conflict studies at the UN-mandated University for Peace in Costa Rica. She specializes in decolonizing peace, postliberal peace, and resilience. She published *Decolonizing Peace* (2012), and she is the author of *Voice from Post-Saddam Iraq: Living with Terrorism, Insurgency, and New Forms of Tyranny* (2008).

Serge Frolov, PhD, is associate professor and Nate and Ann Levine Endowed Chair in Jewish Studies at the Department of Religious Studies at Southern Methodist University. His main research areas include biblical hermeneutics and theology, post-Holocaust theology, and Jewish history and thought. He has published a monograph on the opening chapters of the Book of Samuel, a commentary on the Book of Judges, and more than two hundred articles.

Susanne Johnson, PhD, is associate professor of Christian education at Perkins School of Theology, Southern Methodist University, Dallas, Texas. Her scholarly interests include the intersectionality of class, gender, and race, informed by critical theory and postcolonial thought, with a particular focus on class and power. Publications include chapters in *Children, Youth, and Spirituality in a Troubling World* and *Redemptive Transformation in Practical Theology: Essays in Honor of James E. Loder*. She is past president of the Religious Education Association and the Association of Practical Theology.

Gordene MacKenzie, PhD, is associate professor and chair of the women's and gender studies department at Merrimack College in North Andover, Massachusetts. She co-produced and co-hosted, with her partner Nancy Nangeroni, GenderTalk Radio and GenderVision, and, also with Nancy, co-produced several short documentaries, including *In Memory of Rita* and *Rally for Transgender Rights*. Among her publications are *Transgender Nation* (1994), "Performing Trans Lesbian" (coauthored with Nancy Nangeroni—2002), and "From Sensationalism to Education: Media Coverage of the Murder of US Transwomen of Color" (coauthored with Mary Marcel—2009).

Pamela Milne, PhD, is professor of the Hebrew Bible at the Faculty of Arts and Social Sciences at the University of Windsor in Windsor, Ontario, Canada. Her scholarly interests include feminist critical analysis of the Hebrew Bible, the impact of the biblical tradition on women's lives, and employment equity in the Canadian university context. Among her publications are the following articles: "Doing Feminist Biblical Criticism in a Women's Studies Context" (2011), "Son of a Prostitute and Daughter of a Warrior: What Do You Think the Story in Judges 11 Means?" (2009), and "Administrative Pimping for Fame and Profit" (1995).

Qudsia Mirza, PhD, is associate lecturer at the School of Law at Birkbeck College of the University of London. Her research interests include Islamic law, feminist legal theory, and human rights law, as well as the relationship between English and Islamic laws in the British and wider European context. Among her publications are *Islamic Feminism and the Law* (coeditor—2013) and "Islam and Gender Equality" in *Law and Rights: Global Perspectives on Constitutionalism and Governance* (2008).

Nancy Nangeroni is chair of the Massachusetts Transgender Political Coalition. She co-hosted GenderTalk Radio for eleven years and led the candlelight vigil that inspired the International Transgender Day of Remembrance. Among her publications are "Herland" (2006), "Rita Hester's Murder and the Language of Respect" (1999), and "Fighting for Our Own Reflection: Groundbreaking Film and Video Festival Moves Transgender Lives Center Screen" (1999).

Joerg Rieger, PhD, is Wendland-Cook Professor of Constructive Theology at Perkins School of Theology, Southern Methodist University, Dallas, Texas. He brings together theology and the struggles for justice and liberation that mark our age. Among his books are *Occupy Religion: Theology of the Multitude* (with Kwok Pui-lan—2012), *Globalization and Theology* (2010), *No Rising Tide: Theology, Economics, and the Future* (2009), and *Christ and Empire: From Paul to Postcolonial Times* (2007).

Susanne Scholz, PhD, is associate professor of the Old Testament at Perkins School of Theology, Southern Methodist University, Dallas, Texas. Her main research interests are in feminist hermeneutics of Hebrew Bible/Old Testament studies, epistemologies and sociologies of biblical interpretation, and cultural and literary methodologies. Among her publications are *Sacred Witness: Rape in the Hebrew Bible* (2010), *Introducing the Women's Hebrew Bible* (2007), *Biblical Studies Alternatively: An Introductory Reader* (2003), *Zwischenräume: Deutsche feministische Theologinnen im Ausland* (coeditor—2000), and *Rape Plots: A Feminist Cultural Study of Genesis 34* (2000).

Isam Shihada, PhD, is associate professor in the English department at Al Aqsa University in the Gaza Strip, where he specializes in late nineteenth- and early twentieth-century fiction and gender studies. He was a visiting scholar at Southern Methodist University under the sponsorship of the Institute of International Education's Scholar Rescue Fund from 2010 to 2012. His research interests focus on Arab women writers in English translation and comparative literature. Among his publications are *A Feminist Perspective: Thomas Hardy* (2001), as well as "Patriarchy and Sexual Politics in Nawal El Saadawi's *Woman at Point Zero*" and "Engendering War in Hanan Al Shaykh's *The Story of Zahra*."

Nikky-Guninder Kaur Singh, PhD, is chair of the Department of Religious Studies and Crawford Family Professor at Colby College. She has published extensively in the field of Sikhism. Her books include *Of Sacred and Secular Desire* (2012), *Sikhism: An Introduction* (2011), *The Birth of the Khalsa* (2005), and *The Feminine Principle in the Sikh Vision of the Transcendent* (1993).

Sze-kar Wan, PhD, is professor of the New Testament at Perkins School of Theology, Southern Methodist University, Dallas, Texas. His interests include Second Temple Judaism, postcolonial hermeneutics, Chinese Christianity and philosophical traditions, and political theology. He is author and editor of *Power in Weakness* and *The Bible and Modern China*.